It Should Never Happen Again

To my parents, Lois and Ian,
and all those other parents of later developing offspring, who kept faith

It Should Never Happen Again

The Failure of Inquiries
and Commissions to Enhance
Risk Governance

MIKE LAUDER

Routledge
Taylor & Francis Group

LONDON AND NEW YORK

First published 2013 by Gower Publishing

Published 2016 by Routledge
2 Park Square, Milton Park, Abingdon, Oxfordshire OX14 4RN
711 Third Avenue, New York, NY 10017, USA

First issued in paperback 2016

Routledge is an imprint of the Taylor & Francis Group, an informa business

Gower Applied Business Research
Our programme provides leaders, practitioners, scholars and researchers with thought provoking, cutting edge books that combine conceptual insights, interdisciplinary rigour and practical relevance in key areas of business and management.

British Library Cataloguing in Publication Data
A catalogue record for this book is available from the British Library.

Library of Congress Cataloging-in-Publication Data
Lauder, Mike.
 It should never happen again : the failure of inquiries and commissions to improve risk governance / by Mike Lauder.
  pages cm
 Includes bibliographical references and index.
 ISBN 978-1-4724-1385-7 (hardback)
1. Risk management. 2. Crisis management. 3. Governmental investigations. 4. Accidents--Prevention. I. Title.

 HD61.L377 2013
 338.5--dc23

                                                          2013011907

ISBN 13: 978-1-138-27099-2 (pbk)
ISBN 13: 978-1-4724-1385-7 (hbk)

Contents

List of Figures

List of Tables

Prologue

As this book is about examining failure, let me open with one of my own. When trying to get this book published I received a number of rejections which explained why my proposal did not sit within the publisher's area of interest. I was duly crushed and yet I picked myself up and tried someone else. One of the rejection letters stated, "My feeling is that your proposal is far too academic: you note that the book opens with a review of the relevant academic literature. It also covers a range of inquires (sic), not all of which are directly relevant to a business environment." My immediate thought was, "He needs to read my book to understand why he is so wrong in this instance." (I have to note that his other reasons were quite valid!) What I also noted was that I had failed in my task of communicating why this book was relevant to a business environment. If academic knowledge on business and organisation is not relevant what is the point of it? The challenge for academics is to make their work relevant and digestible.

The second point is that the letter writer had fallen prey to *distancing by differentiation*; that is, by seeing the difference between the inquiries listed and the business environment. However, the governance of *risk* is a universal problem faced by those in charge of all large organisations no matter the type. The issue for them all is how they might prevent unwanted occurrences that have a catastrophic effect from happening in remote and distant parts of their organisation. To do this they need to learn from others whether they are academics or practitioners, they need to broaden their minds about where they might gain valuable lessons, they must think about why some lessons may be relevant to them rather than finding reasons to ignore them. Having read this book, I hope you will agree.

As a society we seem to be beset by tragedy despite the considerable effort made to avoid such events. These events come in many forms. They may range from failure in the transport network, failures of industrial processes, failures within the delivery of services and criminal attacks on society, to failures of society itself, such as when a member or members feel so alienated that they see attacks on fellow citizens as being the most appropriate way forward. Such events are greeted with expressions of great distress and exultations that "this must never happen again". Earnest reports are written, countless hours, days, weeks or years of effort to research and understand what has happened and why it might have happened are undertaken and countless resources are expended to change systems and improve training all in an effort to prevent such things happening again. But they do happen again. Amongst all the questions asked, one seems to be missing. That is, is the way we investigate such events useful and do the recommendations delivered help us prevent, or even significantly reduce the *risk* of, the next crisis or tragedy?

Even at this point we have a problem. The problem starts for me when I try to define precisely what I want to talk about. As in many other walks of life, where there is great expertise there is great segregation of disciplines. In general the disciplines that my work embraces are project risk management, operational risk management (encompassing *enterprise risk management*), accident investigation and prevention, crisis management, *resilience engineering, high reliability organisations*, and that which relates to *normal accident theory*. Each discipline has its own lexicon of terminology and these have their own taxonomy of terms which inevitably clash or contradict those of other disciplines. This makes the reading of these bodies of work very confusing for a generalist. My task is therefore to fuse all this work under a single umbrella in such a way that it is of benefit to the generalist.

As a convenient umbrella I would give the subject that I am addressing the label *risk management*. At the start of my research I tried to define the terms *risk management* and *risk* itself. In the end I gave up. Having found 43 different definitions of risk and a dozen definitions of risk management, I decided that I needed a new approach. I used the logic that by trying to define these terms in a single way, by insinuation, I would be saying that everyone else was wrong. I felt that this would be too big a step to take. Instead I opted to categorise how others had used these terms. This did not however narrow down what was being discussed. In the end I would describe the issue in question as being *the unwanted*; that is the potential for manifestations of *the unwanted* that might occur during the pursuit of some other aim. To borrow a phrase from Erik Hollnagel, it is the other side of the coin to *performance management*. I know that specialists from all the said disciplines will howl with derision at such a crass summary however it is, to me, the most suitable term to embrace what all these disciplines are discussing. For those of you who would like to see how I arrived at this position I would refer you to my doctoral thesis. For the normal reader I would suggest that you go nowhere near it for as my wife and my other proof-readers can attest, it could not be categorised as a good read!

In this book I have tried to distil and lay out what we know and how we use, or do not use, this knowledge in our attempts to forestall the next tragedy. I focus on how we examine these issues in the public forum as it is this that stimulates the public debate. Our opinions are likely to be forged by the results of public inquiries and the press comments that follow. It is less likely that people will go to the academic journals and other publications in order to develop a deeper understanding of the underlying issues. In this book I attempt to bring together both of these worlds. I start by outlining what is available within the academic literature that might be of interest to practitioners. I then examine how inquiries analyse these events in order that we might learn from them and what might prevent us from learning from them. I lay out my thoughts over six chapters.

In Chapter 1 I have tried to set out the context in which any such debate needs to be set. Life is complicated and so the context is also complicated. While we may desire to find the "one true cause", this rarely exists. While we, in the west, may wish the world was clear and controllable, we need to grasp the role that ambiguity, complexity and luck[1] has in shaping our lives. As part of this discussion, I look at our ability to understand and manage such situations through the use of mental models. While living with this perspective may be very uncomfortable, it may give us a more realistic understanding of what is achievable.

In Chapter 2 I look at current academic research. I have tried to reflect the effort and intelligence that has gone into analysing what can go wrong and what is needed to prevent it happening again. I explore these ideas based around the triptych of see, appreciate and act as these are all necessary if accidents are to be avoided. By the end of the chapter, I provide a mental model (based around 20 questions) of how people might use the existing knowledge to develop a better understanding of how to militate against unwanted occurrences in all their forms. The research focuses on the executive board level and their role of *risk governance*.

In Chapter 3, I develop the mental model that underlies the conduct of public inquiries that I see implicit in the recommendations from a number (20) of high-profile inquiries. This work indicates that there is a preference for 23 different types of recommendations.

In Chapter 4, I examine whether the recommendations could be deemed adequate or inadequate-to-purpose. In this chapter I examine the analytical perspective used to create recommendations and some of the tests that need to be applied to them before they are published. Throughout, my analysis is oriented to whether the recommendations meet the needs of learning to ensure such things never happen again.

Chapter 5 looks at the formulation of recommendations. In this chapter I examine who might decide on what recommendations to make and the effect that this might have and then I look at what we might learn about the writing of recommendations both from academic work and from practice and the tests that might be used to steer them towards adequacy. I close the chapter by offering guidelines for the production of recommendations.

Finally, Chapter 6 looks at what might influence the way ahead. I look at the need for inquiries into the conduct of inquiries, the effect that taking a judicial perspective may have on our ability to learn from these events. I finally summarise why we may fail to learn from these experiences.

Throughout this book I have used italics for a specific purpose. This is to signify that the term that I have italicised has a defined academic meaning that is much richer than the words, in themselves, might imply and that is specifically relevant to its usage in the book. I italicise these phrases to warn my readers that they should resist any temptation to give such phrases new meanings or to use them in new ways not previously implied, for to do so would complicate this discussion even more!

In this book I have looked to explore whether we can do better in the future. When I say "we" I look to the many parts of society that are involved. This would include: those in business and government who set these inquiries, those who conduct inquiries, those in the media and academia who comment, those required to act as a result and finally the public who individually and collectively set the context and the expectations for such work. In this book I look to contrast what we know (looking at both academic work and practice) with how this knowledge is or is not used in our attempts to prevent tragedies and disasters reoccurring and here I focus on inquiries that set themselves this aim. I would hope that those people who set up inquiries and comment on their findings may take a moment to read this offering and reflect on their own actions. For those of you who read such reports I would hope that this book might help you to re-evaluate what has been recommended, to decide for yourselves whether the exercise has constituted a good use of public resources and whether it provides valuable insight that might help others to prevent such events occurring within their own field of endeavour.

Endnote

1   For a very good exploration of the idea of luck and the role it plays in our lives, I would recommend that you read the book *Luck* by Ed Smith. This book warns of the detriment effect on a society where, due to the absence of the construct of luck, blame and suspicion infuse everything we do.

Although we all know that we don't learn from just doing things right, but rather from doing the right things and having the mental space to make mistakes and learn from them, we recoil when things go badly wrong. In this magnificent book, Mike Lauder precisely (and with painful accuracy) points out how we miss the opportunity to learn from incidents and mistakes over and over again. Mike masters the art of transforming an extremely complex topic into a practical, relevant and absorbing text. Based on both an extensive academic and practical knowledge of the field, he underpins his arguments with real life examples and empirically proven evidence. This book is a must read for policy makers, emergency service leaders, mayors and governors, as well as leaders in various fields of risk management, as Mike's knowledge and insights – when applied with courage and rigour – will definitely help to forestall the next tragedy.

Hugo Marynissen, Managing Partner,
Crisis Management Consultancy

1

The Complexity of Everyday Life

Introduction

"This must never happen again" is a cry often heard when someone or some group calls for an inquiry: unfortunately it, or something similar, often does but why? The desire that it "never happens again" is often accompanied by the desire "to learn from this tragedy". However as Professor Brian Toft points out in his book *Learning from Disasters*[1] we (organisations and society in general) continue to fail to learn from such events. Inquiries regularly lament such failures. For example, the Columbia Accident Investigation Board (CAIB) stated:

> When changes are put in place, the risk of error initially increases, as old ways of doing things compete with new. Institutional memory is lost as personnel and records are moved and replaced. Changing the structure of organizations is complicated by external political and budgetary constraints, the inability of leaders to conceive of the full ramifications of their actions, the vested interests of insiders, and the failure to learn from the past.[2]

After citing the CAIB Haddon–Cave stated:

> Changing the structure of organisations is complicated by external budgetary and political constraints, the inability of leaders to conceive the full ramifications of their actions, and the failure to learn from the past.[3]

A report by the Chief Medical officer (Liam Donaldson) in 2000 said:

> Most distressing of all, such failures often have a familiar ring, displaying strong similarities to incidents which have occurred before

and in some cases almost exactly replicating them. Many could be avoided if only the lessons of experience were properly learned.[4]

A report by the House of Commons, Public Administration Select Committee[5] states that "preventing recurrence through learning lessons is a key success criterion for inquiries" but "that it is perhaps easier to identify lessons than to learn and act upon them". Lord Donaldson adds that, "In one sense, 'whistleblowing' can be seen as evidence of a failure to learn."[6] So we can see that inquiries are held, large amounts of time and money are expended and we fail to learn and similar events happen again. This lamentable occurrence begs the question, "Why?"

Here is one example in order to set the scene for the rest of the book. On 1 June 2009, an Airbus A330-203 (registered F-GZCP) operated by Air France vanished while flying from Rio de Janeiro to Paris; its flight number was AF447. The investigation and report produced exemplified all that is good about air accident investigation. The persistence, tenacity and skills of the investigators are to be admired. This work was rounded off by a clear and comprehensive report. However the report held an uncomfortable truth. This truth was that the direction and recommendations from previous reports had had a significant role to play in this accident.

There can be no doubt about the role such accident investigations have played in making air travel safer. Many valuable lessons had been learnt over time. The technology used and the understanding of human behaviour have both been advanced by their work. However, what might be described as "the direction of travel" of this work has led the aviation industry into new areas of vulnerability. I look at two:

The first is the complexity of modern aircraft. Design has been improved, redundancies within systems have multiplied and automation has been used in order to prevent human error. The result of this trend is more complex systems where it is proving harder to spot mistakes in design, construction and maintenance prior to an accident. Some now argue that all that is occurring is that the mistakes which used to be made by the pilots are now made at the design stage. This is therefore not risk reduction but just risk transfer. Mistakes are still made that cause accidents, it is just that they now take place within a different discipline.

The second issue is pilot skills. As the systems on the aircraft, when working, can fly the plane within tighter parameters than the pilots (thereby saving fuel and money), they are used more often to fly routine sectors. In his book *Antifragile*, Nicholas Taleb, stressing a similar theme, quotes the US Federal Aviation Administration as saying, "Pilots often 'abdicate too much responsibility to automated systems.'"[7] This is seen to reduce a pilot's inherent flying skills. As many of the systems are automated, the pilot becomes more akin to a system controller; the job of the pilot becomes one where they are required to arbitrate between system conflicts. To do this in real-time they will need to know the system design and weakness as well as, if not better, than the designer. The training required for their system management skills conflicts with their inherent flying skills (the proof for this lies within the ideas of "the magical number seven" and work on the viability of multi-skilling which I address later in the book). As a result there are conflicts between what system designers and operators require from modern pilots and, when the moment comes (as in AF447), the pilots were not able to comprehend and cope with the situation they face.

So who learns the lessons of flight AF447? While those directly involved will, we have to question whether these lessons will be applied to other areas of human endeavour. If they do, how will those who should learn from these events? How should those who examine these issues change the way they look at these issues in light of what we have learnt from Flight AF447? These are the types of question that I hope this book will inspire others to ask.

In this section, I start by looking at the practical problems under consideration. I then articulate the context in which this book is set and finally I will elaborate on my starting point which is within the overall concept of *risk management*.

LEARNING FROM THE TRAGEDIES OF LIFE

The problems at the heart of this matter are those corporate or societal failures that provoke enough vocal (or statutory) concern that it is decided that the source of the failure needs to be formally examined. These failures can come in many forms, some well known and widely reviewed and others less so. Amongst the best known and most widely researched events are:

- the Three Mile Island (1979) and the Chernobyl nuclear accident (1986);

- the chemical spill at Bhopal, India (1984);

- the destruction of the NASA Challenger (1986) and Columbia (2003) shuttle spacecraft;

- the Exxon Valdez (1989) and Deepwater Horizon (2010) oil spills;

- business failures such as Barings Bank (1995), Enron (2001), Worldcom (2002) the 2008 banking crisis;

- the 9/11 attacks on the USA in 2001.

Other equally interesting and informative, but not so widely researched, domestic and international inquiries include:

- the Laming report in 2003 into the death of a child;

- the Smith report in 2005 into the activity of a doctor who had been found guilty of killing his patients;

- the loss of the RAF Nimrod MR2 Aircraft XV230 in Afghanistan in 2006;

- the Donaghy report in 2009 into the underlying causes of fatal accidents within the UK construction industry;

- the attacks by Anders Breivik in Norway which took place in 2011.

As a result of these events and many other events that most people will have never heard of, codes of conduct and management systems have been devised as a way to enhance the effectiveness of management and prevent such events happening again. However, there are questions about whether the system that is currently in place works. For example, Unite's Scottish Secretary, Pat Rafferty, said:

> Time and time again we have been shocked by disasters such as the (tugboat) Flying Phantom and then angered by a system which has no defined structure to prevent a repeat of such an incident.[8]

The questions therefore become: "What is this system that fails?" and "Why does the system fail?" There is not space in this book to explore or even describe the system in place and all its intricacies. For the purpose of this book I shall give it the label of *risk management* which I see as embracing all the related disciplines of safety science, crisis management, business continuity, organisational resilience and *high reliability* to name but a few. However to call this collection "a system" is to stretch a point; I see a more accurate description as being a maelstrom. Within this maelstrom are processes which attempt to learn from the tragedies and disasters which befall us in order to prevent incidents reoccurring.

Erik Hollnagel,[9] a highly respected author in this area, provides a history of accident analysis. In his text he explains how initially accidents were seen as an "act of God", and how this evolved into a hunt for "cause and effect" linkages which, in their turn, were considered to be too limited by the underlying assumption of a "closed system". Hollnagel's argument is based on the concept that "open systems" are subjected to the influences (both weak and strong) of everything within their environment; this work might be seen to be part of what is referred to as a socio-technical design school of thought. Other academics[10] also reject the "cause–effect" model as being too simplistic and use a system methodology in order to capture the complexity of interactions. Established authorities on management of risk[11] also use a systems-type framework to provide "a structural tool to illustrate the ... process, and not (as) an empirical model of how (in his case) communication is factually organised".[12] While Hollnagel and the others limit their theorising to the accident field and related subjects, I extend this logic to cover wider aspects of risk management in its most general sense. While it might not be clear from Pat Rafferty's statement exactly what he meant by the term "system", for the purpose of this book the idea is used in its broadest term of how things influence one another whether by design or not.

The aim of this book is to explore one particular aspect of this subject, the inquiry. I will examine whether some aspects of the inquiry itself may diminish the potential societal wide learning despite the resources expended. At this stage, I will be even more explicit about the focus of my interest which is our ability to learn from such events and to prevent their reoccurrence. Some inquiries are set up for the sole purpose of examining what happened and "to produce a full public account"; these are not designed as part of a learning process and are therefore not of primary interest to me except for where their processes provide examples of practices worth noting. Other inquiries produce findings and recommendations that are very specific to an industry or are focused on the explicit actions of a person involved within a particular discipline. I see these recommendations as being technical issues which have little to teach those outside the defined context. My focus is however on the lessons from inquiries that might help managers and executives who are required to oversee extensive and diverse portfolios of activities to prevent disasters within their organisations. In this book I am looking at the interplay between those who do and those who inquire in order to identify potential barriers to effective communications between these two groups. These, and related reports, provide the starting point for my work and our discussion of whether such efforts are effective.

RESPONSIBILITY FOR FAILURE

Within the codes of conduct there is reference made to the responsibilities for risk management of those with governance roles. This raises the question as to whether there is a different approach at this level that might attract the label *risk governance* as opposed to *risk management*. The label risk governance was, at the beginning, a speculative proposition based on the differentiation made between management and governance. It was based on the proposition that if management was different from governance, then might there not be a differentiation between *risk management* and a construction given the label *risk governance*? Previous research set out to explore this concept.[13]

Corporate failures have generated a wide body of academic research. My own research used this body of knowledge to explore how others have characterised the failures and the mechanisms leading to those failures. I looked to synthesise these ideas so that they may be useful to those involved in Corporate Governance. The premise behind the research was, "If I knew what had been previously identified about the mechanisms of failure, how might this suggest the risk governance function may be performed?" In this context I use the term *risk governance* to mean the "governance of risk management". To many people in corporate life governance is seen in the context of compliance to regulations as symbolised by Sarbanes-Oxley in the USA; this can be seen in the organisations that advertise themselves as governance experts who generally turn out to be law firms and accountants. In this book my use of the term *governance* is more akin to its use within information technology where the term refers to those one stage removed from the day-to-day management of projects. For me governance is about the indirect lever of control available to executives, shareholders and other stakeholders in an enterprise.

My focus of interest concerns the action that this group can take to prevent unwanted occurrences befalling their enterprise.

The understanding of such events, and therefore where responsibility lies, has moved from the examination of the actions of an individual to the examination of organisations and systems as a whole. Those who examine these events in an effort to prevent the next one found that the actions of the individual were often driven by forces, often unseen, outside of their control. Scott Snook's book on the accidental shootdown of two US Black Hawk helicopters by two US fighters over Northern Iraq in 1991 provides an excellent description of this evolution in practice. Snook explained that his first reaction was to blame the pilots but, as his understanding of the events grew, he saw and understood the forces that had led to those tragic events going back as far as to the fall of the Soviet Union. Snook provides what he calls a "causal map"[14] (see Figure 1.1) which provides a pictorial representation of the influence at work. For me this diagram is important for two reasons. The first is that it shows how complicated the causes of these events really are and the second is that I intend to use the construct of the "map" as a way to illustrate the ideas contained within this book.

The Snook book also sets the scene for another important debate that I shall expand upon in the last chapter. This is the tension between the need to understand the causes of such events, the need of parts of society to allocate blame and where the responsibility lies for trying to prevent them. These factors have to co-exist. Some authors feel that there is now a tendency to understand too much and blame too little; other authors feel the key insights may be lost as those involved have an immediate priority of avoiding any potential jeopardy that might be associated with the blame.

The inquiries that are of most interest to me are those that place a high cost on the public exchequer both to carry out and to implement the recommendations. Also of concern are the recommendations that are implemented based on being politically judicious rather than their other merits. Politicians may elect to use an inquiry more as a short-term catharsis than for its long-term learning value. Barry Turner and Nick Pidgeon offer an important warning. They warn that recommendations are designed to deal with the well-structured problem that was defined and revealed by a disaster, rather than with the ill-structured problem that existed before it occurred.[15] Their point is that unless we, as a society, take the responsibility to evaluate the findings and recommendations of these inquiries with a keen critical eye, we may be led to view our world as a

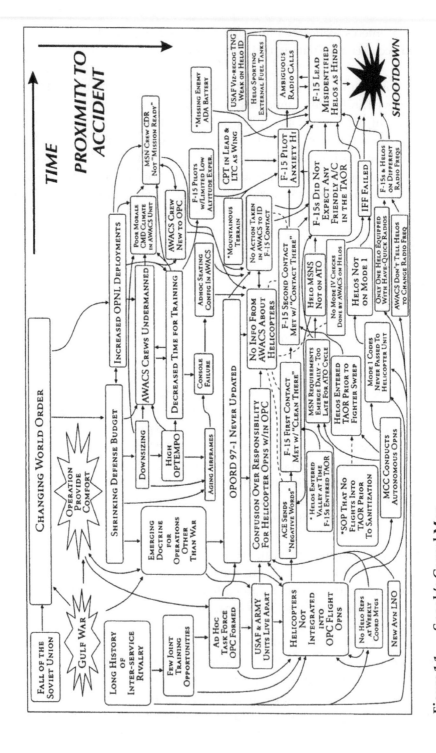

Figure 1.1   Snook's Causal Map

Source: © *Friendly Fire* by Scott A. Snook.

less uncertain and precarious place than it may actually be. In doing so we may build up expectations that erode our own ability to assess the risks we face and then to act appropriately. We start to expect others to do our thinking for us, assessing the risks we face becomes someone else's responsibility to warn and protect us from our own actions. I see this as being a dangerous path to take, fraught with consequences quite contrary to the original intent!

DEVELOPMENT OF OUR THINKING

Alongside the work of academics like Hollnagel and Leveson, Professor James Reason describes how thinking about tragedies such as the ones we have discussed above has developed over the last 50 years. He sees a progress from examining equipment failures, to examining the role of unsafe acts to the part played by systems and cultures.[16] This is important because how we see these events affects what we look for when we try to understand their cause. With systems we see the risk of sub-optimisation. In its simplest terms, this is when a fix to one part of a system has a detrimental effect on another part of the system or to the system performance as a whole. This is a manifestation of unintended consequences of decisions made in good faith.

In terms of our subject, the recommendations of inquiries, my concern is that recommendations, which are made with the best of intent, may have unintended detrimental effects on the system overall. This raises the question as to whether those making recommendations really understand the system they are trying to affect.

Thinking in terms of systems is however very difficult. The alternative is to take an incremental approach where decisions are based on the position arrived at after the last decision. One example of this can be seen in the way case law evolves; another is the trial and error process seen as a key component of *high reliability organisations* (in this latter example it should be noted that errors are an expected part of the overall system). This approach might also be seen as *muddling through* or *disjointed incrementalism* or even *(partisan) mutual adjustment*.[a] *Muddling through* has been described as "to push on to a favourable outcome in a disorganised way."[17] David Hancock described *muddling through* in projects as being where problems are dealt with as they arise in a "whoever

---

a   Within the academic literature there is a difference between *mutual adjustment* and *partisan mutual adjustment*. However for the purpose of this book it is where, in the absence of specific rules and control mechanisms, people adjust their behaviour to accommodate the behaviour of others so that all parties can go about the independent but interdependent business.

shouts the loudest" or makes the "strongest argument" basis. The project meanders through the process until it "arrives" at a solution. Advantages are typically short lived and the disadvantages are that the problem is never "fully" resolved as the solution is constantly changing. Many political problems such as the allocation of budgets and how to provide the best health and education services typically fall into this category.[18]

While in some circumstances an incremental approach has distinct advantages[19] and is the most appropriate way of proceeding, in other circumstances it holds distinct disadvantages. Incrementalism can be seen to induce, amongst other things, *compounded abstraction*[20] and the *problem of induction*.[21] This in turn may both lead to the *garden path fallacy*[b] and unintended consequences. (I will elaborate on these terms later.) Therefore one of the first rules for dealing with unwanted occurrences should surely be "first do no (more) harm". In this area of activity, where we are trying to learn from past experience, we must understand what we are trying to change and how we are trying to change things if we are to see the fundamental causes of problems and fix them.

Use of the Terms

Before we go any further, I want to make clear the way that I use two terms as this is essential to understanding the argument put forward in this book. These terms are *risk management* and *the unwanted*.

RISK PERFORMANCE RELATIONSHIP

The book is written from a *performance management* perspective;[c] that is, the goal is to enable managers to deliver a required outcome while taking the appropriate safeguards necessary to avoid any seen and unforeseen pitfalls along the way. Often risk management is seen as being a separate management discipline, an adjunct to the main management process;[22] I take a different view. I argue that (1) *risk management* needs to be an integral part of management and therefore should be encompassed within the *performance management* sphere and (2) that *performance management* requires the implicit

---

b   Klein (1998), page 70: "Taking one step that seems very straightforward, and then another, and each step makes so much sense that you not notice how far you are getting from the main road."

c   For those who are unfamiliar with this subject might like to browse Mike and Pippa Bourne's book *Handbook of Corporate Performance Management*.

to be made explicit if they are both to be managed effectively. I will start by discussing the place of risk within management.

The relationship between risk and other aspects of management is not settled. The work of Professor James Reason provides an example of the thinking that risk is a separate functional area. Academic and practitioner literature also provides an ambiguous mix involving *performance management, risk management, opportunity management* and *uncertainty management*;[23] they are all used to cover the dialectics of risk–reward which is also articulated as either cost–benefit,[24] upside–downside or opportunity–threat.[25] However, Ramgopal states that, "Strategies for managing project uncertainty cannot be divorced … from strategies for managing the project objectives and associated trade-offs."[26] While Bobker[27] insists that risk should only refer to adverse events, the language is further complicated by such writers as Ward[28] who uses the term *uncertainty management* to embrace *risk management* and *opportunity management*. To others, all management is risk management.[29] Charles Handy, for example, said, "Risk management is not a separate activity from management, it is management … predicting and planning allow prevention … Reaction is a symptom of poor management."[30] Erik Hollnagel is even more succinct, "Instead of seeing success and failure as two separate categories of outcomes … they are but two sides of the same coin."[31] This sees the "risk–reward" dialectic as being the most fundamental of all management dilemmas; that every benefit has associated jeopardy, some of which are obvious and others more difficult to identify. I therefore place the management of risk alongside *performance management*, making them "two sides of the same coin", where *performance management* takes an optimistic benefits-focused approach and *risk management* takes a complimentary but pessimistic jeopardy (or risk)-focused approach. However, for reasons that I will go into next, I feel that using the term risk, in this context, may be misleading.

THE UNWANTED

From the beginning I have a problem in how to refer to *the downside* of the pursuit of any activity. The term *accident* is likely to be rejected by many; for example, the subtitle to a book by Gerstein is "why accidents are rarely accidental".[32] While I might be comfortable to use this label, others might see these events as being preventable and therefore do not view them as being an accident. So, if we are not to use the word accident, how should I refer to these events that will help us visualise and animate the issue?

Patrick Lagadec coined the evocative phrase *brutal audit*[33] to label these crisis events. He says:

> *The events can in some ways be considered as an abrupt and brutal audit: at a moment's notice, everything that was left unprepared becomes a complex problem, and every weakness comes rushing to the forefront. The breech in the defence opened by crisis creates a sort of vacuum … And then into that vacuum is sucked all the forms of difficulty that those involved are then required to face and handle.*

On the other hand Karl Weick[34] described reliability (here characterised as being the absence of *brutal audits*) as a "*dynamic non-event* … dynamic in the sense that it is an ongoing condition" and a "non-event" because nothing adverse happens. Others[35] have extended the definition to safety and here I extend it to *risk management* (as defined above) in general.

There are two important implications of the *dynamic non-event* construct. The first is that, being dynamic, the problem is constantly changing and therefore is unlikely to be identified through static ways of thinking or indicators of risk, that is, they are likely to need dynamic indicators which provide a constantly changing perspective in order to spot an emerging issue. The second, as a non-event, success cannot be judged by absence of problems for the right circumstance or set of circumstances that may not yet have presented themselves. Charles Perrow[36] refers to this as the *Union Carbide Factor*.

Perrow explains that, "It takes just the right combination of circumstances to produce a catastrophe"; he also put it more colourfully, he says, "Accidents are commonplace, but disasters are hard to arrange." To think of it another way, the *Union Carbide Factor* suggests that disasters happen when many unlikely factors align and so we may operate for long periods when such an event might have occurred but has not, some would say, through good fortune. Professor Sidney Dekker uses an adaption of Murphy's law to say the same thing; he says, "Everything that can go wrong usually goes right" yet he goes on to warn, "and then we draw the wrong conclusion."[37] He warns of the *problem of induction* where the imperial evidence won from experience teaches us the wrong lessons. In this case we come to believe we have been doing the right thing when, in truth, we have just been lucky!

Therefore within the ideas conjured up by the word "accident" we see the idea of *brutal audit, dynamic non-events* and good fortune all adding to the mix.

Again, while some might use the word risk for those issues to be managed by risk management, the term *risk* comes loaded with so many meanings I try not to use it at all; I explore these meanings in the next section. As a result of these linguistic gymnastics I will refer to these unwanted circumstances with adverse consequences by the simple label the *unwanted* to embrace all these ideas.

UNDERSTANDING THE TERM RISK

Next we will examine the word *risk*. The word *risk* must be one of the most ambiguous ones in the English language. A reading of many inquiry reports would seem to indicate that many of the protagonists of those events were often talking at cross-purposes and using this term to mean different things. This leads to the danger that resulting recommendations may be misunderstood or, worse, be inappropriate as this fundamental issue was misunderstood. I have described elsewhere[38] how, after the examination of a wide range of literature, I found it a fool's errand to try to come to one agreed definition. The literature examined explored general definitions of *risk management* and the many related areas. These included: (1) accident investigation, (2) crisis management, (3) business continuity management, (4) operational risk management, (5) process risk management, (6) project and programme risk management, (7) resilience, and (8) *high reliability*. Each author used the term to suit their own purpose. I therefore developed a system to categorise the use of the term using a matrix based on concern over time.

The concerns I labelled:

1. **Non-delivery**. Non-delivery covers what might be known as mission failure. This is where an organisation or group fails to deliver all or part of what was intended.

2. **Barrier to delivery**. This category encompasses anything that may prevent the organisation from delivering its intended output.

3. **The unknown**. This category covers both what is unknown and what is uncertain.

4. **The unintended**. The category of unintended includes the problems raised by the interactive complexity within any organisation where the consequences of an action may be different from those intended.

5.   **The unexpected**. The final category of unexpected embraces external influences on the organisation which had not been foreseen or for which mitigation had not been planned.

The second dimension of the matrix had a time-based construct. Using a basic systems structure, the seven temporal categories were seen as: input risks (R1), transformation risks (R2), results (R3), effects (R4), consequences (R5), subsequence (R6), and as an expression of what is acceptable exposure (R7). These were defined as:

- **Input risk**. These are inputs to the system or process.

- **Transformation risk**. These are either break downs of the system or where "normal" interaction produces unforeseen results.

- **Results**. The result is an initial outcome of the mechanism at play on an entity in creating the negative outcome. For example, if the mechanism is the continual flexing of a structure due to natural phenomena such as wind, the result of this may be that the structure becomes stressed.

- **Effect**. The effect is the end product of the result on the entity causing the negative outcome. Building on the stress example, the effect of stress may be structural failure.

- **Consequence**. A consequence is the automatic (cascade) effect that will occur as the end product. Continuing the example, the consequence of part of the structure failing may be the total collapse of the structure.

- **Subsequence**. Subsequence is defined as "the consequence of a decision that follows an unwanted occurrence rather than being part of any cascade of events".

    The term *impact* is reserved for an overarching term that embraces all negative outputs relevant to the matter in hand.

- **Risk exposure**. These are metrics that are used to control the system or process. The controls cover constructs such as risk tolerance, risk exposure or acceptable risks.

The two dimensions (see Table 1.1) provide 35 different usages or meanings for the term *risk*. In every mental model of risk, it needs to be clear how the term is being used.

Table 1.1   Risk Matrix

	Non-Delivery	Barrier to Delivery	The Unknown	The Unexpected	The Unintended
Input (R1)					
Transformation (R2)					
Results (R3)					
Effect (R4)					
Consequence (R5)					
Subsequence (R6)					
Exposure (R7)					

My examination of these uses of the word *risk* made me consider what all these spaces had in common. My conclusion was that they were all unwanted and they all relate to adverse consequences.

PERSPECTIVES OF RISK

Elsewhere[39] I identified that risk management literature divides into three paradigms (three ways of looking at the problem) which I called *line, circle* and *dot*. These metaphorical terms roughly equated to project risk management, process risk management and accident (scenario) risk management (see Table 1.2). The importance of these paradigms is that, while they are interrelated, they are each a particular way of looking at and thinking about risk management issues. Each brings with it its own assumptions, preferences and blind-spots. Therefore those engaged in discussion about risk and related issues need to be aware of which paradigm dominates their thinking, and the thinking of the others involved in the debate, if they are to truly understand and appreciate what each person is contributing.

Table 1.2   Risk Paradigms

	Forward or Backward Looking	Desired or Unwanted Outcome	Chosen or Imposed Outcome	Variance or Invariance of Process	Unique or Recurring
Line	Forward	Desired	Chosen	Variance	Unique
Circle	Forward	Desired	Chosen	Invariance	Recurring
Dot	Backward	Unwanted	Imposed	Variance	Unique

One of the key differences is their assumptions about learning. Within each of these academic risk-based disciplines there are different perspectives as to the gap between understanding and resolution; recommendations and effective action. However this "gap between analysis and implementation is considerable and poorly understood".[40] The impression given by many writers on accidents is that finding the cause of an accident means that an organisation should prevent the next one (writers often express the sentiment that if an organisation had understood the cause of an accident, why did they not prevent it?). Project-based writers are at the opposite end of the spectrum. In their writings they see that understanding an issue is barely a start in trying to resolve it and hence the emphasis on project risk management. There is therefore the potential tension between those perspectives; between those who feel that once the cause is found the job of prevention is near complete and those at the other end of the spectrum who feel that the real work has just begun. These differences have implications for the selection and use of the advice given by experts to inquiries.

Risk Governance

For the purpose of this book, the term *risk governance* is used to denote the activity at board and executive level required by governance "best practice" (as exemplified within the relevant code of governance) to oversee the risk management practice within their organisation.

The issue of leadership is often raised within inquiry reports. This term can be used to cover everything from the control of small teams of frontline workers to the role of the executive board. Where recommendations relating to frontline leaders are often very specific, those referring to the higher echelons are often very vague and the links to specific actions are, at best, tenuous. These responses may be vulnerable to the charge of being a *fantasy document* (a term coined by Clarke and Perrow[41] to mean one which is more a political veneer rather than an effective plan). In order to militate against this charge, an inquiry team might produce their own mental model for how they see the recommendation being turned into effective action.

In this context *risk governance* needs to be related to a high-level risk management function. Again this is not a simple task as there is debate over what the term *risk management* means. BS31100:2008 (the ISO standard) defines *risk management* as the "coordinated activities to direct and control an organization with regard to risk".[42] Other definitions endorsed by the Institute of Risk Management[43] are listed in Table 1.3. Dallas is more specific about what needed to be controlled; he defines *risk management* as, "The process of controlling the impact of risk."[44] Immediately, however, the words "direct" and "control" within the ISO might be seen to be at odds with the UK's Financial Reporting Council's code for Corporate Governance[45] where the same words "direct" and "control" are used to define their concept of "governance".

Table 1.3   Definitions of Risk Management

Institute of Risk Management	Process which aims to help organisations understand, evaluate and take action on all their risks with a view to increasing the probability of success and reducing the likelihood of failure.
HM Treasury	All the processes involved in identifying, assessing and judging risk, assigning ownership, taking actions to mitigate or anticipate them, and monitoring and reviewing progress.
London School of Economics	Selection of those risks a business should take and those which should be avoided or mitigated, followed by action to avoid or reduce risk.
Business Continuity Institute	Culture, process and structures that are put in place to effectively manage potential opportunities and adverse effects.

Rizzi sees governance as a "key, but often neglected component of risk management".[46] My research concentrates on the governance end of the risk management spectrum. Klinke and Renn (the latter a very prominent academic in this field) see three approaches to risk management.[47] These are labelled precautionary-based risk management, risk-based risk management and discourse-based risk management. They summarise the strategies within discourse risk management as (1) consciousness building, (2) confidence building, (3) introducing substitutes, (4) improving knowledge, and (5) contingency management.[48] The premise behind risk discourse can be seen to be that of developing mental models and cross-understanding between interested parties. By 2008 Renn embraces this earlier work within his anthology on "Risk Governance".

As a practitioner, David Hillson sees risk management as providing a framework and common language for dealing with and reacting to uncertainty.[49] This links to my use of mental models. I therefore see a need to attempt to reconcile the mental models of those leading the inquiry with those responsible for the *risk governance* of the target organisations if the inquiry recommendations are to be most effective.

Heuristics and Mental Models

Life is complicated, very complicated. As individuals we all have a limited ability to understand this complexity. This limitation is nicely described by Millar in his article entitled "The magical number seven, plus or minus two". What Miller describes is a limitation of the human brain. In his judgement the human brain could only hold between five and nine ideas at once. Therefore if a problem has more than nine facets, the person cannot consider them all at once but would have to drop one facet in order to embrace another. In short, you can never "consider all the factors involved". This is also important as it would suggest that, if the person has other issues on their mind, their ability to consider multiple factors simultaneously is further reduced. Also important is the fact that as individuals our brains have different levels of "stickiness" – that is, our ability to switch facets also varies; while some can do this very easily others cannot (they obsess about some particular facet). To cope with these limitations humans have developed heuristic forms of thinking.

Heuristics have been described as "rules of thumb" or "short cuts"; they are "informal methods that can be used to rapidly solve problems, form judgements and perform other mental activities",[50] they are "common-sense mechanisms (that process information and help the receiver to draw inferences".[51] There is a large body of work which acknowledges that the use of heuristics is necessary simply in order to act in a timely manner. The alternative would be a full and logical evaluation of every action and the data relevant to it. This approach would be likely to cause all human activity to be afflicted by the paralysis of analysis. A key issue therefore becomes when, in any particular circumstance, heuristics should be replaced by full logical analysis.

One of the keys to heuristics is the idea of mental models. Peter Senge describes a mental model as "our internal pictures of the world, and seeing how they shape our views and actions"[52] made up of "semi-permanent tacit maps" of the world that people hold in their long-term memory, and the short-term perceptions which people build up as part of their everyday reasoning process".[53] Therefore, before we can really understand how we view an issue, we need to understand the mental model that we have subconsciously constructed around it. This understanding is important for a number of reasons. I label these "the Adams Model", "seeing, not seeing", "cross-understanding" and "promoting discourse".

THE ADAMS MODEL

One issue with mental models is the tangibility of the information at the heart of each one. This is a question of how you know what to believe. John Adams provides[54] me, as someone interested in risk management, with one way of differentiating the tangibility of risks. He categorised them as:

- *Directly perceptible risks* are dealt with using judgement – a combination of instinct and experience.

- *"Risk perceived through science ...* to see risks invisible to the naked eye" (instrumented measurement).

- *Virtual risk* – "Where science is inconclusive people are liberated to argue from, and act upon, pre-established beliefs, convictions, prejudices and superstitions. Such risk may or may not be real, but they have real consequence. In the presence of *virtual risk*, what we believe, and whom we believe depends on whom we trust."

As someone also interested in *performance management* I have extended this construct in order to categorise the data that I use to evaluate performance.

- The idea of *directly perceptible risks* translates into *sensual data* which I can touch, feel, smell or count directly using only my senses.

- The idea of risk *perceived through science* translates into *instrumented data* which is data collected and analysed by any form of gauge or other device.

- The idea of *virtual risks* translates into *virtual data* those where you have to rely on the experience, knowledge and judgement of others as the phenomenon is outside your own *seat of understanding*.

These categorisations have implications which need to be considered before the data is used.

- With *sensual data* you have to satisfy yourself that you believe the data that your own senses are providing. You will see the importance of this when we discuss *the bubble* and *cosmological episodes* later in the book.

- With *instrumented data* you have to satisfy yourself that you understand how the instrument works, what it therefore is actually telling you and then whether the instruments are working as designed. One example of where this is important is in drilling operations. During drilling a number of the parameters monitored are only proxy data; that is, by measuring one phenomenon, and then applying a series of assumed associations, you can deduce the state of another. This example is described in some detail by Konrad and Shroder.[55]

- With *virtual data* you have to decide whether you trust the expertise of the person giving the advice or recommendation. Later in the book I give an example of where this was important in one of the cases I examined. This also has implications for whether we learn from inquiries as it comes down to whether we trust the people producing the findings and making the recommendations.

SEEING, NOT SEEING

The idea of mental models is closely linked to the idea of schema,[56] paradigms and worldview. Each provides a way of seeing the world, a "lens" through which we see it. However, as Van de Ven and Poole remind us, "A way of seeing is a way of not seeing",[57] that is, an individual's worldview affects both what they see and what they do not see. It therefore follows that understanding the mental model from which a person sees any subject has a significant effect on the results and recommendations produced. This idea can be seen within the work of *high reliability* theorists who warn against "closed ways of seeing" and recommend being open minded and seeking fresh perspectives (*mindfulness*):[58]

These barriers to seeing are both cultural and managerial. Diane Vaughan points out that, "Aspects of organisational life … created a way of seeing that was simultaneously a way of not seeing hazards."[59] Woods states, "This pattern of seeing the details but being unable to recognise the big picture is commonplace in accidents."[60] Paul Slovic asserts "that people, acting within social organisations, downplay certain risks and emphasise others as a means of maintaining the viability of the organisation".[61] Anomalous events, warning signals and other issues that fall outside the normal cultural lens are therefore readily neglected. While a number of mechanisms may create a cultural blindness to risk, the important issue is that this blindness exists. It is therefore important that individuals understand their own mental model so that they make themselves aware of where their biases (both positive and negative) lie. They need to understand themselves before they can hope that others will understand their perspective on an issue.

WAYS OF VIEWING THE TRUTH

A part of the way people view the world is the way they view what is real, what exists. Academics refer to this as their ontology. This is key to cross-understanding because those holding different ontologies may never agree on what is true. In simple terms, the way we see what is true is a continuum between, at one end, what is referred to as positivism and at the other end as constructionism. At the risk of grossly misrepresenting this complex issue, I will define positivism as seeing the world as an observable reality where the truth can be determined through the scientific methods: this leads to the idea that there is a single truth that can be discovered. For constructionists, on the other hand (and to parody their ideas slightly), it is all in the mind; there is no fixed reality and it is all in the way we view the world. So it can be seen that while a positivist might be searching for the single truth (say for example a "root cause"), the constructionist would be arguing over the nature of what is true! In these circumstances, cross-understanding may be difficult to achieve.

Why is this important? Let us take the case of when the Government Chief Whip (Andrew Mitchell) admitting saying inappropriate things to a policeman at the gate of Downing Street. The case then became whether he had used the word "pleb". The policeman noted that he had, Mr Mitchell denied using the word. The police federation then accused Mr Mitchell of accusing the policeman of lying. If we can take the politics out of this situation, we can see that the police federation were taking the position that there could only be one honest recollection of the events. It does not however take a great step to believe that Mr Mitchell thought he said one thing and for the policeman to hear him say something else. We have all had moments when we have misheard something. Sometimes we realise that what we thought we heard was wrong and we take steps to correct ourselves. Sometimes we do not realise it until later when things do not happen as expected and sometimes we may never realise that it has happened.

Between these two extremes there are many shades of grey, many different beliefs about what really exists. From my own point of view, I see there being a real world that can be deduced by scientific methods. However, determining what is true is more difficult because the way that I see, appreciate and communicate an idea may be different and incompatible with those to whom I am trying to communicate. This would lead to a failure in cross-understanding rather than the realities being different. In addition to this problem we as humans also deal in constructs; an abstract idea which has real consequences. An example of this is the idea of *risk*. What I view as being labelled a risk might be of no consequence to others and therefore not a risk; what others view as being a risk, I might view just as fun! The important point here is that I am sceptical of the idea of determining the truth in any situation, or finding a root cause as this will entail so many individual judgement calls. In order to fully understand a judgement you also need to understand the parameters or criteria used to make the judgement; in terms of any root cause, why the person making the judgement chose to stop at that point. My ontology also leads me to question whether I understand not just what a person is saying but also what they are trying to say or the idea they are trying to communicate. Hence my fixation with cross-understanding! This is also the reason[d] that I write in the first person for as Nicolas Taleb says, "The personal essay form is ideal for the topic of incertitude"[62] and articles written in the third person provide an *illusion of certainty* that is rarely warranted. You see examples of this in authors who, while writing in the third person, reverentially quote themselves as an authority for some particular "truth".

---

d   For anyone interested, my arguments for writing in the first person are set out in more detail in Appendix A to my thesis (Lauder, 2011).

CROSS-UNDERSTANDING

It has been said that no matter what conversation you join, you will always join it in the middle. Once we understand our own viewpoint we can then try to communicate this to others. According to Huber and Lewis:

> Cross-understanding refers to the extent to which group members have an accurate understanding of one another's mental models. Such understanding can evolve through intermember communications ... members' factual knowledge, cause-effect beliefs, sensitivity to the relevance of particular issues, or preferences. Cross-understanding is a group-level, compositional construct.[63]

Cross-understanding needs to be contrasted with "common understanding". Kathleen Sutcliffe warns that an issue with "common understanding" is that "groups sometimes focus only on those perceptions that are held in common" and thereby limit the discussion to areas with which they are all comfortable. She goes on to say, "It is the divergence in information and perceptions, not the commonalities that hold the key to detecting anomalies"[64] and this explains my preference for a cross-understanding approach. Central to any debate is therefore the issue of where different individuals use different mental models and therefore fail to communicate accurately. This might explain why seemingly sound recommendations fail when applied in different circumstances. A clear mental model is therefore the first steps towards good cross-understanding within and between groups.

The difficulties in cross-understanding are highlighted by Nicolas Taleb in the section of his book *Antifragile* which is titled "Domain independence is domain dependent".[65] He gives examples where, "Some people can understand an idea in one domain, say, medicine, and fail to recognise it in another, say, socioeconomic life." Taleb uses the example of how a body responds to the stress of exercise to grow stronger and then explores this idea within a socio-economic context. In this book we are examining the exchange of ideas across four domains (these being politics, the judiciary, academia and practice) that are vital components if lessons are to be learnt from inquiries so that the unwanted incidents "never happen again".

PROMOTING DISCOURSE

Models of any type have both their strengths and their weaknesses for "when you organise, you simplify".[66] The aim of producing explicit mental models is to provide a framework for debate. Karl Weick has stated that, "By placing a meaningful frame around flows of events, (in his case) *normal accident theory* allows people to better grasp and analyse the complexities of technological organisations as they face the unexpected."[67] I am looking to apply the same logic. Weick applauds Perrow's *normal accident theory* for the fact that it frames, it links and it provokes; while noting the warning from Henri Theil that, "Models are to be used, not believed" and from George Box that, "All models are wrong: some models are useful."[68] I have the same ambition as Weick for using explicit mental models. It is to "let people get their bearings when they observe complex organisations that face the unexpected".[69] Weick provides an example of how he used Perrow's 2 x 2 matrix (based on loose or tight coupling within linear or complex transformation systems) to help him "understand how and why the Centre for Disease Control misdiagnosed West Nile virus when it first appeared". He says, "One way we get our bearings in this investigation is to assign the incident to a cell in Perrow's matrix. In a way, it really does not matter where we assign it, because the act of assigning itself gets us talking, digging, comparing, refining, and focusing on the right question."[70] I propose to use the models described in this book in the same way.

Theory into Practice

Inquiries often bring together theory and practice. For example Haddon-Cave[71] used James Reason (a professor of psychology well known for his work on human factors in accidents) as his advisor; Donaghy[72] primarily used Andrew Hale (a professor of safety science) and the Norwegian 22 July Commission had members including a law faculty researcher, a historian and a researcher who specialises in terrorism and terrorist acts. However theory and practice, academics and practitioners are seen to be as compatible as oil and water. There is, not surprisingly, a whole field of academic study that looks at this subject.

Kieser and Leiner[73] make reference to the difficulties in communicating between the academic and practitioner communities; they offer the idea of "bilingualism" and suggest that bilingualism should become an element in PhD programmes to ensure that academics can communicate effectively. Other academics feel such efforts would be a waste of effort as "practitioners are unlikely to understand or appreciate many of the subtleties of the scientific method"[74] and ask, "Should management research be held hostage to people who seem mentally challenged when reading the Harvard Business Review?"[75] There is clear potential difficulty in developing effective cross-understanding between the two. Bilingualism is not however the only problem for cross-understanding between academic and practitioner.

COHERENT WHOLES

An editorial in the *Academy Management Review* in 2011 urged management scholars to take up the challenge of "exploring real-life problems ... by taking down walls and building bridges between perspectives".[76] It went on to suggest that, "Combining multiple theoretical lenses to develop new explanations of management phenomena and solve managerial challenges will continue to be a critical aspect of how research is conducted in our field." He says:

> *This requires a deep discussion of how underlying assumptions can be combined ... the clear articulation of the fit between theories becomes important because readers and reviewers cannot be expected to draw the links that authors may observe, as might be the case in situations where either the phenomena or the underlying assumptions provide such an anchor or starting point ... new theory hinges on the ability of authors to explain how seemingly disparate or unrelated theories fit together to form a coherent whole.*

As we see above, inquiries do lean on academia for support. However, this does raise the question as to whether the research used provides a wide enough perspective to create a *coherent whole*, through synthesis, out of the understanding, models and theories which are to be found in the literature relating to organisations' disasters and failures. Chapter 2 takes a first look at a cross-section of the material that is required to be understood in order to develop the related literature into a *coherent whole*.

This would suggest that any set of issues should not be seen as a list of unrelated items, but rather we should try to explain how they fit together to form a *coherent whole*. This provides links to Perrow's discussion of interactive complexity within *normal accidents*. This complexity is difficult to represent in the linear form provided by the list format.[77] Therefore, there is a need to develop a holistic overview. One option may be to develop the question set in the form of a strategy map;[78] Calandro and Lane[79] have discussed the integration of risk and performance in this format. Another approach may be to take a systems thinking approach such as used by Barber.[80] In the context of this book, the *coherent whole* is provided by the explicit articulation of mental models.

PRACTICAL UTILITY

Corley and Gioia made an important contribution to this debate when they discussed what constitutes a theoretical contribution and the utility of academic work. They distilled existing literature on theoretical contribution and divided it into two dimensions. These are originality and utility. Of the two my interest is in utility. Corley and Gioia[81] further divide utility into two dimensions: scientific or practical.

> *Scientific utility is perceived as an advance that improves conceptual rigor or the specificity of an idea and/or enhances its potential to be operationalized and tested … Theory can advance science by providing cohesion, efficiency, and structure to our research questions and design … In a very practical sense, good theory helps identify what factors should be studied and how and why they are related.*

> *Practical utility is seen as arising when theory can be directly applied to the problems practicing managers and other organizational practitioners face … through "the observation of real-life phenomena, not from 'scholars struggling to find holes in the literature'" … such a practical problem focus is a good way to develop theory per se. Thus, theory directed at practical importance would focus on prescriptions for structuring and organizing around a phenomenon and less on how science can further delineate or understand the phenomenon.*

The focus of this book therefore is the extraction of *practical utility* from the extensive body of research conducted into disaster and other *risk*-orientated events. It is centred on a research approach referred to as scholarship of application,[82] in order to examine the *practical utility* of the previous academic work relating to the subject under consideration.

QUESTIONS NOT ANSWERS

In a complex world individual solutions are unlikely to have a wide applicability. Recognising this, the approach I have taken is not to offer solutions but to provide "good questions" that provoke animated debate. While academics may wish to see the purpose of their work as being to describe, explain, predict and test[83] this may not have the greatest *practical utility*. After the fall of Singapore, Sir Winston Churchill is reported to have said, "I ought to have known ... I ought to have asked."[84] In his acceptance speech to the Academy of Management as its "Executive of the year, 1999",[85] John S. Reed stated:

> We (as managers) have to do two things: we decide what to do, and we try to make it happen. If you boil down all of the practice of business, it is the combination of those two things and the interaction between them that defines the world in which we live.

He goes on to explain that:

> All ... research can do is inform us. It certainly does not give us answers.

Karl Weick sees utility in academic work that "provokes" discussion (it "gets us talking, digging, comparing, refining, and focusing on the right question"[86]). Peng and Dess suggest that scholars "can help managers frame issues, ask the right questions, and question their underlying assumptions".[87] For this to be effective, once again we need to look at the mental models at play.

Understanding the Lessons

The question is whether we can learn lessons from previous disasters. Once again the answer is more complex that a straightforward yes or no. There can be no doubt that all forms of travel are safer now than they once were, and in the western world our buildings do not fall down as often as they once did and our food does not poison us as often as it used to. Those involved can quote seminal moments when fundamental lessons have been learnt and the knowledge has been passed through the related industries thus benefiting future generations. However, planes still crash, buildings do collapse and our food can still kill us. One problem may have been fixed but others have resulted. For example, technology has been used to compensate for the frailty of pilots but now the technology has become so complex that components can be seen to interact disastrously in ways never foreseen.

Those conducting inquiries need to be aware of the unintended consequences of their recommendations. Therefore an important component of their mental model should be the analytical criteria of "first do no harm". Those making recommendations also need to be aware of the ever present danger of the *reverse fallacy* (discussed in more detail later) as the accident may just have happened in a different way.

As the purpose of many inquiries is to discover what happened and to make recommendations to ensure that it will never happen again, it is ironic that such events are unlikely to happen again as each event is unique. Therefore the issue may need to be reframed. One has to question the value of ensuring that the particular accident does not happen again and gear the recommendations towards ensuring that similar events are prevented. This brings into question what academics call "generalisability"; that is whether the circumstances in the future will be close enough for the lesson learnt from one set of circumstances to be applicable to another.

INCLUSIONS AND EXCLUSIONS

The purpose of any discussion is to prepare the parties involved for the decisions ahead; to ensure that their mental frame and the information available to them are appropriate for the decisions that they will need to make. Decision theory gives us an understanding of how individuals may establish such points of reference. No matter what conversation you join, you will always join it in the middle. It is therefore important to establish what running conversation is being joined, define at what point you pick it up and the point at which you will exit so that if you re-join the conversation you are aware that there might be a gap in your comprehension. The concept used in decision theory is that of the start and stop rule. It is thought appropriate to take this concept from decisions theory at this point because, while this chapter does not look at the decision process, the purpose of developing a clear construct of risk is to enable more informed decisions to be taken at some point in the future. Therefore, in simple terms, this is the point from which information is thought irrelevant to the point that no more information is required in order to make a judgement.[88] Snook[89] describes how, in the context of determining the cause of the problem, a person's perspective affects the point at which they stop collecting data: "Trainers stop when they find a weak skill that they can train. Lawyers stop when they find a responsible individual that they can prosecute. Political leaders stop when their constituents stop. Scientists stop when they learn something new" and he points out how this stopping point is an "artificiality".[90] Vaughan, from her experience examining the antecedents to the Challenger accident, warns that NASA's "decision rule had become disassociated from its creators and the engineering process behind its creation".[91] This disassociation led to dysfunctional decision making which was at the heart of the accident. Therefore, my proposition is that, in order to make more informed judgements on risk, those involved need to understand what factors may affect their formulation of start and stop rules appropriate to the issue that they face. As these start and stop rules will exist tacitly, the proposition is that making them explicit would be helpful.

To take this forward we need to examine the types of issues that are likely to affect how the start and stop rules may be generated.

PERCEPTIONAL CONSTRUCT

Paul Slovic argues that risk is a mental construct.[92] If risk is to have meaning, it has to be set in actual circumstances; if the temporal complexity of risk is to have meaning it needs to be set in a context. I have examined the phenomena that frame discussions of risk. This starts with the concept of (1) framing and then looks at (2) boundaries, (3) context, (4) stakeholders and finishes with the place of (5) perceived rewards and jeopardy. In this chapter I cannot hope to explore the detail on each; all I am attempting to do is to justify its inclusion. I will explain each element and then show how it is linked.

Snook says, "The more expected an event, the more easily it is seen or heard."[93] Vaughan adds "how taken-for-granted assumptions, predispositions, scripts, conventions, and classification systems figure into goal orientated behaviour in a pre-rational, pre-conscious manner that precedes and prefigures strategic choice."[94] Nævestad goes a step further and defines frames of reference as, "The context, viewpoint, or set of presuppositions or evaluative criteria within which a person's perception and thinking seem always to occur, and which constrains selectively the course and outcome of these activities."[95] He goes on to say that "This definition emphasizes that our perception and thinking always occur within frames of reference and that these structure our perception and thinking ... Our interpretations and judgments are based on frames of reference."[96] Haddon-Cave provides a clear example of why an understanding of this issue is important. When asking a witness why due notice had not been taken of a previous incident, the witness replied, "We were responding to the fire that we had. There was nothing to arouse our suspicion that we had a particular problem in those areas with fuel leaks."[97] They were not looking; they did not see. Those using this proposed framework need to explore the frame of reference that they are using and therefore need to identify their potential "blind-spots".

Equally, those making the judgement as to what recommendations to produce need to be aware of their own weaknesses and blind-spots. When constructing their mental model they need to consider the framing, the boundaries, the context, stakeholders and their own worldview on the appropriate balance between rewards and jeopardy.

ADOPTING A LENS

For the purpose of this book I will use one particular perspective ("lens") as my point of reference. I will adopt an executive level perspective. I will do this for two reasons both revolving around the idea of the investigator.

The first is the idea of the executive as an investigator. Diane Vaughan[98] and Keith Grint[99] both see a point in any hierarchy of large organisations, where managers move from being "Expert" to being "Investigator"; from no longer dealing with the "Routine" but focusing on the "Novel", not dealing with the "Specifics" but in "Principles"; not looking at the "Full Detail" but managing "By Exception".[100] The idea here links to the construct of decision distancing where "in a six-level hierarchy, there may be a 98 per cent loss of informational content".[101] Central to the issue addressed within this book is therefore how the most appropriate 2 per cent of information is filtered through to top executives and how the executive must become an investigator to ensure that it is the appropriate 2 per cent of information that reaches them.

The second reason for adopting this perspective is that the role of investigator is one that falls to the chair of any inquiry. Many tasked with such work are faced with a new challenge. Rather than just evaluating the evidence presented to them, they also have a responsibility for selecting the evidence that is evaluated. I see any delegation of this responsibility can only be to the detriment of the final recommendations.

Summary

In this first chapter I have tried to explain the context within which this book is set. If we are to learn from previous events we need to appreciate how findings and recommendations are laden with value judgements. We all have our own view of the world and for us to be able to communicate effectively (to develop cross-understanding) we need to understand our own worldview so we can start to appreciate what others might be trying to say. I find the problem of communication is summed up well in the following:

> *What you thought you heard me say*
> *Is not what I thought I said.*
> *What I said was not what I intended to say*
> *which is also not what I meant.*

For inquiry recommendations to be understood fully, the values and rationale behind them need to be made explicit. So far I have provided an introduction to the idea of mental models and why it is important that assumptions and logic contained within any such model are made explicit.

An important aspect of this work is its reflexive nature. That is, looking at the answers through the lens of the material being considered. When considering the construction of mental models, it is necessary to consider what needs to be known and reflecting on what we do using the same knowledge as we use to critique others. In the next chapter I look in more depth at the extensive body of research into the causes of unwanted events and how they may be prevented as a prelude to looking at how this knowledge is or is not used by those conducting inquiries.

Endnotes

1   Toft and Reynolds (2005).
2   CAIB (2003), page 203.
3   Haddon-Cave (2009), page 453.
4   Donaldson (2000).
5   Public Administration Select Committee (2005), HC 51-1.
6   Donaldson (2000), pages 5 and 64.
7   Taleb (2012), page 43.
8   http://www.bbc.co.uk/news/uk-scotland-glasgow-west-20777297, accessed 19 December 2012.
9   Hollnagel et al., (2006), page 9–17.
10   Leveson et al. (2009), page 227; Marais et al. (2004).
11   Renn (2008); Slovic (2000); Waring and Glendon (1998).
12   Renn (2008), page 209.
13   Lauder (2011).
14   Snook (2000), page 21.
15   Turner and Pidgeon (1997).
16   Reason (2008), page 131.
17   Hollnagel (2009), page 44; Reason (2008), page 259.
18   Hancock (2004), page 58.
19   Mintzberg et al. (1998), pages 180–184.
20   Irwin (1977).

21   Taleb (2007), pages 40–41.
22   Reason (1990), page 200.
23   Ward and Chapman (2002), page 1.
24   Gigerenzer (2003), page 76; Sheffi (2005).
25   Browning in Hillson, (2007), page 319.
26   Ramgopal (2003), page 22.
27   Hillson (2007), page 68.
28   Hillson (2007), page 212.
29   Shaw (2005), page 23 cites this as the view of the Canadian risk management pioneer Douglas Barlow.
30   Merna and Al-Thani (2008), page 44.
31   Hollnagel (2009), page 18.
32   Gerstein (2008).
33   Lagadec (1993), page 54.
34   Weick (1987), page 118.
35   Reason (1998), page 294; Gauthereau and Hollnagel (2005), page 129; and Hovden et al. (2010), page 954.
36   Perrow (1999), pages 356 and 398.
37   Dekker (2011), loc 739.
38   Lauder (2011).
39   Lauder (2011), Chapter 3.
40   Carroll and Fahlbruch (2011), page 3.
41   Clarke and Perrow (1996).
42   BS31100:2008 page 2.
43   Hopkin (2010), page 37.
44   Dallas (2006), page 372.
45   FRC (2010).
46   Rizzi (2010), page 312.
47   Klinke and Renn (2001), page 159.
48   Klinke and Renn (2001), page 169.
49   Hillson (2007).
50   Klien (2009), page 307.
51   Renn (2008), page 102.
52   Senge (2007), page 6.
53   Senge (2007), page 237.
54   Adams (2007), pages 38–40.
55   Konrad and Shroder (2011), pages 172–175.
56   Rumelhart (1981).
57   Van de Ven and Poole (1995), page 510. Also see: Perrow (2007), page 74, Blockley (1998), page 78 who cites Turner, Manning (1999), page 285 attributes the idea to Burke, and both Cox et al. (2006), page 1125 and Nævestad (2008), cite Vaughan's work.
58   Weick and Sutcliffe (2007).
59   Vaughan (1996), page 394.
60   Starbuck and Farjoun (2005), page 294.
61   Slovic (2000), page 190.
62   Taleb (2012), page 18.
63   Huber and Lewis (2010), page 7.
64   Sutcliffe (2005), page 421.
65   Taleb (2012), pages 38–40.
66   Weick and Sutcliffe (2007).
67   Weick (2004), page 27.
68   Hubbard (2009), page 213.
69   Weick (2004), page 27.
70   Weick (2004), page 27.
71   Haddon-Cave (2009).

72 Donaghy (2009).
73 Kieser and Leiner (2009).
74 Baldridge et al. (2004), page 1073.
75 Mckelvey (2006), page 823.
76 Editor AMR (2011), page 11.
77 Perrow (1999).
78 Kaplan and Norton (2004).
79 Calandro and Lane (2006).
80 Barber (2008).
81 Corley and Gioia (2011), page 18.
82 Boyer (1990), pages 21–23.
83 Yin (2003), pages 3–27.
84 Weick and Sutcliffe (2007), page 84.
85 Huff (2000).
86 Weick (2004).
87 Peng and Dess (2010), page 287.
88 Todd and Gigerenzer (2003), page 149.
89 Snook (2000), page 219.
90 Snook, (2000), page 189.
91 Vaughan (1996), page 391.
92 Slovic (2000).
93 Snook (2000), page 80.
94 Vaughan (1996) page 405.
95 Nævestad (2009), page 157.
96 Nævestad, (2009), page 158.
97 Haddon-Cave (2009), page 162.
98 Vaughan (1996), page 94.
99 Grint (2010).
100 The former are provided by Grint and the final one by Vaughan.
101 Smart and Vertinsky (1977), page 326.

2

What Do We Know?

In this chapter I look to set the scene for the rest of the book. I set a summary of what we know from academic literature about what might cause unwanted occurrences and how they might be prevented. At the end of this chapter I present 20 questions that I consider encompass all of this work; I offer this as a way for those with *risk governance* roles to keep these issues constantly in their mind. This chapter is a summary of the work I did as part of my doctoral thesis. For the purpose of this book, the purpose of this chapter is to enable readers to compare what we (as a society) do know with what is used by those conducting inquiries.

We need to note from the start that this is an extensive body of work and therefore we cannot possibly hope to do justice to it in this one chapter. What I have tried to do is to identify general themes within the work so that this can be contrasted with the understanding applied to public inquiries. How I arrived at this point is explained elsewhere[1] and so I will not repeat it here. What is important is that we start this discussion from a common point.

My point of departure is that I see all activity as having a purpose which is meant to provide a benefit to those undertaking it. Whether the purpose and benefits are clear to or understood by others is another question; this is addressed later. Within management there are four classic benefits, any of which can be used to justify an activity. These are (1) to make money, (2) to save money, (3) to meet strategic objectives, and (4) to conform to the law or regulations. While each can be used to justify activity, their pursuit can also be seen as a classical form of failure. *Production pressure*, budget cuts, hubris and the incorrect application of rules (or often it is the application of rules in the wrong situation) are commonly cited as causes of unwanted events. This suggests that even the pursuit of a seemingly legitimate objective can, in itself, cause problems.

Other often cited causes are *poor leadership, poor training* and *poor communications*. However, while there are many more cited within the literature, what we look for will affect what we see. What we look for will depend on the mental model we have before we start. The aim of this chapter is to provide an initial summary of the literature in order to feed nascent mental models of this subject. So, what do we already know? I start by looking at the idea of foresight and this is followed by an exploration of the thinking behind why we may fail to act appropriately; why we miss the available clues.

Failure of Foresight

Investigations of organisational failure have often laid the blame on *failure of foresight*. Toft and Reynolds list one general type of recommendation from public inquiries into accidents as "foresight recommendations (that are made) ... in an attempt to forestall problems which could arise in the future".[2] One such example from the UK is Haddon-Cave who evoked *failure of foresight*, both directly[3] and indirectly, saying, "if he had given careful thought"[4] as a contributory cause of the crash of Royal Air Force aircraft, Nimrod XV230. Similarly, the Challenger Accident Inquiry Board (CAIB) report said, "Both accidents (Shuttles Challenger and Columbia) were 'failures of foresight' in which history played a prominent role."[5]

The CAIB used Turner's definition of *failure of foresight* as do other academics.[6] Turner defined it as "a long incubation period in which hazards and warning signs prior to the accident were either ignored or misinterpreted".[7] The need for foresight is espoused across a wide range of academic literature. However, Pidgeon and O'Leary believe that, "Few would probably disagree that foresight is limited and as such the identification of warning in advance of a major failure is problematic"; they also warn that "the identification of system vulnerability in foresight sets an epistemologically impossible task"[8] for how can you know something before it happens.

Stockholm provides us with the purpose of foresight. He states that, "Understanding the underlying causes of our current performance and our part in that performance provides us the insight necessary to resolve existing problems and the foresight necessary to prevent developing problems."[9] The sentiment "that organisations fail to learn" is held by many.[10] Those familiar with *organisational learning* literature will understand that, within that literature, learning consists of two distinct parts: understanding and implementation (adoption of organisations' routines), but this distinction is not always clear. The foresight provided by understanding, however, does not necessarily lead to successful prevention, although it is the assumption of some commentators that the first should "automatically" lead to the other.

There are some proposed tests of foresight. These tests are questions that may be added to the risk assessment process. However, these tests are often set in the context of hindsight. One such example is the question, "Did the individual involved in the incident engage in behaviour that others (when asked individually) recognize as being likely to increase the probability of making a safety critical error?"[11] This is indicative of the majority of the debate to date. The main focus of academia has been to examine the mechanisms that are at the heart of crises and accidents. This work has the benefit of hindsight in the quest to develop understanding. Unfortunately for managers, this facility is not open to them as they manage their organisation. This chapter therefore will concentrate on questions that can be used with foresight. It looks at what questions might be asked and how the emerging context may aid or hinder the conceptualisation of potentially unwanted and damaging occurrences.

PURSUIT OF FORESIGHT

Foresight is not about predicting the future, it concerns logical plausibility. However, for practitioners the scope is ever expanding. As accident inquiries seek to allocate blame based on more tenuous causal linkages, consideration may need to be given to what Weick has labelled *failure of imagination*;[12] that is, what "might happen" even when people have no idea beforehand how it may happen. Foresight might be seen to be focused on the process by which organisations monitor and evaluate that which is changing around them so that they might react appropriately. While some question whether accurate foresight is possible, it is in the nature of mankind to try. While there are many courses of action open to those who try, this research focused on the potential barriers to acting appropriately whereby clues may go unseen or unappreciated. Despite issues of dysfunctional momentum and the extremely difficult cognitive work required to forestall failure, there being no agreement on taxonomy, the need for better conceptual models and processes to make systems more transparent, some authors provide recommendations of how this might be achieved. The work suggests that a mind open to emergent trends, a process that continuously monitors all identified hazards, the expectation of instability of processes, and the need for emerging measures of how and where the system may become brittle, might help. It reminds us that we do not necessarily notice as things change despite, or because of, oversight, checks and balances, and strong cultural norms. It suggests that there may be issues around *organisational learning* and communication, involving information difficulties/impairments exacerbated by organisational politics.[13] Research also recommends the better use of data and the involvement of relevant stakeholders in order to solicit fresh perspectives. The picture created is, as yet, piecemeal; it is not anywhere near comprehensive. In the next section I look at what else might be included in such discussion.

METHODOLOGY

For the purpose of this chapter, the label *unwanted* will be retained; it should be assumed to include the *unwanted* at any part of a transformation process. The literature that most closely relates to this conception of risk ("the unwanted nightmare") is the literature about accidents. This is because the accident literature espouses its purpose as being twofold: (1) to determine the cause and (2) to prevent future accidents. This second purpose is the one that most closely relates to the purpose of risk management ("action taken now to limit the impact of *the unwanted* in the future") and is the focus of this chapter.

Lagadec points out that executives are not able to limit exposure to risk to one specific area, they have to be alert to *the unwanted* emerging from any area of their organisation or from any cause. He says an expert "can be satisfied with making very specific, limited diagnoses, while (decision makers) must integrate many elements".[14] This is why my analysis focuses at the level of *risk governance*.

The phenomena discussed in this chapter emerged from the inductive research of *risk governance*. The research focused on the body of existing knowledge pertaining to risk (in its widest sense) and the relevant literature was reviewed. This included project management, operational risk management (encompassing *enterprise risk management*), accident investigation and prevention, crisis management, resilience engineering, *high reliability organisations*, and that which relates to *normal accident theory*.

The research extracted the phenomena cited by the authors as having been found to have caused *the unwanted* occurrences. Over 250 phenomena were identified; this was far too many to make a viable mental model. A winnowing process therefore took place that identified duplicated coding and overlaps between phenomena, and finally they were grouped under related headings.

The existing body of knowledge was synthesised to produce a workable number of categories, while trying not to lose the richness of the full body of work. Twenty-four categories were identified which were seen to embrace all of the existing knowledge. It was, however, accepted that even this may not provide practitioners with an appropriate portal through which to access the existing knowledge. Therefore I looked for a triptych of main headings under which to group the categories.

SEE, APPRECIATE, ACT

The research showed that the prevention of *failure of foresight* required three processes to be integrated. These processes were embraced within a number of triptychs that existed in the literature (see Table 2.1); once alert to these sequences they can be recognized in other forms, such as, data, inference, project or even see, emphasise, worry. In the end the triptych that I chose to use was (1) "Failure to See", (2) "Failure to Appreciate", and (3) "Failure to Act". The importance of this triptych can be seen later, for when an individual is criticised "for not acting", we can see that consideration needs to be given to whether they should have seen the crisis coming and whether they would have appreciated what the information they were seeing was trying to tell them. For this reason, it is important to appreciate the derivation of this triptych.

Table 2.1   Triptych Options

1.	Seeing/knowing/responding (Roe and Schulman, 2008:159)
2.	Detecting the problem/representing the problem/generating new courses of action (Klein, 1998:135)
3.	Detect/misrepresent/notice weaknesses (Klein, 1998:275)
4.	Framing/knowing/responding (Roe and Schulman, 2008:7)
5.	Meaning/interpretations/action (Van de Ven, 2007:26)
6.	Measure/understand/manage (Coleman, 2011:26)
7.	Share/interpret/construct (Van de Ven, 2007:26)
8.	Transfer/interpret/implement (Van de Ven, 2007:25)

The genesis of the first heading, "Failure to See" came from the idea that "seeing is a way of not seeing"[15] which is examined in more detail later in the chapter. The heading was used to capture any phenomena relating to the receiving of warning signals. The genesis of the second heading, "Failure to Appreciate" was Diane Vaughan's reference to the idea of *seat of understanding*.[16] The heading was used to capture any phenomena relating to comprehending the value of warning signals. Finally the heading "Failure to Act" came from the repeated queries by authors as to why individuals, who had had a warning, had failed to prevent a disaster. The heading was used to capture any phenomena relating to the action stimulated by warning signals. Similar categorisation had also been used by Turner where he wrote about *emergent dangers*;[17] he said, "Another problem which recurs at many points in the three reports is that of a failure to see or to appreciate fully the magnitude of some emergent danger." Power also used similar categorisation; he said, "And yet ... an intensified concern for organisational process may also incubate risks of its own, not least the failure to see, imagine or act upon the 'bigger picture'."[18] So between them, the two authors have used failure to see, imagine, appreciate and act. I did not use the heading *failure of imagination*, not because the idea is not important,[19] but because phenomena that might have been placed under this heading seemed to fall more naturally into the debate about not seeing warning signals or appreciating what they meant.

The results of the induction process are described below. The chapter describes each grouping and shows how they are clustered under each heading. The chapter concludes each grouping with an abstraction of the ideas that are seen to be central. The 24 abstractions are offered as a distillation of the body of existing knowledge available to practice.

Missing the Clues

In this section, I look at the literature for clues as to what might explain the mental processes which contribute to the acceptance or rejection of potential signals of failure. The factors are grouped into three areas: (1) Failure to See the signals, (2) Failure to Appreciate the significance of signals, and (3) Failure to Act appropriately based on a model where individuals fail to perceive or recognise warnings or assess and respond adequately.[20] The concept of *mindfulness* has been used to provide additional definition to this description. "Failure to See" the signals would embrace the mindful ideas of "preoccupation with failure" and "sensitivity to operations".[21] "Failure to Appreciate" the significance of signals would also embrace *reluctance to simplify* and *deference to expertise*.[22] "Failure to Act" would embrace *commitment to resilience*.[23] These relationships will be described in more detail below. The key assessment criteria when looking at each concept in the literature is the idea of foresight/hindsight. It is whether the concept can be invoked before the event, or are the associated "start rules" so non-specific that they can only be applied in hindsight?

It should also be noted that the literature does not provide a clean separation between the three issues and descriptions can become circular and so there is overlap between sections as theories merge.

FAILURE TO SEE

I start by looking at the concept of "Failure to See" the signals. Under this heading I look at nine subject areas. These are (1) *mindfulness*, (2) the inconceivable, (3) barriers to seeing, (4) denial, (5) context, (6) categorisation of signals, (7) the learning of lessons, (8) data sources and communication, and (9) recognising themselves as an "error-inducing" organisation.

Within *mindfulness*, Weick and Sutcliffe talk of "preoccupation with failure" and "sensitivity to operations". Under "preoccupation with failure"[24] they advocate the framing of organisational activity within a pessimistic (negative) mindset: that is, that every lapse or near miss should be perceived as a forerunner to impending disaster. The organisation should encourage the reporting of errors and that "weak signals of failure required a stronger response". The difficult operational or strategic question then becomes, "Which signals can be safely ignored?" Sensitivity to operations reminds organisations to stay "attentive to the front line, where the real work gets done".[25] While the temptation for any board is, in line with a well-used business mantra, "to stay focused on the core business",[26] Jaques provides an example of why this focus may lead to a failure to see warning signs. He cites the case of the "Dow Corning breast implant controversy … (where) a non-core market which represented a miniscule element of the company's total sales … (drove) a $5 billion dollar corporation into voluntary bankruptcy".[27] The question then becomes, where should top executives be looking for signals of potential failure? The answer "everywhere" may be sound in theory but is impractical. In practice executives need to be clear about their rules for inclusion and exclusion and the risk associated with their delineation.

The debate about the validity of considering the inconceivable would seem to lead directly back to the debate between Perrow's *normal accidents* and those who support the concept of the *high reliability organisation*. While the advocates for each seem to see these as alternatives, in my reading of this body of work I see them, on this subject at least, as being complementary. I read Perrow's *normal accidents* as a warning that as accidents are inevitable, one should think twice (or more) about the potential consequences before using high-risk technology.[a] Accidents can happen at any time (both an accident with a 1:100 calculated probability and a 1:10,000,000 calculated probability might still happen tomorrow, with the former being more likely to have happened within ten years). This does not however mean that there is no point in (1) trying to put off the inevitable or (2) preparing for such eventualities. In doing so, one must understand that, no matter how many precautions are taken, it is not possible to ensure that such an event will not occur. Therefore, the question is, if you use the technology, can you live with the potential consequences? Therefore, it can be concluded that the *normal accident* concept supports the contention that, even if current risk management practices label an event "highly improbable", which therefore may be taken as being inconceivable, where these events have the potential to produce significant damage or harm, they should not be subsequently side-lined or ignored, as seems to be the current practice.

But what of the *high reliability* school of thought? While Perrow focuses on outcomes, I read the *high reliability* theorists as concentrating on the processes necessary to ensure *high reliability*, that is, how to turn the calculated probability of 1:100 to one of 1:10,000,000 or greater. Experience, however, shows that even when the calculated probability is very high, adverse events can still happen. For example, Perrow reports that a specific event of a DC10 aircraft had a calculated probability of less than one in a billion, yet the problem occurred four times in four years.[28] The Haddon-Cave report acknowledged that the Royal Air Force's Nimrod aircraft had flown for 400,000 hours "with *only* four accidents recorded resulting in the loss of an aircraft"[29] (emphasis added). With the eight barriers to failure that had been designed into the drilling operation on BP's Deepwater Horizon rig in the Gulf of Mexico, the blow out that occurred in April 2010 may well have appeared to them to be inconceivable. While it might be argued that these were not *high reliability organisations*, Le Porte does not talk of *high reliability organisations* being error-free.[30] Instead he talks of "examining the conditions which seem substantially to reduce the incidence of regular accidents". He goes on to say, "We accept ... that systems cannot be designed and operated in ways that can guarantee the avoidance of any failures ... it is folly to suppose ... that one can expect to design systems and operate them in failure-free modes for extended periods."[31] Karlene Roberts points out that *high reliability* can be fragile within an organisation: "We should not suppose that because an organization or an industry is highly reliable at time one it will be highly reliable at time two. Reliability enhancement requires constant attention, is expensive, and is very fragile."[32] Therefore, neither the

---

a   In a private email of 1 November, 2010, Professor Perrow kindly confirmed that this reading correctly represented his views.

normal accident concept nor *high reliability* literature supports the notion that occurrences perceived as being inconceivable, can or should be ignored. This now raises the question as to whether that which is "inconceivable" may contribute to *failure of foresight*.

Weick and Sutcliffe recommend a *reluctance to simplify* as part of *mindfulness* because, for organisations, "the world they face is complex, unstable, unknowable and unpredictable".[33] Quoting an editorial in the New Yorker, Paul Slovic described "fail-safe systems failing" as the "unforeseeable … the whispering omen of a hovering future".[34] Standard risk management procedures use heat maps or matrices to help evaluate probability and consequence. The logic goes that those with the greatest probability and the highest consequences are given priority. Closely linked is the construct of "acceptable risk".[35] There is, however, limited debate about how to integrate the concept of acceptability and that of conceivability, leaving the practitioners to find their own solutions,[b] this is more easily judged in hindsight than it is calculated in foresight. I argued that the use of risk indicators should be focused on envisaging the "inconceivable", including the necessity to be ready for the inconceivable at the organisational level,[36] at the operational level,[37] and at the individual level[38] as the inconceivable can and does still occur. The question for the executive is therefore, "Of those issues that we have labelled so improbable as to be 'inconceivable', which still have such potentially serious consequences (the unacceptable) that we must stay mindful of them?"

The barriers to recognising what one sees is a fundamental issue in respect of *failure of foresight*. These barriers might be created within the individual or the organisation. An individual's perception of risk also provides reasons why signals may be missed. There are many texts that investigate risk perception[39] and so the argument will not be repeated here. Three aspects are, however, highlighted here: personal association, timeframe and tangibility. That which affects a person directly is seen to be privileged over that which affects others, the short term is privileged over the long term and the tangible privileged over the intangible. John Adams[40] provides a taxonomy which groups risks as ranging from the tangible, through those visible through science, to the virtual; James Reason[41] categorises errors as ranging from behavioural and the contextual to the conceptual. Both of these categorisations can be seen to range from the tangible to the abstract (the more ambiguous). Within organisations, these barriers are both cultural and managerial. Vaughan points out that, "Aspects of organisational

---

b   For example, when Radell in Smith and Elliot (2006:296) talks of "keeping storming within the boundaries of acceptable risk".

life … created a way of seeing that was simultaneously a way of not seeing hazards."[42] (The idea that "seeing is a way of not seeing" has already been introduced). Woods states, "This pattern of seeing the details but being unable to recognise the big picture is commonplace in accidents."[43] Slovic asserts "that people, acting within social organisations, downplay certain risks and emphasise others as a means of maintaining the viability of the organisation".[44] Smith puts the point slightly differently when he talks of "experience as an inhibitor";[45] Klein agrees that, "Experience can sometimes interfere with problem detection."[46] The final example I use is Pidgeon who explains how cultures may desensitise our perceptions and thus create "blind-spots".[47] Managerial blind-spots are created by phenomena such as the *fallacy of complete reporting*[48] and *structural secrecy.*[49] Anomalous events, warning signals and other issues that fall outside the normal cultural lens are readily neglected. While a number of mechanisms may create a cultural blindness to risk, the important issue is that this blindness exists. Therefore, executive teams need to make themselves aware of the personal and organisational filters that might inhibit their seeing warnings available to them.

Linked to the previous issues is one of denial. This subject has been raised by many of those writing in the context of *failure of foresight*. The symptoms of denial can be seen in what has been called *myth management* and *fantasy documents*. Vaughan[50] uses the term *myth management* to describe obtaining "legitimacy (and thus resources) by projecting and living up to a cultural image". These myths can be perpetuated by what Clarke and Perrow called *fantasy documents*.[51] These are plans that "are neither wholly believed nor disbelieved…(they) cover extremely improbable events. They are tested against reality only rarely…(they) are likely to draw from a quite unrealistic view or model of organisations". For those engaged in risk discourse, these phenomena should alert them to the potential gap between how the executives view their organisations and what really exists. Executives should therefore be concerned to ensure that *fantasies* do not enter into their systems. They therefore need to assess whether their plans and policies, which are a product of their bureaucratic process, are likely to withstand "an abrupt and *brutal audit*"[52] which would become very clear in hindsight.

Context is an important consideration for *failure of foresight*. The context adds complexity. Lagadec suggests that, "Geographic, cognitive, historical, political, cultural and symbolic factors all shape events."[53] Reason explains how apparently simple problems have a multiplicity of alternatives.[54] His example is of a bolt with eight nuts labelled "A" to "H"; Reason points out that there is one way to assemble them correctly and over 40,000 ways (factor 8) to get it wrong.

This points to the fact that while performance indicators (such as "profit") may be able to be relatively static, the significant unwanted occurrence may, in this example, be one of 40,000 issues; when NASA lost the Shuttle Columbia, it was not that they were unaware of the problem with the heat resistant tiles but that it was but one of 4,222 issues at that time classified as critical.[55] For foresight, the relevance is that it is an issue of assessing the workload of any part of any system. For hindsight, this raises questions of the validity of any comments about managerial competence if the factor or workload is not considered. With so many potential problems arising from so many potential sources, executives cannot be expected to cover them all. They can, however, expect to be questioned on why they decided what they did. Therefore, executives need to establish what risks are "acceptable" to them and why, and then test their reasoning to ensure that it is robust and not a "fantasy".

Warning signals may come in many different forms and be of different strengths. A number of writers have developed labels for signals of risk. The terms are described in Table 2.2. I would draw your attention here to the term *weak signal* the missing of which is often presented as the reason for *the unwanted* happening; readers may like to note that *weak signals* are but one type of signal that may mislead or confuse decision makers. Executives therefore need to be aware of the various forms if they are to be able to identify each as they appear. These categories can be used as part of the foresight process. As part of any risk discourse, executives need to be aware of the incoming data and need to be able to assess it against signal types in order to understand its relevance (both positive and negative) and be able to justify its inclusion or exclusion from the debate.

Table 2.2   Signal Types

Type of Signal	Description of Signal	Source
Strong Signal	Irrefutable evidence able to alter an organisational paradigm. "Signal, too strong to explain away, refute, or deny." "A signal that ... overturned the scientific paradigm."	Vaughan, 1996:364, 379
Routine Signals	"An anomaly that occurs in a predictable manner." "These that occur frequently ... even when acknowledged to be inherently serious, loses some of its seriousness as similar events occur in sequence and methods of assessing and responding to them stabilize."	Vaughan, 1996:246 Vaughan, 1997:87
Loss of Salience	Warning signs lose their potency: As a result of research which "Normalises Deviance." These facts were known in the company, and by hindsight they are easy to understand as indicators that process safety was seriously at risk. Nevertheless, this was not leading to appropriate action. Clearly the meaning of these events was not fully understood.	Vaughan, 1996:244, 397 Zwetsloot, 2009:498

Table 2.2   Continued

Type of Signal	Description of Signal	Source
Weak Signals	"Warning signals very close to the normal background noise." "Suspected (but un-proven) correlation", "information is informal and/ or ambiguous." One that was unclear, or one that, after analysis, seemed such an improbable event that working engineers believed there was little probability of it recurring.	Lagadec, 1993:47 Vaughan, 1996:245, 262, 355 Vaughan, 1997:87
Mixed Signals	"Signals of potential danger were followed by signals that all was well, reinforcing the belief in acceptable risk."	Vaughan, 1996:245–263
Messy Signals	"Ambiguity of information. Ambiguity means that the same information has multiple (and sometimes conflicting) meanings. Environments and situations that are unpredictable and rapidly changing provide unclear, messy signals, so that people can draw different yet equally plausible conclusions from observing the same 'objective' data."	Sutcliffe, 2005:421
Decoy Signals	The investigation revealed that the entire industry's attention was drawn towards mining safety and that tip safety was hardly on the agenda. Mining safety worked as a "decoy problem", obscuring the more serious problems looming in the background.[56] "Decoy problems" that draw attention away from more serious problems elsewhere.	Rijpma, 1997:21 Turner and Pigeon, 1997:42
Missing Signals	Where organisations' barriers prevent salient information being added to the conversation.	Vaughan, 1996:349, 356,358,359
Silent Evidence	"People in other locations had potentially useful information and opinions that they did not enter into the conversation." "Organisations work very hard at silencing people."	Vaughan, 1997:93 Kerfoot, 2003:294
Misinterpreted Signals	Mean one thing; understood to mean the reverse.	Vaughan, 1996:315
True but Useless Information	Often a lack of information drives those affected to fill the void ... with inexact or irrelevant data seized at random. Where data are collected because they are available, not because they are relevant.	Lagadec, 1993:81 Grint, 2010

Having raised earlier the construct of *distancing through differencing* (where individuals fail to see the similarities between their own position and that experienced by others and therefore fail to see the lessons to be learnt), this phenomenon is now linked to benchmarking (learning from the experience of others). The lessons may come from external organisations, from near misses or from accidents. In addition, there are the *forgotten lessons*; these can be seen to be closely related to signals that have *lost saliency*. The mechanism might be such factors as *drift* which is discussed later. Other mechanisms that might cause lessons to be missed are *management distancing* and *inattentional blindness*. James Reason explains *management distancing*.[57] He says, "The human controllers of … systems have become remote from the processes they manipulate and, in many cases, from the hazards that potentially endanger their operations. Both this distancing effect and the rarity of bad events make it very easy to not be afraid, as evident at the Chernobyl nuclear power station." The term *inattentional blindness*[58] describes the visual perception of unexpected objects. Mack and Rock concluded that, where an occurrence is unexpected, observers fail to notice it even when the occurrence is fully visible. This is because the observer's attention is already engaged on other aspects of what is in front of them. (The link to the phenomenon of *decoy signals* may be noted.) The question for the executive is therefore whether they are seeing all the lessons that are available to them and whether they understand, and therefore take into account, factors that might be working against them in this regard.

The theme of this section has been the examination of data sources and communication. This is not a simple problem. For example:

> The facts in this case "were known in the company, and by hindsight they are easy to understand as indicators that process safety was seriously at risk. Nevertheless, this was not leading to appropriate action. Clearly the meaning of these events was not fully understood by many company people, especially the higher managers who have the primary responsibility for safety."[59]

Communications are often cited as being a general issue but the question becomes whether one can judge, at the time, whether what your organisation is doing is good enough. There are many potential causes of *failure of communications*. The issue might be that the executives think they know more than they do know (Westrum's fallacies of *centrality* and *incomplete reporting*),[60] that staff are reluctant to "speak truth unto power" (the *unrocked boat*[61] or *taboo data*),[62] or that there are flaws in reporting systems (whether these are internal issues or failures with external auditing or regulatory bodies). The concern is that these failures can only be judged in hindsight. The constant question for an executive is therefore whether the right information is getting to the right people within the right timeframe and how they would know if it was not before it was too late.

Throughout his book on *normal accidents*, Perrow points to factors that may indicate an "error-inducing organisation"; the relevant characteristics are set out in Table 2.3. Erik Hollnagel sees five classic patterns[63] as the basis for his analysis. These are: (1) a drift towards failure as defences are eroded in the face of *production pressure*, (2) taking past success as reason to be confident, (3) fragmented problem solving clouds the big picture, (4) not revising assessments as new evidence accumulates, and (5) breakdowns at organisational boundaries. Woods, in the case of NASA, cites, "Insufficient time to reflect on unintended consequences of day-to-day decisions, insufficient time and workforce available to provide the levels of checks and balances normally found, breakdowns in inter-group communications, too much emphasis on cost and schedule reduction."[64] While others may add to this list, together these authors provide a rich picture of factors, which those taking part in risk discourse may use in order to generate foresight about their organisation.

Table 2.3   Error-inducing Organisations

Page	Factor
p.176	authoritarian organisational structure (centralisation of power)
p.367	group and power interests
p.370	latency period may be longer than any decision-maker's career
p.176 and p.230	ambiguous cognitive model; that enables an inaccurate mental model to be created
p.176	dysfunctional systems/processes
p.246–247	"forced errors" – ("do wrong or be sacked")
p.187	("prescribed") behaviour is hard to enforce
p.189	a system that does not breed cooperation
p.176	economic pressure to perform (production pressure)
p.175	failure appears to be continuous, but recovery is possible
p.176	complex equipment, barely maintained
p.192	blame transfer outwards from centre

Note: Page references refer to Perrow, *Normal Accidents* (1999).

The question for those conducting risk discourse is whether they have clear evidence that they do not fall into this category of organisation.

In summary, I have explored nine groups of issues that may contribute to "Failure to See" warning signs. Each of these raises questions for an executive who wishes to be alert to such warnings in order to forestall a *failure of foresight*. The *risk governance* considerations that emerge from the literature pertinent to "Failure to See" are summarised in Table 2.4.

Table 2.4   Forestalling Failure to See

1.	To be clear about their rules for inclusion and exclusion of subject areas and the risk(s) associated with their delineation.
2.	Awareness of those issues that are labelled so improbable as to be "inconceivable", which still have such potentially serious consequences (the unacceptable) that we must stay mindful of them.
3.	To make themselves aware of the personal and organisational filters that might inhibit their seeing warnings available to them.
4.	To assess whether their plans and policies, which are a product of their bureaucratic process, are likely to withstand "an abrupt and *brutal audit*".
5.	To establish what risks are "acceptable" to them and why, and then test their reasoning to ensure that it is robust and not a "fantasy".
6.	To be aware of the incoming data and need to be able to assess it against signal types in order to understand its relevance (either positive or negative) and be able to justify its inclusion or exclusion from the debate.
7.	To question whether they are seeing all the lessons that are available to them and whether they understand, and therefore take into account, factors that might be working against them in this regard.
8.	To question whether the right information is getting to the right people within the right timeframe and how they would know if it was not before it was too late.
9.	To question whether there is clear evidence that they do not fall into the category of an "error-inducing" organisation.

FAILURE TO APPRECIATE

In this next section I now examine why signals that have been seen may fail to be appreciated as being significant. Under this heading I look at six issues. These are (1) *mindfulness*, (2) the messenger, (3) synthesis, (4) interpretation of data, (5) drift, and (6) situational comprehension.

Within *mindfulness*, Weick and Sutcliffe talk of *reluctance to simplify* and *deference to expertise*; these may be seen to contribute to a "Failure to Appreciate". Under *reluctance to simplify* Weick and Sutcliffe describe how "people simplify in order to stay focused on a handful of key issues and key indicators" and how, in their view, *high reliability organisations* need to "take deliberate steps to create more complete and nuanced pictures of what they face of ... the complex ... and the unpredictable".[65] The perils that emerge are also encapsulated within the construct of "taming wicked/messy issues".[66] Weick and Sutcliffe however acknowledge that "when you organise, you simplify". There is a large body of work which acknowledges that the use of heuristics is necessary simply in order to act in a timely manner. This, coupled with Ockham's razor and Miller's "Magical Number 7", militates against any espoused *reluctance to simplify*.

The question therefore becomes one of how to create the appropriate balance; to simplify the issue enough to be able to conceptualise it but not too much so you fail to appreciate its significance. The question for the executive is therefore to judge whether they have enough relevant detail to enable them to appreciate the complexity of the mechanisms acting at the time.

Under *deference to expertise,* Weick and Sutcliffe talk of how, "Rigid hierarchies have their own special vulnerability to error".[67] The errors include both a failure to recognise a problem and a Failure to Act appropriately. Vaughan provides the phrase *seat of understanding*[68] which I have defined (based on work by Klein)[69] to mean having the training, knowledge, experience and current data required to make the appropriate judgements. Structure, culture, power and politics have all been found to militate against judgements and decisions falling to those most appropriate. This issue is debated within the *high reliability organisation* area as the balance between centralisation and decentralisation. The debate involves factors such as where power and authority lies, where does expertise and detailed knowledge lie, the timeliness, completeness and understanding of new data. These rational factors compete with more irrational ones such as hierarchy, need for control, ego and hubris. The question for those conducting risk discourse is therefore how to judge the most appropriate level within their organisations for decisions to fall, given the need for the appropriate *seat of understanding,* resource power and need to act in a timely manner.

In the appreciation of a signal, the messenger may be as important as the message. This is especially relevant when discussing what Adams labelled as *virtual risks*; here one is reliant on the expertise and understanding of others. These messengers might fall into three categories: "heroes", "Cassandras" and those who "cry wolf". Heroes are those whose warnings are heeded and *the unwanted* is prevented, Cassandras are those who provide valid warning but are ignored and those who cry wolf are those who provide false warnings (heeded or unheeded). While in hindsight it becomes very clear into which category each warning falls, in foresight it is not so clear. For risk discourse the question therefore becomes whether the messenger (source of any data) is having an effect on how the data is viewed and, if so, whether this can be judged to be "rational" and therefore "valid".

After the data has been gathered and recognised as being important then there is a need to synthesise it to ascertain its full value. As important as this process is, there is little literature debating the relative merits of the various forms of synthesis available. Most of the academic literature that relates to risk management and synthesis is looking at the research methodology used in academic papers. Those that are addressing the synthesis of risk data tend to favour mathematically based solutions. There is little work addressing the collation and synthesis of ideas necessary in the formative stages of risk discourse. Karl Weick describes *failure of imagination*[70] and notes from the 9/11 Commission Report that, "Imagination is not a gift usually associated with bureaucracies."[71] While this could have been included under the heading of barriers, it is included here because, in order to counteract failures of imagination, Weick, based on the concept of *mindfulness*, suggests the replacement of "deductive thinking with abductive thinking, shifting a culture of analysis towards a culture of imagination ... (a) focus on sense-making rather than decision making".[72] The danger at the other end of this dimension is that individuals use existing rules or regulations as an excuse for poor analysis or thinking.[73] The question for risk discourse is to discuss what method of analysis would be most appropriate to the problem at hand and whether a formal system of analysis may "reduce the effect of personal bias".[74]

Interpretation of the signals (of potential dangers) is subject to errors shaped by a still wider system that includes history, competition, scarcity, bureaucratic procedures, power, rules and norms, hierarchy, culture and patterns of information.[75] Linked to Vaughan's summation of factors that shape interpretation are Perrow's categorisation of victims into four groups[76] and the clear difference in viewing perspective of the insider versus outsiders.[77] These provide an initial choice of perspectives from which to start discussions of risk. Each may provide a separate starting point for the discourse thus providing the *requisite variety*[c] suggested necessary for a richer analysis. Also linked to the debate on interpretation of signals are factors such as whether a scientific or intuitive approach is used,[78] hubris,[79] the *problem of induction*[80] and "fallacy of centrality".[81] The question for those involved in risk discourse is to discuss which factors might be acted on and affect the perceptions that contribute to how they appreciate the signals available to them.

Central to Turner's ideas of disaster development is the construct of a gap, "Discrepancy between the way the world is thought to operate and the way it really is rarely developed instantaneously."[82] This is the gap that enables the "incubation" of *the unwanted*, the period where discrepancies "accumulate unnoticed". "The phenomena of drift ... is a common theme in organisational literature".[83] Farjoun talks of "safety drift"[84] while Weick and Sutcliffe[85] talk of a "drift into automatic processes" as organisations become mindless. Snook's

---

c   Nævestad traces the "law of requisite variety" back to Ashby (1956) where he suggests that "only variety can control variety".

construct of *practical drift* is a more detailed description. *Practical drift* is "the slow, steady uncoupling of local practice from written procedures" such as in the case where two US air force fighters shot down two US Army helicopters over northern Iraq in 1994 killing 26 peacekeepers. *Practical drift* provides a mechanism by which gaps occur; this is seen to be a particular issue where there is "local adaptation (that) can lead to global disconnects".[86] In the context of this chapter, it would seem potentially more likely where management has moved from the expert to the investigator, as described above. Related to *practical drift* is Vaughan's construct of the *normalisation of deviance*. This theory describes a mechanism where "signals of potential danger (are) normalised"[87] or become regarded as being normal, that is, to lose their salience. Vaughan describes sophisticated and nuanced mechanisms that include three factors: *organisational culture, culture of production* and *structural secrecy*. Each of these factors is described in its own chapter. Snook sees the difference between *practical drift* and *normalisation of deviance* as being that the latter has to do with how the environment affects policy and the former has to do with coordination.[88] Snook sees the flip side of *practical drift* as being *practical sailing* which can be summarised as the successful *mutual adjustment* of autonomous bodies; where local adjustment within a global framework is successful rather than a failure as it is more often than not (I cover this later in the book). The question for those involved in risk discourse is how to recognise each form of drift as it occurs. While in hindsight this may be clear, this is a different matter in foresight, even when those involved know what to look for.

Seat of understanding is linked to "situational comprehension". Whereas *seat of understanding* is about the person's endogenous disposition, situational comprehension is about the exogenous factors that play on their ability to comprehend what is happening around them. For the purpose of this chapter, situational comprehension has been divided into two of its aspects; the first is the situation itself and the second is how those involved receive the relevant data. The situation itself may be one that is stable, a well tried and tested system which is thought to be well understood. At the other end of the perspective is the new or novel situation. Here the literature has made us aware of two phenomena of interest. They are the *liability of newness* and *unruly technology*. Vaughan extends the idea of *liability of newness* from its original context but reminds us that the *liability of newness* includes the necessity of generating and learning new roles; it has costs in time, worry, conflict and inefficiency; there is an absence of standard routines[89] and that they therefore require interpretive flexibility in the absence of appropriate guidelines; that unexpected glitches are commonplace and need debugging through use; that there are likely to be extensive system-wide problems with technological components; and, that practical rules, based on experience, supplement and take precedence over technical decision making and formal universal rules.[90] There is therefore a high degree of reliance on human interaction with the system that might fail. Mechanisms of failure have been described by Rochlin and Weick. Rochlin describes the concept of "having the bubble".[91] The bubble is where a person who has the appropriate *seat of understanding* has a temporary comprehension of a complex and dynamic situation. The system expects the person to become fatigued or have lapses and at that moment they have to call "lost the bubble" and a deputy, who has been shadowing the situation, steps in. This process demonstrated to Rochlin a clear understanding of the strengths and weaknesses of human comprehension in such circumstances. Closely aligned to the bubble is the phenomenon of *cosmological episodes*. Weick describes a *cosmological episode* as occurring "when people suddenly and deeply feel that the universe is no longer a rational, orderly system. What makes such an episode so shattering is the sense of what is occurring and the means to rebuild that sense collapse together".[92] While Stein[93] contrasts the Three Mile Island incident with Apollo 13's safe return to earth in order to understand how to prevent such a collapse of comprehension, there needs to be questions for those involved in risk discourse about how well they understand their system, who will have to handle potential crises and whether they are mentally equipped to do so.

In summary, we have explored six areas that may contribute to a "Failure to Appreciate" warning signs. The considerations for *failure of foresight* that emerge from the literature pertinent to "Failure to Appreciate" are summarised in Table 2.5 which can now be added to the issues pertinent to "Failure to See".

Table 2.5   Forestalling Failure to Appreciate

10.	The question for the executive is therefore to judge whether they have enough relevant detail to enable them to appreciate the complexity of the mechanisms acting at the time.
11.	To judge the most appropriate level within their organisation for decisions to fall, given the need for the appropriate *seat of understanding*, resource power and the need to act in a timely manner.
12.	To question whether the messenger (source of any data) is having an effect on how the data is viewed and, if so, whether this can be judged to be "rational" and therefore "valid".
13.	To discuss what method of analysis would be most appropriate to the problem at hand and whether a formal system of analysis may help to reduce the effect of personal bias.
14.	To discuss which factors might be acting on and affecting the perceptions that contribute to how they appreciate the signals available to them.
15.	How to recognise "drift" as it occurs.
16.	To question how well they understand their system, who will have to handle potential crises and whether they are mentally equipped to do so.

FAILURE TO ACT

Finally, after having looked at Failure to See and Failure to Appreciate, now we look at reasons for failing to act appropriately. Under this heading we look at a further eight issues. These are (1) *commitment to resilience*, (2) alternative options, (3) rule-based or knowledge-based action, (4) the mechanisms of cohesion, (5) *unresponsive bystander*, (6) group dynamics, (7) *amoral calculation*, and (8) failures of *organisational learning.*

Weick and Sutcliffe highlight the need for *commitment to resilience*. Weick and Sutcliffe make clear what they mean: they say, "To be resilient is to be mindful about errors that have already occurred and to correct them before they worsen and cause more harm."[94] Here we see the need to act (appropriately). They also say:

> *The ability to cope with the unexpected requires a different mind-set than to anticipate its occurrence. The mind-set for anticipation is one that favours precise identification of possible difficulties so that specific remedies can be designed or recalled. A commitment to resilience is quite different.*

This is consistent with Wildavsky's definitions. He says, "Anticipation is a mode of control by a central mind: efforts are made to predict and prevent potential dangers before damage is done"; whereas, "Resilience is the capacity to cope with unanticipated dangers after they have become manifest, learning to bounce back."[95] This may be restated as anticipation results in a specific "plan B" whereas resilience requires capacity (buffer/unused capability) with which to respond. In other disciplines this differentiation is not used. This usage of the terms can be contrasted with Schulman where he describes *anticipation* as "an approach that equates reliability to invariance" and *resilience* as the capability of "responding to, rather than trying to weed out, the unexpected would be the ultimate safeguard of stable performance".[96] Hollnagel says, "Resilience is therefore the ability to create foresight – to anticipate the changing shape of risk, before failure and harm occurs".[97] To them, anticipation is part of resilience. Therefore as different disciplines define these terms in different ways, two practical questions arise. The first is whether those involved in the risk discourse are clear about how they use the terms, and the second is whether they are clear about the way in which they plan to act (have a plan B or buffer capacity) as they discuss their options.

The second issue is the discussion of options. As part of the discussion of any series of options, it is usual to discuss the advantages and disadvantages of each. Where these options are discussed, this is mostly limited to process rather than discussions of unwanted outcomes or the unintended consequences associated with each option. This may lead to inappropriate action being taken. There is no differentiation between the disadvantages when implementing an option and the potential jeopardy associated with an option. There may therefore be an advantage in more clearly differentiating between process and outcome when considering what action should be taken. Weick warns, in the context of enactment, of the relationship between action, inaction, understanding, misunderstanding, appropriate and inappropriate action.[98] This part of the discourse may be aided by consideration of an appropriate quadrant analysis tool. Based on the basic "advantages" and "disadvantages", Vaughan's construct of "Bright" and "Dark sides",[99] the *high reliability organisation/normal accident* differentiation between process and outcome, a revised grid is offered in Table 2.6. Failure to appreciate the differences may lead to a Failure to Act appropriately.

Table 2.6   Options Quadrant Analysis

	Processes	Outcome
"Bright side"	Advantages	Benefits
"Dark side"	Disadvantages	Jeopardy

The question that therefore arises is whether those involved in the risk discourse are clear about the action required (process) and to what end (outcome), and the jeopardy associated with each.

Many commentators privilege a rule-based approach for action. Inquiry reports often recommend the tightening of rules and so do some academics.[d] Linked directly to this is the assumption often that if rules are broken, it is always inappropriate or wrong. Dekker points out that often "formal rules follow practice that had already evolved"[100] with all the induction issues that involves. Hirschhorn debates the practicality of *verbatim compliance*[101] in the context of nuclear power stations and concludes that management need to develop two classes of procedure. The first is "broad in scope and applied

---

d   See for example Hopkins (2008); Flavell-While (2009) reports a discussion on the practicality of
     a rule-based approach between Hopkins and Peter Webb.

to a wide range of circumstance" and strictly applied. The second is detailed and specific, employees are free to vary it "as long as they fulfil its intention". This links to Schulman's[102] discussion of the same subject. He argues that while much of the previous organisational theory would mean that "it is reasonable to expect a high degree of rigidity and formal rules", he advocates caution in the use of such an approach. Reason[103] debates Rouse's model which included when the use of rules may be appropriate, and added to the discussion can be the phenomena of the *liability of newness* or *unruly technology*.[104] The debate on how rule-based and knowledge-based procedures might be intertwined within the organisation is too extensive to do it justice here and is worthy of a fuller synthesis in its own right. However, even though rules and regulations do provide a starting point for any debate on drift, the validity of rules should not be taken at face value. Therefore, any debate on actions based upon existing rules and regulations also needs to debate how the context or situation might have evolved since the rule was written, in what direction, and whether they need to catch up with practice or practice needs to be reined in by the rules. They therefore need to consider whether the rule has become time-expired, whether it is appropriate for the circumstance, whether the action required is clear and whether the direction is "absolute" or "guidance". For example, within the UK, the Highway Code may be issued as a source of guidance however it is advisable to comply with it! This needs to be done even before consideration of the expertise and competence of the rule writers. Those engaged in risk discourse need to be aware of the strengths and limitations of rule-based and knowledge-based approaches and be clear when each should be applied within their organisation.

Linked to this action is the issue of how to ensure that the most appropriate mechanism of cohesion/coordination is applied in the circumstances. Roberts[105] and Weick[106] are examples of authors who use the terminology of pooled, sequential and reciprocal interdependence based on work by Thompson.[107] Snook characterised these as coordination by standards, coordination by plans and *mutual adjustment*.[108] Linked closely to the mechanism of coordination is the use of rule-based or knowledge-based actions. While accident inquiries often recommend a tightening of rules (with little debate over their advantages and disadvantages), as stated above, there is a substantial body of literature that warns of some of the downsides of relying on rules to ensure safety and reliability. The question for those involved in risk discourse is therefore to debate the appropriate use of these five mechanisms (standards, plans, *mutual adjustment*, rules and experience) and how to enhance each and safeguard the organisation against the weakness of each.

The fifth issue has been referred to as the *unresponsive bystander*. Snook and Connor talk of *structurally induced inaction*[109] and refer to work by Latané and Darley;[110] Ghaffarzadegan refers to this phenomenon as *social shirking*.[111] Snook and Connor also refer to later work by Latané and Nidd which sets down the four conditions under which "bystanders" might intervene.[112] These are that they "notice the event", perceive it as requiring action, feel responsible for taking action (or not, such as when someone else is in charge, better qualified or has the time) and feel that they have the skills and resources necessary to be effective. Snook and Connor then relate this to decision making within an organisation. They assert that "three psychological processes tend to decrease the likelihood of intervention".[113] The first is the potential embarrassment of failure. The second is that individuals look to clues from those around them on how to act (what Ghaffarzadegan called *pluralistic ignorance*[114] – "when bystanders assume nothing is wrong because nobody else appears concerned") and the third is where responsibility is defused. *Bystander syndrome* came to public attention in the UK in early 2013 when people start to question how Jimmy Savile had avoided detection as a sex-attacker for nearly half a century.[e] The question that therefore arises is whether those involved in the risk discourse are conscious of the potential for inaction by themselves as individuals and of the group overall and what mechanisms they may put in place to guard against these issues.

Sixth, group dynamics have been clearly shown to have a role in causing a Failure to Act appropriately. The ones that I will cover here are *groupthink*, *folly* and *risky shift*. The first of these, *groupthink*, has received wide coverage. While the term was coined by William Whyte in *Fortune* magazine,[115] the first major studies are attributed to Janis in the 1970s. Over time eight symptoms have been identified and mitigation processes have been developed. In summary these symptoms are: an illusion of invulnerability, rationalising away warnings, an unquestioned belief in the morality of the group, stereotyping of adversaries, direct pressure to conform, self-censorship of "deviant" ideas, illusions of unanimity and self-appointed *mindguards*. While scholars still debate the exact nature of the phenomenon, there is sufficient evidence to suggest that decision-making groups need to be aware of *groupthink*'s insidious effects on effective decision making. Not so well known is the related phenomenon of *folly* as articulated by a historian, Barbara Tuchman.[116] Her criteria for *folly* are: (1) the action was perceived as counter-productive in its own time, not requiring hindsight, (2)

---

e   http://www.newstatesman.com/broadcast/2013/01/savile-denialism-and-grooming-nation-delusion. Access 20 January 2013.

feasible alternatives were available, (3) the fallacy should be that of a group, persisting over generations of leaders, (4) the role of "Wooden-Headedness" (a source of self-deception), and (5) the role played by *Cognitive Dissonance*.[117] Enzer provides a clearly related example of *folly* from the development of US energy policy in the 1970s; he states, "Today's (written in 1980) energy situation is the result of a *failure of foresight*, not because current conditions could not be anticipated, but because the United States did not act ... At the time, many people not only predicted today's energy situation, but also foresaw that energy conditions would continue to deteriorate."[118] The final issue is *risky shift* which is where, 'The result of group polarization is a failure to take into account the true risk of a course of action followed by a shift towards riskier decision making."[119] *Groupthink*, *folly* and *risky shift* have all been identified as risk factors within the decision-making process of groups. Where there is potential for decisions to have disastrous consequences, those involved in risk discourse should debate whether their group is taking any steps to guard against the threats created by these group dynamics.

Seventh is the concept of *amoral calculation* in the face of *production pressures*. Vaughan describes *amoral calculation* as the "rational calculation of cost and opportunities"[120] which values "economic success more highly than the well-being of workers, consumers or the general public". In the case of the shuttle Challenger, as in many other cases, the violation of rules[121] is seen to be a symptom. This phenomenon has also been referred to as "good people doing dirty work". Research suggests "that culture, structure, and other organisational factors, in combination, may create a worldview that constrains people from acknowledging their work as 'dirty' ... Plus, rather than contemplating or devising a deviant strategy for achieving the organisational goals and then invoking techniques of neutralising in order to proceed with it or rationalising it afterwards, they never see it as deviant in the first place".[122] Snook suggests however that "individual responsibility is not ignored"[123] and that the issues should be framed more on the lines of "good people struggling to make sense" rather than as "bad ones making good decisions". Perrow uses the term *Executive Failure*[124] where they "knowingly take risks in violation of regulatory law"[125] in order to maximise profit. "This entailed a risk ... that, (in the circumstance he describes) for about a decade ... paid off." Here we see the interaction between *production pressure*, consequences over time and their effects on different stakeholder constituencies. The current risk management procedures which allow exclusions on the grounds of improbability or on cost–benefit may be used as a rational justification for such *amoral calculations*; the Ford Pinto case provides such an example. In this case the company "decided not to buffer the fuel tank" [126] as "the costs of compensation for burn victims were 'outweighed' by the costs of improvements to the vehicle".[127] These cases however need to be separate from what Kakabadse describes as the "dark side of leadership"[128] which are enacted when people with socio/psychopathic traits take control of organisations. This becomes a wider issue of governance rather than being an issue of *failure of foresight*. The question therefore becomes whether those involved in risk discourse are clear that the criteria they use for making decisions may not be viewed by others, at some later stage, to be amoral.

Finally, I return to the issue of *organisational learning*. A common question in the literature is about why organisations fail to learn from the past; why, when the potential for disaster is clear, the appropriate action was not taken. Smith and Elliot state that, "There is a growing body of evidence that organizations are resistant to learning from crisis"[129] and emphasise that *organisational learning* is not only about understanding of causes and mechanisms but also the requirement for the "full cultural adjustment"[130] necessary to prevent the next unwanted event. As stated in the introduction to this chapter, the issue with *organisational learning* is therefore not only the "why" something occurs but a full understanding of the "how" to prevent it. This is therefore a much more demanding standard than is presented by the need to understand "why" something has occurred (as difficult as this question in itself might be to answer). Therefore, the questions for those conducting the risk discourse are not only what might occur (including the inconceivable) but also (1) what might cause it, (2) how might it be prevented, (3) is the necessary process in place, (4) are our people effectively trained, (5) do they have the necessary resources, (6) will they recognise the problem should it arise, (7) will they see the right action to take, (8) will they implement the necessary action appropriately, and (9) will we get the same answers if we ask these questions tomorrow?

In summary, I have explored eight areas that may contribute to a "Failure to Act (appropriately)" on warning signs. The considerations for *failure of foresight* that emerge from the literature pertinent to "Failure to Act" are summarised in Table 2.7 now providing those tasked with *risk governance* a total of 24 themes for their consideration.

Table 2.7   Forestalling Failure to Act

17.	Define the group's understanding of the terms "anticipation" and "resilience". Define whether the action needed is to create a "plan B" or to generate buffer capacity.
18.	Is the action required about process or outcome and is the jeopardy associated with each of them clear?
19.	To be aware of the strengths and limitations of rule-based and knowledge-based approaches and be clear when each should be applied within their organisation.
20.	To debate the appropriate use of the five mechanisms of action and coordination (standards, plans, *mutual adjustment*, rules and experience) and how to enhance each and safeguard the organisation against the weakness of each.
21.	To be aware of the factors affecting the potential for inaction by themselves as individuals and of the group overall and what mechanisms they may put in place to guard against this issue.
22.	To debate whether their group is taking any steps to guard against the threats created by group dynamics.
23.	To debate whether the criteria being used for making decisions may not be viewed by others, at some later stage, to be amoral.
24.	What might occur (including the inconceivable): (1) what might cause it, (2) how might we prevent it, (3) is the necessary process in place, (4) are our people effectively trained, (5) do they have the necessary resources, (6) will they recognise the problem should it arise, (7) will they see the right action to take, (8) will they implement the necessary action appropriately, and (9) will we get the same answers if we ask these questions tomorrow?

Discussion

So far in this chapter, I have provided an indication of the amount of research that is relevant to the issue of *failure of foresight* and have attempted to construct it as a *coherent whole*. The availability and accessibility of this research to practitioners, in its original form, is questionable. There are many competing claims, with apparent overlaps and contradictions. Research is still required to collate the available work, to contrast the competing claims and to validate their utility if our understanding of what can go wrong is to be used more effectively to forestall failures of foresight. However, those passing judgement should be aware of the general thrust of the debate, rather than relying on a particular vignette, if their recommendations are to provide real value to society.

It is also clear from the literature described above that top executives with responsibilities for *risk governance* are "distanced" from the frontline activity and that relevant data is filtered as the information is passed to them and as their directions are passed out to their organisation. Adams provides a useful categorisation in this context. Adams describes three levels of data that affect the perception of, in his case, risk as (1) perceived directly, (2) perceived through science (where there is a direct link between the measurement and the phenomenon), and (3) *virtual risks* (where proxies are measured and judgements then have to be made about the state of the phenomenon of interest).[131] The mechanisms of upward filtering have been discussed and given such labels as *structural secrecy* and *operational secrecy*; this is labelled *reporting cascade*. However, as Vaughan[132] and Grint[133] have pointed out, top executives examine issues by exception and look at principles; the label *organisation filter* represents where the executive's span of responsibility has become such that the executive moves from being, in Grint's words, "expert to investigator". At this point the executive creates their own conceptualisation, which may or may not be accurate, based on the information they receive and their existing understanding of the mechanisms operating within their organisation that produce the outcomes required (the "envisaged end state"). The executive then issues directions, which are translated into operational activity and cascaded through the organisation in order to revise the operational routine required. We need to examine the implications this has for the mechanism by which their general directions are transformed into detailed action at lower levels. A related question is whether, in their conceptualisation of issues, top executives have a detailed vision of how they expect their direction to avoid failures and be interpreted and translated into action at the lower levels of their organisation, or how they envisage the weaknesses in this process and identify the potential for gaps to occur within which disasters have space to incubate. This potential mechanism of failure (communications barriers) deserves more detailed research and may be part of the answer to why organisations fail to learn. The issues are summarised in Figure 2.1.

A key issue arises out of the constructive tension between theory and practice, between academia and practitioners. This has been highlighted by Elliot where he states that "crisis management (theory) into practice is very difficult".[134] He recognises that "the priority of much research (is) dealing with complex constructs at a more theoretical level", that "much that is written on practice is based upon flimsy, possibly anecdotal evidence"[135] and therefore that research on practice should now be exercised with the same rigour as the research into theory. This points to the privileging within academia of the "why" question[136] whereas practice is more concerned with "how"; the assumption of some academics who appear to have an expectation is that because the "why" can be articulated, the "how" will naturally follow. Where accident prevention does not follow, managers are labelled "sloppy" or some other such adjective and accused of *failure of foresight*. When Elliot joins with Smith in the final chapter of their book, they acknowledge the importance of theory and

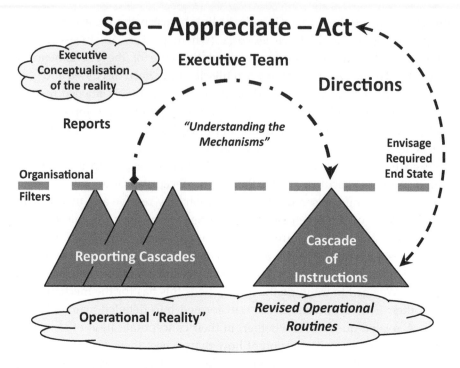

Figure 2.1   Communications Barriers

"that theory and practice are inextricably interwoven", they acknowledge that there remains a critical tension between the two. They highlight the fact that "there is often no evidence" on which to base decisions and therefore on which to act.

Practical Utility

So far in this chapter I have provided an overview of the research significant to those concerned with preventing *the unwanted* and *failure of foresight* as being relevant to *risk governance*. What the review does reveal is that many of the ideas so far developed, particularly by those examining the causes of accidents, require hindsight.

The chapter has also identified a reflexive dimension to this task. For example, one of the tenets of *mindfulness* is the *reluctance to simplify*. This work identified over 200 factors that previous research would suggest are relevant to *failure of foresight*. The prospect of developing a mental model with over 100 variables is daunting. However, not to consider such an option would be to deny ourselves *mindfulness*. Now that the literature has been synthesised to the degree that it has, the synthesis needs to be developed into an explicit (mental) model. It is accepted that this will only provide a rudimentary expression of the complexity and subtlety of thought contained within the original implicit model. Having developed 24 themes, the next step is to see whether this might become the basis for an executive's (the investigator's) mental model suitable for those with *risk governance* roles; that is, to give this work some *practical utility*. [137]

In line with the idea of "investigator", the themes were reworded as questions and relationships between the questions were identified and mapped. To enhance the development of *cross-understanding*, I tested the questions on a sample of 21 people operating in or advising executive teams. By using this approach the questions were refined and the mental model was seen by the respondents to have resonance and *practical utility*. The *practical utility* envisaged is that the questions provoke thinking about the issues and provide an introduction to the body of knowledge that exists on this subject.

The final respondents were asked to comment on the *practical utility* of questions against three criteria based on work by Platts.[138] These criteria were:

- Usability became "I understood the question at face value".

- Utility became "the question provided a useful prompt to my thinking".

- Feasibility became "I could use the question as part of a risk-based discussion".

In order to address the issue of learning, the respondents were asked to respond to the statement, "I see benefit from learning more on the issues that underlie the question."

As a result of the interviews, the original 24 themes were reduced to 20 questions, grouped under four headings. These headings emerged during the process; they were "the problem", "the group", "the process" and "summarising questions".

A summary of results are presented under the four headings of "usability", "utility", "feasibility" and "learning". The results contained many contradictory views, which I made no attempt to reconcile. From the outset, it was accepted that there was unlikely to be a definitive set of questions. It is envisaged that the most that can be achieved is that the majority of the questions have *practical utility* to some respondents.

USABILITY

The issue of usability is whether the question was understood as presented and here I encountered what has been described as "the limitation of language".[139] I saw how an individual's worldview, temporary or fundamental, clearly affected the way they interpreted individual words. The main issues around usability concerned their cognitive focus and the use of specific wording within their individual context. A substantial number of the comments on usability came down to the specific wording of the questions in the context specific to the respondent. The conclusion reached was that no wording would satisfy everyone. The ambition was therefore for most of the questions to have meaning to most respondents. Taking into account the comments received, the questions could however still be improved.

UTILITY

The issue of utility was whether the questions provided a useful prompt to thinking. Here I saw three issues highlighted. The first was the range of divergent views amongst respondents. The second was the issue of the questions being "utopian" in design. The third and final issue was an issue about "utility for whom?"

There was considerable disagreement about utility between the respondents. This can be demonstrated in the debate over Questions 19 and 20, the summarising questions. A number of those interviewed saw these questions as being key therefore making the others redundant. Others equally strongly suggested the two final questions were not needed as all the issues had been covered in the previous 18 questions. In the end, this issue came down to one of perspective.

The issue of perspective also arose around the wording of the questions. The ambition of the questions was seen, by some, to limit their utility. The questions were designed to focus on the "desired end state", this was seen by some to be utopian and therefore lacked the pragmatism needed "in the real world".

Part of the debate on utility revolved around the question "Having utility for whom?" The results demonstrated different interpretations of the questions. The first interpretation was whether the questions prompted the respondent into thinking differently. Several disagreed that the questions had prompted their thinking because they were already very aware of the issues involved. Those that disagreed with utility for this reason were then asked about the questions' wider utility. The ambition was again for most of the questions to provoke new thinking in most respondents. A number of those interviewed acknowledged that some of the questions had made them "squirm" which had alerted them to investigate, within themselves, what had created this *cognitive dissonance*.

The conclusion reached on utility was that not all the questions could be expected to provoke new thinking in the same way in everyone who sees them but, as a question set, they worked.

FEASIBILITY

The issue of feasibility was whether the questions could be used as part of a discussion on the risks that face their organisations. The results demonstrated that, in general, they could. Three main issues were raised by respondents.

The first was the political sensitivity of the issues in the questions. The feasibility of some questions was tempered by organisational politics, as one interviewee said, "You ask some absolutely spot on questions but it is an issue of how honest can you be."

The second was the potentially virtuous circle between academic and practical work enabling a difficult issue to be raised in an abstract, and therefore acceptable, way because it has been identified elsewhere as being a potential issue.

The final issue was the potential ways of employing the questions and whether they could or should be used all at once. The respondents debated the feasibility of using all the questions at once. There was concern that they may be used "unthinkingly" as a checklist, which would hinder rather than promote the new thinking required. Interviewees warned against this approach and emphasised the need therefore for the questions to be open in design rather than being able to be answered with a yes/no reply. They agreed that, to enhance this approach, the questions should provoke respondents to seek to provide evidence to support their views or assumptions, rather than relying on assertions. Their responses show a range of potential ways to use the questions to stimulate thinking and to resist the temptation to turn them into a process.

The conclusion reached on feasibility was that all the questions could be used under the right circumstances. As the questions do not constitute a process, respondents were left free to use the questions when they seemed appropriate. My interviewees offered a range of ways this may be done, demonstrating the great flexibility in their use.

FUTURE LEARNING

A secondary purpose of the questions proposed by this research was to provide access (a "portal") into the extensive body of existing knowledge on risk. The conclusion drawn from this research is that there may be a limited appetite to learn about the background research that underpins the questions. Even those with a self-declared "appetite to learn" showed little inclination to examine, what to them is, the raw material. Therefore, it might be concluded that, a valuable area for future research would be to examine how the material that exists might be taught to practitioners. It would appear that little of the general *practical utility* of the existing research has been realised. This finding may also be seen to have implications for trying to promote learning from inquiries.

Reshaping the Questions

The conclusion that I reached at this point was that, while the questions can be refined, they did have potential *practical utility*. However it is important to remember when shaping the questions that these questions should not be seen as being definitive. No question should be seen to be privileged over another. They are not designed to provide the final answer but should be seen as a catalyst to the start of a debate about risk within an organisation. As a result of discussions with respondents, a number of design parameters emerged for the questions if their *practical utility* was to be maximised:

- While each question has been derived from a rich source of ideas, for clarity each question should contain a single clear idea. Where compound questions are required, each part of the question should be clearly separated.

- The question should ask, or at least imply, that the evidence on which the judgement is made should be made explicit rather than those individuals involved relying on intuitive judgement. This is to ensure all underlying assumptions are aired and debated, which in turn, would enhance shared understanding within the group.

- The use of the negative question was deliberately used in order to challenge the "positive perspective" often held by senior management (this has been referred to as "optimism bias").

- The questions, to them, were not always clear in the way the terms "executive" and "the board" were used. The intent of this research is to focus on those with governance responsibilities whether this is as a "unitary board" or in organisations that have distinctively separate roles such as those of the executive or as a board member. Therefore the term "board/executive" was adopted to capture both cases.

The final form of the questions is given in Table 2.8. The 24 themes become 20 questions by combining the three issues relating to see, appreciate and act into Question 7 and combining data and the people assessing it in Question 9.

Table 2.8   Final Question Formulation

	The Problems
1.	Where do we need to have clear and fully justifiable criteria for which events or scenarios are **included in** and **excluded from** our risk management process?
2.	While we normally monitor "**outcomes**" ("end"), where do we need to monitor the "**processes**" ("means") that might create unacceptable outcomes?
3.	What risks are "**acceptable**" to us and why; how have we tested our reasoning for both core and non-core activity (against both internal and external yardsticks) to ensure that our reasoning is robust?
4.	Of those issues that we judge to be so improbable as to be "inconceivable", which of these still have such **potentially serious consequences** (unacceptable) that we must stay alert to them?
5.	What evidence do we have that we have a shared understanding about: (1) when we will prepare an alternative plan (anticipation); (2) when we will set aside reserve capacity (resilience); (3) where we just react to situations (reactive)?
6.	How might our approach to **risk taking be stifling** our organisation?

Table 2.8   Continued

The Group
7.	Are we aware of what factors might: (1) inhibit us from **taking note of warning signs;** (2) **affect our perception** of them; (3) **restrain us from acting** upon them?
8.	**How well do we understand** our system's operating modes (routine, high tempo, emergency and maintenance) and manage the transition between them? How well do we know those who will have to handle potential crises and are we sure they are equipped to do so?
9.	How do we judge the most **appropriate level** within our organisation for decisions to be made and whether each **decision maker** has the appropriate intuitive understanding of the issues, the organisation and its resources, and the ability to act in a timely manner?
10.	What proof is there that we are conscious of the **dynamics** and personal interactions that might cause our board and executive **team** to be **dysfunctional** (thereby generating risk) and what are we doing to ensure that we do not fall into these traps?

The Process
11.	How can we be sure that we have a culture that takes every key **opportunity to learn** from unwanted events experienced within the organisation (accidents and near-misses) and from the experience of other organisations?
12.	How do we, as the board/executive group and as an organisation, ensure that we are getting **the appropriate and relevant data** to feed into our risk discourse? How do we judge appropriate and relevant?
13.	How do we judge whether the way we **analyse risk** is appropriate to the risks we face?
14.	What might give us confidence that after an unwanted event our **decision making will stand up**, in hindsight, to critical **external scrutiny**?
15.	How do we ensure that all the members of the board/executive have a **shared view and understanding** of the organisation, the way it works and its risks?
16.	What evidence can be provided that our **plans and policies** are **robust enough** to withstand a disruptive event?
17.	How might we notice where an **emerging gap** between our practice and our formal procedures becomes a potential source of risk?
18.	When would we expect our people to use their **experience and intuition** rather than adhering strictly to written plans or standards; when might this **cause problems**? Where might our "**rule-book**" actually hamper the achievement of our organisational goals?

Summarising Questions
19.	What "**unwanted**" occurrences (including those perceived as "**inconceivable**") might affect our organisation?
20.	What evidence exists to show that our organisation's culture, structure or processes do NOT **provoke errors** or rule violations?

Related Risk Governance Issues

As discussed earlier, an important aspect of this work is its reflexive nature – looking at the answers through the lens of the material being considered. The research into risk has identified a number of behaviours amongst decision makers that might aggravate or mitigate potential risks. It is important for those involved in *risk governance* to be aware of these issues. The answers provided by respondents therefore cannot just be taken at face value; not only does consideration need to be given to what they were trying to say and what they were trying to avoid saying, but the answers need to be considered in the light of knowledge gained from previous research into risk. This includes such issues as hubris, denial, *cognitive dissonance, management distancing* and distancing by differentiation, to name but a few of the issues that emerged during the interviews.

Therefore, in order to fully understand the findings of this research, readers need to consider some of the other issues raised. These come under six headings of (1) level of expertise, (2) failing to ask, (3) knowing, but not acting, (4) attitude towards the questions, (5) desire to learn, and (6) liability v. risk.

LEVEL OF EXPERTISE

As there is a wide range of expertise amongst practitioners of risk management, there is therefore a question about at whom the questions were aimed. The answer is that the questions are aimed at the non-risk expert; this is seen to be the executive who has had no formal training in risk management or who has not specialised in the consideration of risk. (A rudimentary scale is proposed in Table 2.9. The groupings are seen to have varying degrees of training, education, experience and specialisations in matters of risk.) These executives rely on their general experience and knowledge to make sound judgements on matters of risk. The implication of this is that the questions must therefore be phrased using language that is designed to be clear and have no terms that have very specific meanings to some parts of the risk management community.

It is envisaged that, while the basic questions should have *practical utility* to the intuitive user, they should also provide a portal to the more detailed research that lies behind the questions. Other users, with more experience and knowledge, may use their understanding to adapt the questions to their audience, incorporating more detail. They may become aware of areas of existing knowledge with which they had not previously been made familiar. The details are provided with the aim of enhancing the knowledge of those with experience or seen as being experts.

Table 2.9   Scale of Users

Scale of Users	Description
Intuitive User	No training and uses their own general ability and experience in order to make judgements in respect of risk.
Trained or Experienced User	While they may have some general training, they have mainly learned the craft of risk management through extensive trial and error.
Subject Matter Expert (SME)	Has received some formal training, or through extensive practical experience of managing a specific risk speciality.
Multidiscipline SME	Has training and or experience of a number of recognised risk management disciplines.
Scholar/Practitioner	Has extensive knowledge of the research and theory that underlie risk management practice and has extensive practical experience.
Academic	Has extensive knowledge of the research and theory that underlie risk management practice but has little practical know-how.

The purpose of these categories is to stimulate users to ask themselves: "Where would I place myself: (1) an intuitive user, (2) an experienced user, (3) an SME, of which risk discipline(s), (4) scholar? What does this tell me about my actual level of knowledge and the gaps in my knowledge and how does this correspond to my assumptions about my knowledge and practice?"

In summary, the relationship between practitioner and knowledge can be seen to be multifaceted. It is therefore unlikely that any single framework can be optimised for all potential audiences. This work tries to link detailed research with intuitive users. However, no matter what level of expertise a person has, they are still seen to need to ask the right questions, be open to the data they receive and be prepared to acknowledge the limits of their own knowledge.

FAILURE TO ASK

A key issue is the willingness or the ability of those involved in this process to ask difficult and challenging questions. The "failure to ask" was a major theme of the discussions; for example one respondent suggested that, because he was in a heavily regulated industry, he relied on the regulatory process to detect irregularities. This reliance upon regulatory systems comes as a stark contrast to findings within the literature. Amongst others, Diane Vaughan's discussion of the Challenger Accident and Charles Perrow's discussion about how to reduce society's vulnerabilities,[140] both debated the role of regulators and found them wanting for a variety of reasons. These writers both cite political, structural and social limitations to all types of regulatory systems and point out that all the available options have their inherent weaknesses. In all these circumstances, it is the assumption that what is done is adequate but it can be seen to present an unmonitored potential source of vulnerability. But just asking might also not be enough.

KNOWING, BUT NOT ACTING

The key issue for any such thinking framework is whether knowing leads to action. The purpose of these questions is to prompt more detailed thinking and reflection on particular areas that may generate risk. Any such questions need to prompt more than just an acceptance that the questions have utility. Users need to approach such issues, not with a question about whether they are addressing the particular issue, but questioning whether they are doing "what is appropriate in the circumstances", that is, not only are they doing enough but, given the circumstances, are they doing too much? This behaviour may be seen to be consistent with concerns expressed within the literature about the tendency of individuals to deny issues that are relevant to them or trying to "distance" themselves from the issue's relevance. It is also a key concern of this work as expressed in the relationship between "seeing, appreciating and acting". It might therefore be seen that it is not (just) about asking the right questions, it is about how you build them into the management's (process).

One person interviewed for this research provided evidence that thinking differently does not necessarily lead to doing things differently. While he said that the questions had provoked him to think differently, and in his role as a school governor he would probably use the questions, he did not see himself using them in his core business. When asked to explain "why not?", he took some time to consider his answer and then acknowledged that there was no reason why not; this would seem to demonstrate that cultural norms and "ways of doing" are much harder to change than simply providing new ways of thinking. It can be seen that this issue also has implications for whether we can learn lessons from inquiries and then put them into practice.

ATTITUDE TOWARDS THE QUESTIONS

The interviews revealed that attitude is as important as the questions. When it came to examining the questions, attitudes ranged from those who found reasons for not using the questions as prompts to their thinking, to those who found the exercise stimulating. Comments on attitude can be separated into two groups. The first is the attitude of the individual respondents and the second is the attitude of the groups with whom they work.

One interviewee, paraphrasing A.E. Housman, stated that while consideration of the questions may "just take a moment of thought, a moment can be a long time and thinking is difficult". Therefore, the attitude with which an individual approaches these questions is as important as the questions themselves, as is the individual's desire to learn. An exercise such as this is therefore unlikely to be an easy one.

Group dynamic and social norms are also likely to affect the *practical utility* of such questions. As individuals combine into groups or teams, group dynamics and social norms have an effect on the behaviour of boards and executive teams. Another interviewee clearly differentiated between boards she would take part in, where such questions are asked, rather than those either run by "alpha males … who want to exert themselves" or boards composed of "dead white males" (a caricature of where *requisite variety* is lacking) where the challenge of such questions would be unacceptable. The questions are therefore more likely to have *practical utility* for groups that welcome constructive challenge.

No set of questions, by themselves, can transform a process, let alone a process of *risk governance*. The potential users of such questions have to be open minded enough to want to accept the challenge presented by any such questions. The *practical utility* of any such set of questions should not therefore be judged by the willingness of any particular population to adopt them.

DESIRE TO LEARN

An important consideration on whether practitioners will learn is their desire to learn. The difference in the appetite to learning of board/executive members was clear to see in the responses received. These answers should be seen in the light of those who indicated a reluctance to learn from others who were missing the opportunity to benefit more cheaply than would be the case if they had their own organisational disaster. What this evidence does suggest is that an organisation's ability to learn from the work of others is likely to be limited by their attitude to learning rather than the availability of the relevant information.

It might be assumed that at the national level there would be a uniform desire to learn from past mistakes and to transfer these lessons to all those who might benefit. This is not the case. Some national systems work against the opportunity to learn from disasters and crises. For example, I understand that within Belgium the content of inquiry reports is confidential and so it is forbidden by law to share with others the conclusions and recommendations of these interventions.

Whatever the good intentions, and the espoused belief in the value of learning from the experience of others, the comments of interviewees reflect observations made elsewhere that this might not always be the case. For example Daniel Ellsberg, reflecting on his own experience when he published the "Pentagon Papers", describes *an anti-learning mechanism* he found within government. He says:

> *Avoiding improved performance is not the point of the mechanism. But because studying present and past faulty decision-making risks may invite blame and organisational, political, perhaps even legal penalties, those outcomes "outweigh" the benefits of clearly understanding what needs to be changed within the organisation.*[141]

It can therefore be seen that a desire to learn may not be enough. There also needs to be a system put in place that promotes such learning.

LIABILITY V. RISK

In his discussion of *normal accidents*, Charles Perrow expressed the view that he saw that there was sometimes a conflict between the work of lawyers, trying to limit liability and the efforts required for effective risk management. Perrow's comments related particularly to the shipping industry; it was evident from comments made to me during my research that the problem still exists in the industry today. One interviewee also expressed concern that the legal process of discovery, for cases of litigation, provides an incentive to organisations to reduce the documentation and explicit evaluations necessary for effective risk management. A second interviewee commented that organisations run by "lawyers and economists", where they rely on rules, have a tendency to fall prey to the "law of unintended consequences". In addition, one potential respondent withdrew from the research after advice from his in-house counsel who suggested that such work might conflict with the interest of his company. Here is seen the conflict between candour, learning and liability as an issue which is likely to be even more prevalent within inquiries.

Those people engaged in *risk governance* therefore need to consider the extent to which the interests of liability mitigation may militate against effective risk management. In his discussion of iatrogenics (literally translated as "caused by the healer"), Nicholas Taleb describes how, within medicine, issues of liability may induce practitioners to intervene with a patient in their own interest rather than in the interest of their patients. In these cases, the risk to the patient of the intervention outweighs the potential gain, however for the doctor, intervention may be the better option as it reduces the likelihood of their being sued for negligence.[142] Where this is described as an issue of agency, moral hazard or risk transfer, this suggests that there may be serious conflicts between different components of risk management. This should, in turn, alert us to there being the potential that other unseen conflicts may exist within the overall concept of Risk Management.

THE EXPLICIT MENTAL MODEL

The 20 questions provide us with the basis of our mental model. This is illustrated in Figure 2.2. It is based, for its greater simplicity, on the strategy map format. This format provides the opportunity to illustrate the potential interactions between the questions. At this stage, which connections are annotated is thought not to be important; what is important is that they "provoke" thinking, which they get "us talking, digging, comparing, refining, and focusing on the right question"[143] and make us reconsider how we evaluate the world around us.

Summary

In this chapter I have tried to provide a flavour of the extensive knowledge contained within academic literature which relates to why *the unwanted* might occur and I see this as being essential knowledge for anyone who is trying to determine the cause of any particular event. This is especially true if they are also suggesting lessons that may be learnt from such events.

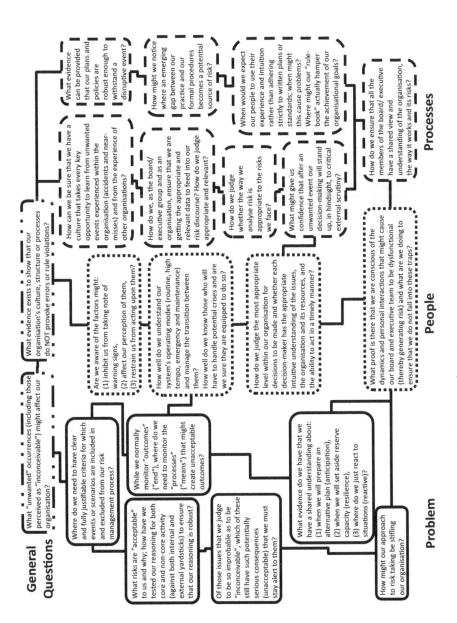

Figure 2.2   Schematic of "20 Questions"

Examining this literature highlights one key but depressing fact. The issue for risk management is that it does not seem to matter what is done well, what is important are the weaknesses within any system. This means that it is not necessarily the "big risks" that will cause the catastrophic unwanted occurrence. According to chaos theory, it may be the small issue that is easily overlooked; more poetically, "the kingdom may be lost for the want of a nail". It is through these weaknesses, or vulnerabilities, that *the unwanted* may occur. This might be summed up in the cliché that "a chain is only as strong as its weakest link" but I prefer to use the metaphor of a leaking roof. For those who have had a leaky roof will know that, while the structure may look sound, every time it rains the drip appears. Efforts are made to find and fix the fault but the drip persists. After several unsuccessful attempts to fix the drip, one day it just stops. This metaphor represents how, in a complex system, the cause and effect may be difficult to establish and therefore the appropriate corrective action hard to determine. The weakness in the metaphor is the idea that the roof tiles are static. A more realistic representation of organisations would be to consider the rafters as the structure of the organisation, the underlay as the policies, procedures and culture while the tiles are the individuals. Now imagine trying to find and fix a leak where every tile has independent thought, a will and is able to take autonomous action. To me this is now a more accurate representation of the risk management problem; it represents all the parts of the organisation that are working well, working as planned, and trying to identify where weaknesses exist or where parts are not working in the way they should be. Therefore when considering risk management we need to recognise that it is not what we do well that is important, but rather the gaps, the weaknesses, the blind-spots and the vulnerabilities.

Overall, the research was about knowledge transfer between the academic community and practitioners. The final list of 20 questions is aimed at those who are described, for the purpose of this chapter, as the intuitive user. This person is least likely to be versed in the theoretical knowledge that underpins risk management practices. It is accepted that no single set of questions will be perfect for all contexts (an 80 per cent fit would therefore be seen as the target).

In this chapter we have seen that there is a body of relevant academic work which has *practical utility*. I developed 24 themes and operationalised them into 20 provocative open questions appropriate to those at executive (investigator) level in *risk governance* roles. The questions have been arranged under the four main headings of "The Problems", "The Group", "The Process" and "Summarising Questions" to make them easier to use. By being aware of the issues raised by each theme those investigating unwanted occurrences may see issues that they may previously have not appreciated as being significant.

The mental model created by the questions is illustrated in the schematic at Figure 2.2. This constructs a *coherent whole* out of the widely diverse literature that, in turn, provides a portal back into the literature. The questions look to expose underlying assumptions and hidden evidence but this will only happen if the individual approaches them with the appropriate attitude.

One question now raised is the value to be placed on the research that underlies this summary. If this research is deemed to be significant and valuable then should those conducting inquiries have a professional duty of care that requires them to be familiar with this material before passing judgement? If this is deemed unnecessary, why do we as a society spend so many resources in this area? This shall be discussed further in the final chapter. My next step is to examine how those conducting inquiries might conceptualise the problem.

Endnotes

1	Lauder (2011), Chapter 5.
2	Toft and Reynolds (2005), page 49.
3	Haddon-Cave (2009), page 331.
4	Haddon-Cave (2009), page 375.
5	CAIB (2003), page 195.
6	Such as Vaughan (1996), page 411 and Barton and Sutcliffe (2010), page 72.
7	Turner (1978), page 51.
8	Pidgeon and O'Leary (2000), page 21.
9	Stockholm (2011), page 46.
10	Such as Schobel and Manzey (2011), page 47; Elliott et al. (2000), Weir (2002) and Qureshi (2007).
11	US DOE (2009), page 96.
12	Weick (2005).
13	Pidgeon and O'Leary (2000), page 15.
14	Lagadec (1993), page xxiv.
15	Van de Ven and Poole (1995).
16	Vaughan (1996).
17	Turner (1976b), page 391.
18	Power (2004), page 44.
19	See Weick, (1989 and 2005).
20	Turner (1976b), page 391.
21	Weick and Sutcliffe, (2007), pages 9 and 12 respectively.
22	Weick and Sutcliffe, (2007), pages 10 and 15 respectively.
23	Weick and Sutcliffe, (2007), pages 14.
24	Weick and Sutcliffe (2007), page 9.
25	Weick and Sutcliffe (2007), page 12.

26   Peters and Waterman (2004) and see Minns's (2010), page 22 "findings confirm that a common approach is to focus on core business".

27   Jaques (2010), pages 475–476.

28   Perrow (1999), page 139.

29   Haddon-Cave (2009), page 21.

30   Le Porte (1994), page 207.

31   Le Porte (1994), page 209.

32   Bourrier (2005), page 95.

33   Weick and Sutcliffe (2007), page 10.

34   Slovic (2000), page 198.

35   As described, for example, by Heimann (1997) or Fischhoff et al. (1981).

36   Farjoun (2010), page 210.

37   Weick (2010), page 540.

38   Cullen (2001a), page 70.

39   Such as Slovic (2000).

40   Adams (2007).

41   Reason (1990), pages 12–13.

42   Vaughan (1996), page 394.

43   In Starbuck and Farjoun (2005), page 294.

44   Slovic (2000), page 190.

45   Smith (2004), page 357.

46   Klein et al. (2005), page 22.

47   Pidgeon (1998), page 100.

48   Westrum (1982), page 391.

49   Vaughan (1996), page 242.

50   Vaughan (1996), page 212.

51   Clarke and Perrow (1996).

52   Lagadec (1993), page 54.

53   Lagadec (1993), page 20.

54   Reason (1997), page 93.

55   Dunbar and Garud (2005), page 209.

56   Turner (1978).

57   Reason (1998), page 296.

58   Coined by Mack and Rock (1998).

59   Zwetsloot (2009), page 496.

60   Westrum (1982).

61   Reason (1997), page 6.

62   Kutsch and Hall (2010), page 247.

63   Hollnagel (1993).

64   Woods (2009), page 499.

65   Weick and Sutcliffe (2007), page 10.

66   See Grint (2010) or Hancock and Holt (2003).

67   Weick and Sutcliffe (2007), page 15.

68   Vaughan (1996), pages 261 and 363.

69   Klein et al. (2005).

70   Weick (2005).

71   9/11 Commission Report (2005), page 425.

72   Weick (2005), page 436.

73   Toft and Reynolds (2005), page 103.

74   Elliot (2006), page 403.

75   Vaughan (1996), page 415.

76   Perrow (1999), page 67.

77   See Vaughan (1996), page 406 and Boin and Schulman (2008), page 1054.

78   An issue prominent within Vaughan (1996).

79   See Weick (1997), page 401; Taleb et al. (2009), page 81.

80 See Snook (2000), pages 3 and 214; Taleb (2007), pages 27 and 41; Easterby-Smith et al. (2008), pages 15–106.
81 For the concept see Westrum (1982), page 393; for a practical example see Snook (2000), page 177.
82 Turner (1976a), page 758.
83 Snook (2000), page 196.
84 Farjoun (2005), pages 60–80.
85 Weick and Sutcliffe (2007), page 9.
86 Snook (2000).
87 Vaughan (1996), page xiv.
88 Snook (2000), page 223.
89 Vaughan (1996), page 275.
90 Vaughan (1996), page 140.
91 Rochlin (1991), page 117.
92 Weick (1993), page 633.
93 Stein (2004).
94 Weick and Sutcliffe (2007), page 68.
95 Schulman (1993), page 368.
96 In an edited volume on *Resilience Engineering,* Hollnagel et al. (2006), page 6.
97 Weick (1988), page 307.
98 Weick (1988), page 307.
99 Vaughan (1999).
100 Dekker (2011), loc 3182.
101 Hirschhorn (1993), page 148.
102 Schulman (1993), pages 357–358.
103 Reason (1990), pages 44–46.
104 Vaughan (1996).
105 Roberts (1990).
106 Weick (2005).
107 Thompson (1967).
108 Snook (2000), page 153.
109 Snook and Connor (2006), page 182.
110 Latané and Darley (1970).
111 Ghaffarzadegan (2008), page 1675.
112 Latané and Nidd (1981), page 308.
113 Snook and Connor (2006), page 183.
114 Ghaffarzadegan (2008), page 1676.
115 Whyte (1952).
116 Tuchman (1984).
117 Tuchman (1984), pages 2, 4–5 and 280.
118 Enzer (1980), page 12.
119 Choo (2008), page 41.
120 Vaughan (1996), page 35.
121 Vaughan (1996), pages 57 and 278.
122 Vaughan (1996), page 408.
123 Snook (2000), page 207.
124 Perrow (2007), page 146.
125 Perrow (2007), page 167.
126 Perrow (1999), page 310.
127 Smith in Smith and Elliott (2006), page 156.
128 Kakabadse (2010).
129 Smith and Elliot (2007), page 519.
130 Smith and Elliot (2007), page 52.
131 Adams (2007), page 38.
132 Vaughan (1996), page 94 and 259.

133   Grint (2010).
134   Elliot (2006), page 394.
135   Elliot (2006), page 396.
136   Van de Ven (1989), page 486.
137   Corley and Gioia (2011).
138   Platts (1993).
139   Woolgar (1980).
140   Perrow (2007).
141   Gerstein (2008), page x.
142   Taleb (2012), page 345.
143   Weick (2004).

3

What Inquiry Reports Report

Up to this point we have looked at the mental model that might be created from knowledge of the literature relating to disasters and other unwanted occurrences appropriate to those in *risk governance* roles. It's now time to start examining the mental model of those conducting inquires. It is however outside the scope of this book to look at the actual mental model used by any specific inquiry team. It is my intention to define the tacit mental model that is implied by a selection of inquiry recommendations.

Before we look at the recommendations, we need to debate which part of the inquiry report provides the best opportunity to disseminate the lessons learned. All inquiry reports can be, for the purpose of this work, divided into three parts. These are the main text, the findings and the recommendations. While the richest understanding of any event can only be gained by reading the whole report, we would be deluding ourselves to think that this will be done by anyone other than those directly affected or those who take a specific interest in these issues. No general manager has the time, or probably the inclination, to spend the effort required to read and digest these intense pieces of writing. While the findings are generally more succinct, they are probably also overlooked. Generally it is the recommendations that receive the greatest publicity and receive coverage by the media. Therefore, it is the recommendations on which, at this point, I will concentrate.

In this chapter I intend to divine the mental model adopted by those conducting boards of inquiry from the recommendations they propose. I will start by describing the method I have used.

Method

The method that I used to divine the mental model was inductive. I grouped the recommendations by their perceived purpose. Each purpose was given a label and each label was defined; academics might refer to this process as "coding" the recommendations. It took the analysis of the recommendations of six inquiry reports for the labels to settle into a pattern and another six for the definitions to settle ("settle" is defined as requiring no more adjustment or adaptation).

LIST OF REPORTS

The reports analysed are listed in Table 3.1. They were chosen initially for their prominence within the literature and then to create a spread between subject areas and national perspectives. Other reports were reviewed but, for various reasons were not included in the final list. For example:

The Sheen report (1987) into the Zeebrugge ferry disaster was analysed as it is considered to be a seminal piece of work which advanced our understanding and the practice of accident investigation. However, due to its format and narrative nature it was not clear what was comment, a finding or a recommendation. To avoid misrepresentation of the report's intent, it was therefore excluded from further analysis.

The report by Prof Brain Toft "into the adverse incident that occurred at Queen's Medical Centre, Nottingham, 4th January 2001",[1] which examined a very specific activity with a very specific setting (the administration of intrathecal chemotherapy within a hospital setting) and, as a result, 40 of the 56 recommendations concerned proscriptive changes to procedures and required competencies (therefore coded as "Technical [1]"). While important within its own context, I felt that the report was not representative and so would distort the results of my small sample.

The Hutton report decided that it was unnecessary "to make any express recommendations because (he had) no doubt that the BBC and the Government will take note of the criticisms which (he had) made"[2]

Dame Janet Smith's report[3] into the activities of Harold Shipman was produced in six parts. These covered the number of potential victims, the police investigation, the work of coroners, the control of drugs, complaint handling and finally the inquiry considered the number of victims earlier in Shipman's career. Reports 1, 2 and 6 offered no recommendations. Report 3 offered 48, report 4 offered 33 and report 5 offered 109 and so only these latter three reports are included in the analysis.

The Coroner's report[4] on the 2005 "7/7" attacks in London was also reviewed. This contained nine recommendations all of which could be categorised as "further review"; this did not, in itself, add any new understanding of the inquiry mental model. It was therefore not included within this part of my analysis.

At this point I would also like to acknowledge that I have only read part of the Norwegian 22 July Commission and that was the part published in English. This extract did include the recommendations. This highlights two points. The first is that, as previously stated, many see the recommendations as being the critical part of a report maybe without appreciating that to learn we need to understand fully why something has been recommended and the circumstances that prevailed at the time. Therefore recommendations without the necessary explanation militate against the report's full potential to teach valuable lessons. The second point is that while much of the academic work on this subject area is published in English, as are many but not all inquiry reports, I can only wonder what lessons are lost due to the lack of a common language.

Table 3.1   List of Inquiry Reports

US – Roger's Commission (1986) – Challenger Accident
UK – Taylor (1989 and 1990) – Hillsborough Tragedy
UK – Donaldson (2000) – NHS Training
UK – Cullen Inquiry Parts 1 & 2 (2001) – Railing Crash
US – Presidential Commission (2002) – 9/11 attack
US – Presidential Commission (2003) – Columbia Accident
UK – Laming (2003) – Death of V. Climbie
UK – Smith (2005) – Activity of Dr Shipman (I analysed three of her reports)
US – Baker (2007) – BP Texas City Accident
UK – Woolf (2008) – Ethics at BAE
UK – Haddon-Cave (2009) – Crash of RAF Nimrod XV230
UK – Walker (2009) – 2008 Banking Crisis
UK – Donaghy (2009) – Death of Construction Workers
Aus – Borthwick (2010) – Montara Oil Spill
US – Presidential Commission (2011) – BP Deepwater Horizon
UK – FSA (2011) – RBS Failure
Fr – BEA (2012) – Crash of Flight AF447
Nor – 22 July Commission (2012) – Attacks in Olso and at Utoya Island

The fact that some key reports are not included in this part of the analysis does not mean that they have nothing to add to our understanding of this subject. The work here aims to produce a representative mental model rather than a definitive one. A definitive proof would require the use of a much larger sample and a much more detailed statistical analysis. It is for others to decide whether this work would add further value.

FUNCTIONAL CATEGORIES

The labels and their definitions divined by the analysis are set out in Table 3.2. The labels were chosen for their specificity and without any intent to provide any implied judgement. However, I recognise that some terms may have, in the view of some readers, implied connotations; I would ask that they be taken as neutral.

Table 3.2   Recommendation Labels and Definitions

Definition	Label (Code)
These recommendations affect how external stakeholders (those outside the immediate management structure), oversee activities in order to ensure that the required benefits are delivered.	Governance
These recommendations propose that the purpose of the system be confirmed or redefined.	Purpose
These recommendations propose that an activity be planned or the related documentation be reviewed/improved (updated to ensure that they are not *fantasy documents*) either at the: • conceptual/policy level; • strategic or operational level; • procedural, protocols ("good practice") and process level; • analysis and design stage.	Planning [1] Planning [2] Planning [3] Planning [4]
These recommendations require political rather than bureaucratic skills to accomplish: • resource prioritisation; • changes to powers and power structures; • changes to legislation or regulations.	Political [1] Political [2] Political [3]
These recommendations propose new or enhanced capabilities, whether they relate to: • general cultural traits; • knowledge, skills, and related *organisational learning* and training; • systems, services, technology or equipment.	Capability [1] Capability [2] Capability [3]
These recommendations affect how internal stakeholders ensure the efficient and effective delivery of defined benefits through: • a supervisory function (internal governance); • direct action (scrutiny, control and communication); • personal appraisals including the evaluation of competence or conduct.	Performance Management [1] Performance Management [2] Performance Management [3]

Definition	Label (Code)
These recommendations affect: • structures or arrangements; • authority, roles, duties and responsibilities; • audit, compliance or regulatory activity; • definition of terms; that are required to deliver a defined benefit.	Bureaucracy [1] Bureaucracy [2] Bureaucracy [3] Bureaucracy [4]
These recommendations propose new or revised: • formal definition, documentation and communication of the standards (or guidance) to which a routine is to be performed; • competencies required by personnel needed to conduct a specific task.	Standards [1] Standards [2]
These recommendations propose specific technical changes to: • formal processes; • Infrastructure, machinery, technology or method; in order to ensure that the technology is safer or more reliable.	Technical [1] Technical [2]
These recommendations propose further "consideration" or analysis of specific subject matter; they indicate that the inquiry has identified an issue but does not wish to offer advice as to how the issue should be addressed.	Further Review
These recommendations require no action but pass a judgement.	Comment
These recommendations remind the recipients of a particular requirement of a routine or aspect of their role.	**Admonish**

Results

The details of the coding exercise are summarised in the Annex. It can be seen that no report made recommendations that fall into every category. The mental model identified is therefore based on a synthesis of all of the reports. I do not claim that this mental model was used by any of the report authors. I would go further the other way and suggest that the authors were not aware of the mental model that underlay their analysis.

PRIMARY AND SECONDARY PURPOSES

The purpose of recommendations can be complex. This can be illustrated using Hallet's nine recommendations on the "7/7" attacks (see Table 3.3). I see the need to identify both a primary and secondary purpose of recommendations. The primary purpose (the action required by the target audience) of all nine recommendations was further review (worded as "consideration", "be examined" or "reconsider"). These are in bold text in the table. The differentiation comes at what each review needs to examine. This I have called the secondary purpose; these are italicised in the table. They fall into three categories: the planning of procedures and protocols (Recommendations 1, 2, 4, 5 and 6), improved training (Recommendations 3 and 8) and new capabilities (Recommendations 7 and 9). In the case of

Recommendation 9, the recommendation is specific about what needs to be reviewed. In this case the review needs to consider how the capability should be funded.

Table 3.3   Hallet's 7/7 Recommendations

	Recommendation	Comment
1.	I recommend that **consideration be given** to whether the *procedures* can be improved to ensure that "human sources" who are asked to view photographs are shown copies of the photographs of the best possible quality, consistent with operational sensitivities.	Further review *Planning [3]*
2.	I recommend that *procedures* **be examined** by the Security Service to establish if there is room for further improvement in the recording of decisions relating to the assessment of targets.	Further review *Planning [3]*
3.	I recommend that the London Resilience Team **reviews** *the provision* of inter-agency major incident training for frontline staff, particularly with reference to the London Underground.	Further review *Capability [2]*
4.	I recommend that TfL and the London Resilience Team **review** *the protocols* by which TfL (i) is alerted to major incidents declared by the emergency services that affect the underground network, and (ii) informs the emergency services of an emergency on its own network (including the issuing of a "Code Amber" or a "Code Red", or the ordering of an evacuation).	Further review *Planning [3]*
5.	I recommend that TfL and the London Resilience Team **review** *the procedures* by which (i) a common initial rendezvous point is established, and its location communicated to all the arriving emergency services, and (ii) the initial rendezvous point is permanently manned by an appropriate member of London Underground.	Further review *Planning [3]*
6.	I recommend that TfL and the London Resilience Team **review** *the procedures* by which confirmation is sought on behalf of any or all of the emergency services that the traction current is off, and by which that confirmation is disseminated.	Further review *Planning [3]*
7.	I recommend that TfL (i) **reconsider whether** it is practicable *to provide first aid equipment* on underground trains, either in the driver's cab or at some other suitable location, and (ii) **carry out a further review** of station *stretchers* to confirm whether they are suitable for use on both stations and trains.	Further review *Capability [3]*
8.	I recommend that the LAS, together with the Barts and London NHS Trust (on behalf of the LAA) **review** *existing training* in relation to multi casualty triage (that is, the process of triage sieve) in particular with respect to the role of basic medical intervention.	Further review *Capability [2]*
9.	I recommend that the Department of Health, the Mayor of London, the London Resilience Team and any other relevant bodies **review** the *emergency medical care* of the type provided by LAA and MERIT and, in particular (i) its capability, and (ii) its *funding*.	Further review *Capability [3] Political [1]*

The size of the recommendation itself cannot be seen as an indication of its complexity. Here are two examples, both from the Laming report. The first example shows a long simple recommendation (Table 3.4) while the second is relatively short and complex (Table 3.5).

Table 3.4   Laming (2003) Recommendation 13

The Department of Health should amalgamate the current Working Together and the National Assessment Framework documents into one simplified document. The document should tackle the following six aspects in a clear and practical way:

1. It must establish a "common language" for use across all agencies to help those agencies to identify who they are concerned about, why they are concerned, who is best placed to respond to those concerns, and what outcome is being sought from any planned response.
2. It must disseminate a best practice approach by social services to receiving and managing information about children at the "front door".
3. It must make clear in cases that fall short of an immediately identifiable section 47 label that the seeking or refusal of parental permission must not restrict the initial information gathering and sharing. This should, if necessary, include talking to the child.
4. It must prescribe a clear step-by-step guide on how to manage a case through either a section 17 or a section 47 track, with built-in systems for case monitoring and review.
5. It must replace the child protection register with a more effective system. Case conferences should remain, but the focus must no longer be on whether to register or not. Instead, the focus should be on establishing an agreed plan to safeguard and promote the welfare of the particular child.
6. The new guidance should include some consistency in the application of both section 17 and section 47 (paragraph 17.111).

Laming's Recommendation 13 is concerned with the creation of a National Framework document. This is conceived as being neither procedural nor an operational plan and therefore is given the label Planning 1. The rest of the recommendation details what is to be included in the framework.

Table 3.5   Laming (2003) Recommendation 27

Chief executives and lead members of local authorities with social services responsibilities must ensure that children's services are explicitly included in their authority's list of priorities and operational plans (paragraph 5.4).

Laming's Recommendation 27 is concerned with *performance management* in that someone is required to ensure that something happens but at a level above day-to-day responsibility. This level is seen as *governance* and so is given the primary label "Performance Management [1]". As the recommendation allocates responsibility to a particular party, it receives a secondary label of "bureaucracy [2]", because it suggests a change of priorities so it receives the secondary label of "Political [1]" and as it relates to operational plans it also receives a secondary label of "Planning [2]".

During the coding process all the recommendations were coded to show both their primary and secondary purposes. The mental model however was constructed from an analysis of the primary purposes only. While I accept that this may not portray the full mental model used in each case, it does give us the basic building blocks. Based on the logic of cross-understanding, each mental model will be a unique combination of the building blocks and the way the blocks are connected. The question therefore that needs to be asked is whether we have a structure that enables the necessary cross-understanding to be built between all engaged parties?

BASIC MENTAL MODEL

It can be assumed that the basic premise of any mental model that underlies an inquiry is that if the organisation had taken due care over each of the components identified, then the disaster would not have occurred. This is similar to the construct of *Critical Success Factors* where *Critical Success Factors* are defined as those things that need to go right for success to be achieved. In this sense, many recommendations can also be seen to be *Critical Success Factors*. However, there are three types of the recommendations, which, while being essential to the mental model, cannot be considered to be *Critical Success Factors*. These are Comments, Further Review and Admonish which are therefore seen as being peripheral issues.

The basic construct of the model (see Figure 3.1) is the separation of the organisation (represented by the main oval) and the external environment. In the external environment lies the external governance. The interplay between the external environment and the organisation is represented by the intended outcomes which are the benefits that the organisation seeks to deliver to the external environment. The politics and the capability are often bought in from the outside. The remaining factors are all considered internal to the organisation. Taking a systems view, all the factors will be linked or will interact in some way or other. These interactions are represented by the arrows. Figure 3.1 represents my (cross-) understanding of the mental model being used by those, as a body, conducting inquiries.

As stated previously, no model is accurate but some are useful: the purpose of this model is to stimulate debate amongst interested parties as to how they see the interconnectedness and the relative importance of each element.

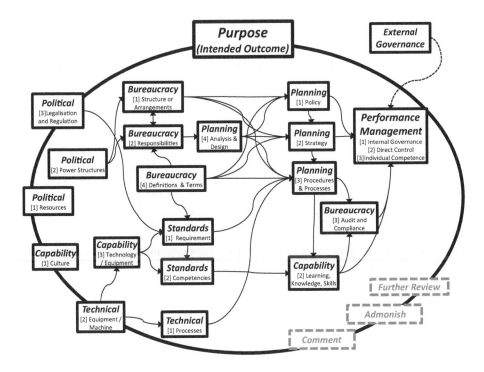

Figure 3.1   Basic Mental Model

RELATIVE IMPORTANCE OF EACH FACTOR

One way of assessing the relative importance of each factor is to see how often it attracted a recommendation. To this end, 1,130 recommendations, in 20 reports, were analysed. The highest number of recommendations in any one report was 162 and the lowest was ten; the average number was 56.5.

Table 3.6 sets out the total number of recommendations that attracted each label, its average against the total number and an adjusted average. The adjusted average is the average number of recommendations based on the percentage of the recommendations given that label in each report; this removes the bias given to a particular label by the reports with the most recommendations. Details of the averaging exercise can be found in the Annex.

Table 3.6   Result Statistics

	Label (Code)	Total Number	Average	Adjusted Average
1.	Governance	7	0.62	0.73
2.	Purpose	4	0.35	0.36
3.	Planning [1]	19	1.68	2.41
4.	Planning [2]	24	2.12	2.84
5.	Planning [3]	42	3.72	3.75
6.	Planning [4]	9	0.80	0.75
7.	Political [1]	30	2.65	3.28
8.	Political [2]	23	2.04	1.34
9.	Political [3]	40	3.54	3.81
10.	Capability [1]	9	0.80	1.46
11.	Capability [2]	48	4.25	4.64
12.	Capability [3]	114	10.09	12.37
13.	Performance Management [1]	41	3.63	4.62
14.	Performance Management [2]	59	5.22	7.33
15.	Performance Management [3]	13	1.15	0.99
16.	Bureaucracy [1]	111	9.82	7.77
17.	Bureaucracy [2]	93	8.23	7.73
18.	Bureaucracy [3]	18	1.59	1.16
19.	Bureaucracy [4]	9	0.80	0.58
20.	Standards [1]	56	4.96	5.20
21.	Standards [2]	4	0.35	0.48
22.	Technical [1]	145	12.83	9.03
23.	Technical [2]	31	2.74	3.28
24.	Comment	22	1.95	1.13
25.	Further Review	127	11.24	10.18
26.	Admonish	32	2.83	2.83

The effect of adjusting the average can be clearly seen in Figure 3.2; this also shows a consistency in the distribution of the labels used between the two different averages. While there is a general levelling, the pattern of use remains clear. The labels that represent the most popular types of recommendations remain consistent.

The six most popular labels (according to adjusted average), in descending order, are:

1. At 12.37 per cent is Capability [3] – propose new or enhanced capabilities, whether they relate to systems, services, technology or equipment.

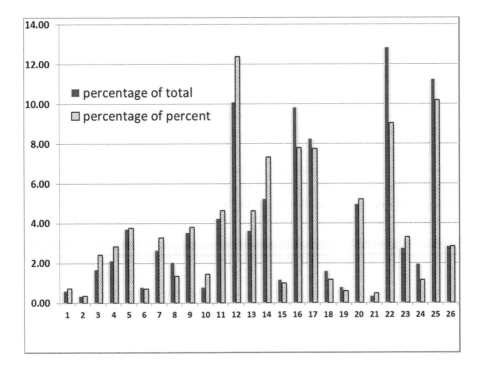

Figure 3.2   Chart of Percentages

2.   At 10.18 per cent is Further Review – they indicate that the inquiry has identified an issue but does not wish to offer advice as to how the issue should be addressed.

3.   At 9.03 per cent is Technical [1] – they offer specific changes to existing procedures.

4.   At 7.77 per cent is Bureaucracy [1] – they suggest changes to structures or arrangements.

5.   At 7.73 per cent is Bureaucracy [2] – they suggest changes to authority, roles and responsibilities.

6.   At 7.33 per cent is Performance Management [2] – they suggest changes to how internal stakeholders ensure the efficient and effective delivery of defined benefits through direct action (scrutiny, control and communication and so on).

The remaining labels all have below 5.5 per cent of the total number of recommendations.

This would seem to tell us that the most pressing issue is a lack of appropriate capability. Organisations are trying to carry out tasks for which they are not equipped. However, reflecting on Chapter 2, we know that new capabilities bring new risks (*liability of newness*) and so these recommendations may, in themselves, be the source of the next disaster. The Taylor reports on Hillsborough made 30 recommendations that required new capabilities. These ranged from new cutting equipment, closed-circuit television, interactive signing, fully equipped ambulances, to first aid rooms and control rooms. All of these require skills to operate and maintain, all of which adds complexity to the operating environment. The extrapolation of a finding made by Haddon-Cave provides a further guide to good practice. Haddon-Cave criticised[5] Sir Sam Cowan for failing to carry out a risk assessment in light of the changes he proposed. To be consistent with this finding, inquiries should also be required to subject their recommendations to a risk assessment in order to ensure that they do not incite unintended consequences.

The fact that a call for further reviews is the second most common recommendation would suggest that, even after months of study, there are critical issues which remain unresolved, for which the most appropriate course of action still remains unknown. This would suggest that the situation faced by those involved contained ambiguities which remained unclear even after a considerable period of reflection let alone at the time.

The final three most frequent recommendations would seem to be interrelated. They focus on structures and arrangements, roles and responsibilities and how they are executed. This would seem to place greater focus on good management design rather than knowledge and skills; they focus on the bureaucracy rather than the skills and ability of the individual to perform the function required of them.

I see two ways of looking at the frequency at which recommendations are made. The first is that they represent the weakest areas within the system. The second is that they represent the factors that those making the recommendations see as being most important in ensuring that *the unwanted* does not occur. At this stage I am not clear which of these it is. However, if it is the latter, then it is interesting to note that the top two represent the need for capability or knowledge that did not exist at the time, which puts the attribution of blame in a whole new light!

My findings raise two points. The first is whether those conducting inquiries have the same understanding about what is required to prevent these occurrences as do those who have executive responsibility. The second is that if there is a gulf between the two, and this causes management to react specifically to recommendations for political reasons rather than believing that they may actually help, this might be a significant reason why society does not seem to learn from the experience of others.

INQUIRY MENTAL MODEL CRITICAL SUCCESS FACTORS

Individuals have their own way of seeing the connections between the factors and will set their own priorities. It will take intensive discussion for individuals to come to understand how others perceive the links therefore I see little point in trying to establish a definitive set of links at this stage. However, it is possible to be clear about what each factor entails and to offer some logic for each link in order to provide others with a starting point for their own debate. I will examine each factor in turn.

Governance issues affect how external stakeholders (those outside the immediate management structure), oversee activities to ensure that the required benefits are delivered in an appropriate manner. These stakeholders may range from non-executive directors, shareholders, regulators or governing body, to the public or society in general. While issues of governance may relate to any part of an organisation or its activities, the main link is seen to be to the *performance management* processes.

The second set of labels I have used to group the recommendations relates the activity of planning and documenting the activity required to deliver the required benefit. The key theme of this work is to ensure that plans do not just become *fantasy documents*. The labels identify four levels of planning activity.

The first level of planning looks at the conceptual or policy-level documents. These are likely to be aspirational and set the context for organisational activity. In themselves these documents are likely to have only tenuous links to any activity directly related to accidents. From a risk management perspective, where relevant, they should articulate how policy relates to the prevention of unwanted outcomes. They should also articulate what the policy means for planning at the strategic or operational levels.

The second level of planning looks at the strategic or operational level. These plans set out, at the higher levels, how a benefit will be delivered. Here again the links between plans and the final actions may be very tenuous. These plans generally are important as they set priorities and the resources that the organisation allocates to delivering a benefit. These plans will need to be linked to the relevant processes and procedures.

The third level of planning looks at the procedural and process level; these are more likely to have a direct effect on whether an unwanted occurrence happens or not. However, *verbatim compliance* with rules and procedures do not in all circumstances prevent unwanted occurrences happening for all the reasons stated previously. Therefore rules and procedures need not only to be connected to compliance issues but also to the learning, knowledge and skills required to understand and use the tools and equipment provided, and the standards to which they must work.

The fourth level of planning looks at the analysis and design stages. Plans do not just write themselves. Implicit in the planning process is the analysis and design required prior to any plan being written. The stage therefore needs to be linked to the writing of plans at each level.

Management at all levels also needs to be managed. This is done through what I have labelled *performance management*. Each level needs to be linked directly or indirectly to the appropriate level of *performance management*.

I have labelled three types of recommendation as political. These recommendations require the political[a] skill of negotiation rather than bureaucratic or managerial organisational skills to accomplish their goals.

The first political level concerns resource prioritisation. I have called this political as resource allocation is rarely made solely on the basis of need built on objective criteria. In reality resource allocation is a process of negation between competing interest groups. The allocation of resource pervades everything that an organisation does.

The second political level concerns changes to power structures. Organisational structures and related power structures are developed during negotiations between individuals and interest groups both inside

---

a   Defined as "relating to a person or organisations status or influence". See Fowler's *Pocket Oxford Dictionary* (1984).

and outside the organisation. These power structures are linked to the bureaucracy structures and responsibilities developed by the organisation.

The third political level concerns changes to legislation or regulations. While some of the regulations may be internal to the organisations, much will be based on legislation or regulation which requires negotiation with other interested parties. These negotiations are often long and protracted and are therefore unlikely to be easy to achieve. The recommendations are seen to be the basis for the standards set within organisations.

The next set of labels defining recommendations relates to new or enhanced capabilities required to deliver the desired benefit. Again this is divided into three levels.

The first level of capability concerns general cultural traits. These relate to the espoused norms within an organisation. While they relate to what is generally acceptable within the specific organisation, their link to specific action may be tenuous. Also an organisation may espouse one set of values and practise another. As such the culture that drives an organisation can be seen to be an all pervasive part of the capability that links to the way everything is done within the organisation.

The second level of capability is far more tangible. This concerns knowledge, skills and the organisation's ability to learn and then transfer this learning to its staff. The placing of this factor in the model is based on the belief that it is people that deliver benefits and all the rest of the organisation is about properly enabling the people to deliver the benefits desired by an external party. This capability links to compliance, where particular activities need to be monitored specifically, or to *performance management* in general.

The third level of capability concerns systems, services, technology or equipment required to deliver the benefits desired by external parties. These capabilities relate to all the inanimate (non-human) parts of the organisation which often drive not only the competencies required to operate them but they will dictate, by their operating envelope, the standards of what they will deliver.

The fifth group of recommendations affects how internal stakeholders ensure the efficient and effective delivery of defined benefits; I have labelled this as *performance management*. Here again there are three defined levels that are intertwined.

> The first level of *performance management* concerns a supervisory function. This embraces both corporate governance and project/programme governance. In both these cases the responsibility is one step removed from the day-to-day management of the activity. These are the *Investigators*; the people who need to have a solid *seat of understanding* in order to ask incisive questions of those with the direct responsibility for delivering the benefit.

> The second level of *performance management* concerns direct action (direction, scrutiny, control and communications) required to not only deliver the defined benefit but also to ensure that unwanted occurrences are avoided. This requires not only the review of day-to-day activities but also ensuring those regulatory and legal requirements are satisfied.

> The third level of *performance management* concerns personal appraisals including the evaluation of competence or conduct. This includes not only the management appraisal of individual staff on a day-to-day and annual basis but it also includes the provision and review of specific competencies required by law and regulation for individuals to perform specific functions.

The sixth set of recommendations affects the administrative procedures required by the organisation to manage its own activities or to deliver the defined benefit to external parties. Four categories of activities were identified.

> The first category of bureaucracy concerns structures or arrangements deemed necessary to deliver the benefit; they provide a mechanism for communication and coordination between the various parties involved. It should be noted that they do not in themselves deliver the benefit; they are enablers. As such they may be, in themselves, a cause of unwanted occurrences. They can be seen to link to responsibilities and all levels of planning.

> The second category of bureaucracy concerns authority, roles and responsibilities allocated to individuals and groups. Again this is an important enabler but, in itself, does not ensure that unwanted events do not occur. Roles and responsibilities need to relate to the structure and plans involved in delivery.

The third category of bureaucracy concerns audit or compliance. This relates to the organisation making positive checks to ensure some particular aspect conforms to some pre-set standard. Audit and compliance is however just data that needs to be fed in the *performance management* process where its significance is evaluated and decisions on "what happens next" are taken.

The final category of bureaucracy concerns the need to define specific terms in order to avoid confusion. Once a term has been defined it should (only) be used within any plan or other document to convey the defined meaning.

The seventh set recommendations propose new or revised standards. The recommendations on standards cover two related issues.

The first issue relates to the formulation, definition, documentation and communication of the standards (or guidance) to which a routine is to be performed. These formalised standards are then linked to the written plans, procedures and processes and the competencies necessary to deliver performance commensurate with those standards.

The second issue is the defining of competencies required to deliver results commensurate with the set standards associated with the conduct of a specific task. These competencies then need to be linked to training required to ensure that designated personnel are able to deliver the defined competencies.

The eighth set of recommendations propose specific technical changes to existing systems to ensure that they are safer or more reliable. These recommendations come from outside the organisations and look to learn from the experience in order to adapt:

The first level of technical recommendation concerns specific amendments to formal processes. These therefore need to be linked to the rewriting of procedures and processes.

The second level of technical recommendations concerns specific changes or modification to existing infrastructure, machinery or the technology being used. This factor needs to be linked to the capabilities that exist with the organisation.

There are also three types of recommendations used that do not lead directly to action by those intimately involved in the events. They either ask for further reviews to be conducted, they admonish the protagonist for action or inaction or they pass comment on some aspect of the event.

> Further review recommendations propose that further "consideration" or analysis of specific subject matter is undertaken; they indicate that the inquiry has identified an issue but does not wish or is not able to offer advice at this time as to how the issue should be addressed.

> Some recommendations admonish protagonists for the way they conducted their duties and simply remind them of a particular requirement of their role or aspect of a routine. These simply point to a particular failure.

> Some recommendations are just comments where those conducting the inquiry think it necessary pass a judgement. They require no action.

Finally, there are recommendations that consider the purpose of the system needs examining. While the purpose should be the fundamental driver of organisational design and activity, and therefore needs to link to everything being done, it seems that inquiries rarely consider this factor. For this symbolic reason I have listed it last; from a risk management perspective however, I would consider this factor first.

Discussion

Four points need to be discussed at this point in the debate. These are the omission of consideration of the outcome being pursued, a stratification of the model components, the significance of the wording and whether agreement with the model is necessary for it to have utility.

IMPORTANCE OF OUTCOME

From my sample it would appear that consideration of the intended outcome of the organisation is rare: four of nearly 1,100 recommendations considered it. This is about 0.4 per cent. While this may be the reason an organisation exists, its importance and the pressure that an organisation faces to deliver the benefit and survive are only mentioned when the drive to deliver is seen to be a contributory factor to the accident. In these circumstances the drive is referred to as *production pressure*. For the purpose of risk management however the balance between efficiency/productivity (doing more for less) and going out of business can be a very marginal judgement. The only difference between survival and oblivion may depend on whose luck runs out first. I will give two examples. On the one hand, when investigating *high reliability organisations*, Roe and Schluman seemed surprised at the "frequent mention of the role of 'luck' in maintaining balances in the (electrical) grid during critical periods".[6] On the other, it was ironic that the night that the rig Deepwater Horizon was destroyed by an explosion and fire, there was an executive team on board the rig celebrating a safety milestone of seven years without a single lost-time incident.[7] *Attribution bias* is seen when we attribute our successes to our skills and our failures to bad luck. In overlooking the purpose of any system, inquiries fail to set their work in context and fail to judge where a norm has existed which only in hindsight is seen as a *latent failure;* where the difference between the tragedy happening to your organisation or someone else's comes down to the unfortunate alignment of the necessary factors in one case rather than another; in other words luck. If society wishes to express its disapproval in the form of inquiry findings it is free to do. However, false lessons may be learnt or false expectations may be set if they are not clear whether those involved were uniquely responsible or where the events are but one unfortunate example of a wider potential hazard.

STRATIFICATIONS OF FUNCTIONS

Another issue with the mental model as described above is that it does not make clear the level within society at which it is working. Therefore when we refer to governance it may not be clear whether we are looking at the national level or at community interest in local services. The report by Rita Donaghy[8] provides a useful categorisation where she uses the labels Macro, Mezzo and Micro. These are described as:

1. Macro, for example, society, education, industry, corporate organisation, unions, Health and Safety Executive.

2. Mezzo, for example, project, management and organisation, procurement.

3. Micro, for example, worker, workplace, supervisor.

These categories provide a way to stratify specific issues. I take as an example the skill and training required to deliver effective risk management. While the skills are designed to achieve the same end, no unwanted occurrences, the specific skill and knowledge required at each level will be different. At the Macro level the skill may entail greater conceptualisation of the issues and improving the investigative skill; learning to ask the right questions. At the Mezzo level the skill may focus on coordination and communications to ensure plans are effectively delivered. At the Micro level the training may focus on the specific of certain procedures and the related artisan skills.

In terms of the mental model the constructs of Macro, Mezzo and Micro provide great depth. This stratification can be seen to correspond approximately to the levels defined as Planning 1, 2 and 3, and Performance Management 1, 2 and 3. This would suggest that there may be potential for misunderstanding elsewhere within the model and so cross-understanding may be enhanced by awareness and discussion of the potential Macro, Mezzo and Micro stratification.

SIGNIFICANCE OF WORDING

The wording of recommendations is highly significant. The words selected will have connotations for all that follows. This is an issue of cross-understanding for, what do I think the author meant; what was their intent? Here are two examples. I first contrast "power" with "responsibility" and then contrast "ensure" with "audit".

The word power has connotations of legal authority, the ability to impose the will of those with power on the unwilling. On the other hand the word responsibility is seen to be a step softer. The person with responsibility may not have the power to impose their will and so will have to influence and persuade others in order to fulfil their responsibilities. This will in turn have considerable effect on the system dynamics and the mental model of how the end will be achieved.

With the exception of Table 3.7, the majority of recommendations use the word power to denote a statutory authority; the usage in the examples in Table 3.8 is ambiguous.

Table 3.8 sets outs two recommendations where responsibility suggests power, and where the ability to set standards and to enforce them equates to power. Table 3.7 and Table 3.8 demonstrate a potential cross-over and therefore ambiguity between the use of terms such as power and responsibility.

Table 3.7   Power Recommendations

Walker (2009) Recommendation 22. Voting powers should be exercised ...
Panckhurst (2012) Recommendation 11. Worker participation in health and safety in underground coal mines should be improved through legislative and administrative changes. – allow unions to appoint check inspectors with the same powers as the worker health and safety representatives.

Table 3.8   Responsibility Recommendations

CAIB (2003) Recommendation R7.5–1. Establish an independent Technical Engineering Authority that is responsible for technical requirements and all waivers to them ...
Smith (2005) Report 4 Recommendations 18. ... I suggest that the Healthcare Commission (or, if it comes into being, the controlled drugs inspectorate) should be responsible for approving SOPs for GPs in private practice and for ensuring compliance...

In the same way we can look at the words audit and ensure. The word audit has connotations of checking, of looking at what is happening and reporting back. The word ensure has a fuller flavour. The word ensure has connotations of planning, tasking, monitoring, advising and assessing; in fact all the facets of management. Therefore audit is but one of the steps required to ensure the desired outcome is delivered. The question remains whether these words are meant to have these meanings and are used in this way consistently.

While I am sure that the report authors will have selected their words very carefully, it is not so clear that they were conscious that they used these words in a similar way to other report writers and what they might mean to their potential audiences. If we are to learn more from inquiry recommendations, a conscious effort needs to be made to ensure a consistent lexicon for action is created.

AUDIENCES

Every inquiry report will have two audiences. The first will be those directly involved and the second will be those wishing to learn the lessons that emerge from the events. While it is clear that the reports do address the first audience, it is not so clear that they address the second one. If the authors feel that it is proper to point out that organisations have failed to learn from some previous event then they need to be clear about what they envisage the organisation should have learnt from others and be conscious of the part that they and their predecessors have to play in the process. They need to be aware of the part they have to play in the failure to communicate these lessons. This would suggest that when wording their recommendations they need to be conscious of any lessons learnt which might have a wider application and present them in a way that is digestible to those not directly involved.

FACTORS, WEIGHTING AND UTILITY

If you do not agree with the construct of the mental model presented above, does this matter? I would say not. What is important is that all parties to a particular discussion firstly recognise that they need to make a deliberate effort to develop cross-understanding. After this preparatory work, they need to understand enough about how the other parties view the issue to be able to work towards the same end in the same way.

This work therefore is designed to provide a framework which could be used by others to discuss whether these are the right factors, whether there may be others that are missing and whether the weighting given to each is correct. This work cuts across many individual academic disciplines. I am sure that specialists in each discipline will see much to criticise in my representation of their discipline. I think that this is also likely to be a fair criticism of many managers in general. Therefore when inquiries criticise individuals for a lack of understanding of some area of management, they need to offer a clear analysis of why that person should have known some particular detail of the subject area and in their recommendations explain how this needs to be addressed.

Summary

In this chapter we have examined what inquiry reports report. We have developed a mental model implied by analysis of report recommendations which contrasts with the mental model proposed for executives in *risk governance* roles. We see the relative importance placed on each by the frequency of each type of recommendation and we have discussed some of the implications.

At this point we are now able to contrast the mental model implied by inquiry recommendations with another way of holistically viewing organisations and that is through the lens of *performance management*. We have

26 building blocks. This might be contrasted with *performance management* which by one account had ten. These are to (1) respond to elected officials' and the public's demands for accountability, (2) make budget requests, (3) do internal budgeting, (4) trigger in-depth examinations of performance problems and possible corrections, (5) motivate, (6) contract, (7) evaluate, (8) support strategic planning, (9) communicate better with the public to build public trust, and (10) improve.[9] On the other hand, Behn sees performance measurement used to (1) evaluate, (2) control, (3) budget, (4) motivate, (5) promote, (6) celebrate, (7) learn, and (8) improve.[10] In these differences we can start to see areas where cross-understanding between the two perspectives may be difficult and why communication between the two may, on occasions, fail.

Hatry notes that improving programmes is the fundamental purpose of performance measurement, and all but two of these ten uses – improving accountability and increasing communications with the public – "are intended to make program improvements that lead to improved outcomes".[11] With this we see consistency with the purpose of this discussion; this is to learn and so to improve. Therefore our next step is to examine the quality of the learning building blocks, the recommendations.

Endnotes

1   Toft (2001).
2   Hutton (2004).
3   Dame Janet Smith DBE (2005), www.shipman-inquiry.org.uk/reports.asp, accessed 17 October 2012.
4   Hallett (2005), para.8.
5   Haddon-Cave (2009), page 375, para.13.80.
6   Roe and Schulman (2008), page 72.
7   Konrad and Shroder (2011), page 248.
8   Donaghy (2009), page 7: Part 2 – External Research.
9   Hatry (1999), pages 257.
10   Behn (2003).
11   Hatry (1999), pages 158.

4

Quality of the Recommendations

In the previous chapter we looked to define the implicit mental model that underlies inquiries. This work has identified 26 factors, building blocks, which make up the model. However, we also recognise that each person's model will be unique in its arrangement of and the links envisaged between the blocks. This has implications for the way that individuals understand how others think about these issues. This difference will extend to their opinions about the quality of the recommendations produced. Within *performance management*, one of the criteria for quality often reviewed is value for money. In their 2005 report the Public Administration Select Committee (PASC) discussed this issue at length and raised questions over whether this was being achieved. While I see this as being an important topic, I am not even going to attempt to broach it as it would require more space than we have here and most readers would find the subject too dull; perhaps it is a subject for another day. It should be noted that, in its response to the Committee's report, the Government rejected the need for research into this issue.[1]

When it comes to the quality of recommendations, in this chapter we will consider the question, often used in *performance management* books, "What does 'good' like?" Again, as an individual, our view of what is good is likely to be highly subjective, what we shall do here is to discuss some criteria that might be used as part of any such evaluation.

Findings and Recommendations

Within the idea of "it should never happen again" we see the goal of inquiries as being to turn normal organisations into, in the code used by academics, *high reliability organisations*. Academics however have expressed concern about whether the recommendations as currently formulated will achieve this. For example, Arjen Boin and Paul Schulman[2] "wonder whether the recommendations of the CAIB (the Columbia investigation) report would help NASA become one" (a *high reliability organisation*). At the core of being a *high reliability organisation* is process management. The recommendations, like the recommendations of many inquiries were "of a structural nature. They impose new bureaucratic layers rather than designing intelligent processes".

James Reason has commented on the tendency for inquiries to recommend the "writing (of) another procedure" and the emphasis placed upon "blame and train". He says, "People feel helpless in the face of ever present dangers and, while the familiar reaction to incidents and events, such as writing another procedure and 'blame and train' may not actually make the system more resilient to future organisational accidents, they at the least serve the anxiety reducing function of being seen to do something".[3] In her report Dame Janet Smith recognises the limitation of "yet more procedures". She says, "The main reason why this investigation (into Shipman) failed was that the wrong people were in charge of it." She goes on, "Nowadays, good police practice requires that there should be a protocol for the handling of many types of situation that occur on a regular basis. However, there will always be some sets of circumstances that are new and different from what has happened before. There cannot be a protocol for every eventuality. Some problems can be resolved only by the application of the minds of people with the necessary intelligence and experience."[4] We see from this that inquiry recommendations must be more than offering up new structures and more rules.

If we are to learn from inquiries we need practitioners to take the lessons and apply them to their own circumstances. To do this the lessons must be as clear as possible and communicated in such a way that they will be understood. As I read inquiry recommendations some can seem to be written in a political code which is not meant to be understood by the lay-reader. In truth, I do not know whether this is the case or whether they are just unclear in construct and badly written. Whichever it is, it militates against the aim of preventing such occurrences ever happening again.

In the previous chapter we started to expose the complexities involved in ensuring that "it never happens again". We see that there is a linkage between structure, roles, capability, legislation, regulation, plans, standards, guidance, protocols, procedures, routines, audit and other management supervisory processes (see Figure 4.1). However we are not clear about how those making the recommendations envisage that its substance will prevent the event recurring; we assume that they do because otherwise why would they have made the recommendation. We do not know whether they see all that is required is that specific action or that they envisage a whole chain of other unspecified action as well.

GAPS IN LEARNING

In the lengthy documents that make up inquiry reports there is much detail. There is clear temptation for inquiry teams to pass comments on the many and various aspects that emerge during the course of their inquiry which, in turn, are not followed up with recommendations. While this temptation is quite understandable, it can present problems for those looking to learn from their work. The first issue is that it conflates data, analysis and deductions with potential lessons. The second issue is that, as what might be seen as a throw away comment, it may alienate their audience. The reasons for this are that the value of these recommendations may be difficult to assess and they may be taken just as examples of pomposity. The final issue is that without the lessons being included within the recommendation they are likely to be missed as few people will read the main document. If the panel thinks the issue is important enough to warrant comment, they need to ensure the issue is drawn to the notice of their audience by being included within the recommendations. Such gaps can be seen as evidence that the inquiry team do not see or clearly understand the part they have to play in the learning process.

ADEQUATE-TO-PURPOSE

As concern has been expressed about inquiry recommendations we now have to examine what they should look like. In his paper on "The theory and practice of performance measurement" Pietro Micheli[5] looks at the way we assess the quality of individual and collective efforts. His views on the need for clear mental models are consistent with mine as he states:

> *The relevance and unavoidability of interpretive models in the measurement process also highlight the importance of surfacing mental models in the design and use of PM (performance measurement) systems … since long-term success often depends on the process through which management teams modify and improve the shared mental models of their organizations…*

After examining measurement from three paradigmatic standpoints (metaphysical, representational and relativistic) he states:

> *It would be nonsensical to state that a performance indicator is either "good" or "bad" in absolute terms. Rather, on the bases of its goals and other relevant factors (for example, cost, quality), an indicator could be deemed adequate or inadequate-to-purpose.*

It is therefore this idea of "adequate-to-purpose" that we will examine. To do this we need to ask the question, "What is the purpose of these inquiries?" Here we need to look to both the general and the specific.

Analytical Perspective

As discussed in an earlier chapter our view of the world affects how we see, analyse and evaluate an issue. This idea does not only hold good for us as individuals but also how we as groups, as a society, view issues. We can also see that, over time, the values that we use to evaluate an issue can change. As an example we can track back to Barry Turner's description of *failure of foresight* as:

> *The collapse of precautions that had hitherto been regarded culturally as adequate ... some large-scale disasters that are potentially foreseeable and potentially avoidable, and that, at the same time, are sufficiently unexpected and sufficiently disruptive to provoke a cultural reassessment of the artefacts and precautions available to prevent such occurrences.* [6]

However, Turner's comments were of their time; he wrote this in 1976. He stated that:

> *When a trawler is lost in Arctic fishing grounds, or when a wall collapses onto a firefighting team, there is much less comment than when an accident kills passengers on a suburban commuter train.*

This is no longer the case. In 2010, for example, there were cases in the UK of the fire-service and the police being prosecuted under health and safety regulations, which have had a significant effect on the service provided. Here I quote examples given in the media:

Boy drowned as police support officers "stood by". The parents of a schoolboy who drowned in a pond have demanded to know why two police support officers did not try to save their son.[7]

A volunteer coastguard who was nominated for an award for rescuing a schoolgirl from a cliff has resigned after a row over health and safety. Paul Waugh climbed down to Faye Harrison, 13, who was hanging on by her fingertips and about to fall 200ft … He did not wear safety equipment as it would have taken time to go back to his vehicle which was some distance away. (Waugh) climbed down and held on to her for 30 minutes until she could be winched to safety. Mr Waugh was later told that he had broken rules. The Maritime and Coastguard Agency (MCA) said it was not looking for dead heroes.[8]

Firefighters have been ordered to use "common sense" during emergencies after health and safety rules prevented them rescuing a mother who lay dying in a mine shaft for six hours.[9]

The 7/7 inquest heard how the transport police held back London underground staff from responding to the incident "and (how) nobody was sent to the track for at least 25 minutes" because of the potential danger to the rescuers.[10]

This change in social attitude continues. The Haddon-Cave report and the way UK civilian laws are being used as the benchmark against which military action in combat in Afghanistan are judged may be seen as a continuation of this same trend.

Another shift in public perception was seen in relation to the destruction of the NASA shuttle, Challenger, in 1986. By the time of its tenth and last flight, for political considerations, the shuttle programme was no longer designated as being "experimental"; it became a "bus into space". Public perception moved from the flights being "brave men and women doing extraordinary things" to one where the craft was perceived as being as safe as other forms of air travel. Therefore it was acceptable and safe enough, to take "civilians into space". Therefore when a shuttle exploded, killing its crew and a civilian (Christa McAuliffe) this came as a great shock to the public and the search for someone to blame started. But what short memories we have. By the time Apollo 13 flew, less than ten months after the Apollo 11 mission first landed on the moon, the flights were considered so routine that they no longer received wide coverage by the television networks; it was only after the explosion occurred on-board the spacecraft that the public interest was once again aroused.[11] Public perception about what is extraordinary may be quite short lived.

In October 2012, six Italian Government scientists and one official were sentenced to six years in prison for failing to predict the earthquake that struck L'Aquila in April 2009. The earthquake, which was of 6.3 magnitudes, killed 309 and devastated the city. The scientists and the official were members of the National Commission for the Forecast and Prevention of Major Risks. They were accused of providing "inexact, incomplete, and contradictory" information about the level of risk. This case is not about the scientists' ability to predict earthquakes – it is about their statements communicating the risk of an earthquake; communication is at the bottom of this case. David Spiegelhalter, Professor of the Public Understanding of Risk at Cambridge University, warns of the dangers created by this case:

> It would be terrible if we started practising defensive science and the only statements we made were bland things that never actually drew one conclusion or another. But of course if scientists are worried, that's what will happen. [12]

This would suggest that incidents, such as those in the mind of Turner, would now cause the "cultural reassessment of the artefacts and precautions" of which he had previously spoken. Therefore, there must be questions raised over the exclusions Turner articulated.

> In accounting for failures of foresight, undesirable events known about in advance but which were unavoidable with the resources available can be disregarded. In addition, little time need be spent on catastrophes that were completely unpredictable. Neither of these categories present problems of explanation. In the former case, because of lack of resources, no action was possible. In the latter, no action could have been taken because of a total lack of information or intelligence.[13]

The case for the first exclusion needs to be reviewed because of the concept of *Production pressure*[14] as a source of *the unwanted* occurrence. *Production pressure* is said to be an inappropriate balance between the drive for benefits delivery and the resources (including both time and money) allocated to the task resulting in *the unwanted*, both in terms of outcomes (accidents, disasters or crises) or process. Colligan and Murphy[15] describe how workers are put under "considerable pressure to increase production". This concept is also used by, amongst others, Perrow in his work on *normal accidents,* by Peter Sagan[16] on how "production pressures on lower-level personnel can ... lead to unauthorised or unapproved activity" and by Diane Vaughan[17] in her commentary "the historically accepted explanation of the Challenger launch decision: production pressure and managerial wrongdoing". The issue of whether the "appropriate" resource could have been made available by reprioritisation is a common theme of accident inquiry reports. Therefore, while Turner excluded *production pressure,* in the current context, failures due to an inappropriate allocation of resources are now likely to be labelled a *failure of foresight.*

In the case of the second exclusion, there are questions over what, if anything, might currently be accepted to be "completely unpredictable". Reports from accident inquiries all seem to be able to identify a root cause and they always seem to be able to show that warning signs were available but, for some reason, were missed. Therefore the scope of *failure of foresight* needs to be expanded to include all potential events, no matter what their source or their predictability.

This widening of the *failure of foresight* concept has already happened elsewhere. Vaughan citing Turner states: "'failure of foresight': long incubation periods typified by signals of potential danger that were either ignored or misinterpreted."[18] She does not acknowledge any of Turner's original nuances.

PURPOSE OF INQUIRIES

Within the UK, general statements of purpose are provided by the air, maritime and railways accident investigation boards as well as the health and safety executives. The three accident investigation boards are consistent in their purpose. They are:

> *The purpose of the AAIB is: to improve aviation safety by determining the causes of air accidents and serious incidents and making safety recommendations intended to prevent recurrence ... It is not to apportion blame or liability.*[19]

> *The role of the MAIB is to contribute to safety at sea by determining the causes and circumstances of marine accidents and working with others to reduce the likelihood of such accidents recurring in the future. Accident investigations are conducted solely in the interest of future safety. ... the Branch does not apportion blame.*[20]

The RAIB[21] says: Our purpose for investigating an accident or incident is ... to prevent further accidents from occurring. We achieve this by identifying the causes of accidents and other aspects that made the outcome worse... and are focused solely on safety improvement – we do not apportion blame or liability.

The HSE sees itself as having a different role; it sees its mission as being, "The prevention of death, injury and ill health to those at work and those affected by work activities."[22] They see their purpose as being one of enforcement.[23] As part of this enforcement role they:

- ensure that dutyholders take action to deal immediately with serious risks;

- promote and achieve sustained compliance with the law;

- ensure that dutyholders who breach health and safety requirements, and directors or managers who fail in their responsibilities, may be held to account, which may include bringing alleged offenders before the courts in England and Wales, or recommending prosecution in Scotland, in the circumstances set out later in this policy.

The HSE see the role of the investigation process as being "vital both in the interests of justice and to reduce the likelihood that the outcome of the investigation (including any legal proceedings) can be successfully challenged".[24] The significance of the difference in the emphasis will be examined later in this book.

The House of Commons PASC 2005 report states that, "The term 'independent public inquiry', as it has come to be used in this country, is a loose one ... (and that they) have instead concentrated on those inquiries set up by ministers to investigate specific, often controversial events that have given rise to public concern."[25] The report also says, "For the Government the primary purpose of an inquiry is to prevent recurrence." It is also their view that "the main aim is to learn lessons, not apportion blame".[26] Their concern was that, despite the resources expended on inquires (£300 million since 1990),[27] organisations still failed to learn. The Inquiries Act 2005, which was the consequence of the Select Committee report, emphasised this point in section 2; it stated, "An inquiry panel is not to rule on, and has no power to determine, any person's civil or criminal liability." The act does not however address the issue of blame. This leaves a fine differentiation between blame, responsibility, criticisms and legal (civil or criminal) liability.

The purpose or function of inquiries is not however that straight forward. Sir Ian Kennedy and Lord Howe identified to the Select Committee a number of different functions.[28] Sir Ian Kennedy's list of functions consisted of (1) the recognition and identification of different, genuine perceptions of the truth, (2) learning, (3) healing, (4) catharsis, (5) prescribing, and (6) accountability. Lord Howe's version is listed in Table 4.1.

Table 4.1   Howe's Inquiry Functions

Establishing the facts – providing a full and fair account of what happened, especially in circumstances where the facts are disputed, or the course and causation of events is not clear.
Learning from events – and so helping to prevent their recurrence by synthesising or distilling lessons which can be used to change practice.
Catharsis or therapeutic exposure – providing an opportunity for reconciliation and resolution, by bringing protagonists face to face with each other's perspectives and problems.
Reassurance – rebuilding public confidence after a major failure by showing that the government is making sure it is fully investigated and dealt with.
Accountability, blame and retribution – holding people and organisations to account, and sometimes indirectly contributing to the assignation of blame and to mechanisms for retribution.
Political considerations – serving a wider political agenda for government either in demonstrating that "something is being done" or in providing leverage for change.

With all these competing priorities, there is therefore a danger that the issue of learning is lost.

TERMS OF REFERENCE

Each inquiry is given a specific purpose which is stated in their terms of reference. Some are very brief, such as those given to (1) the Lord Justice Taylor:

> *To inquire into the events at Sheffield Wednesday football ground on 15 April 1989 and to make recommendations about the needs of crowd control and safety at sports events.*

Or (2) Lord Hutton:

> *urgently to conduct an investigation into the circumstances surrounding the death of Dr Kelly.*

In the middle ground are the terms of reference giving to Lord Laming (see Table 4.2).

Table 4.2   Laming's (2003) Terms of Reference

1. To establish the circumstances leading to and surrounding the death of Victoria Climbié.
2. To identify the services sought or required by, or in respect of Victoria Climbié, Marie-Therese Kouao and Carl Manning from local authorities in respect of their social services functions, the Health bodies and the Police between the arrival of Victoria Climbié and Marie-Therese Kouao in England in March 1999 and Victoria Climbié's death in February 2000.
3. To examine the way in which local authorities in respect of their social services functions, the health bodies and the police: (i) responded to those requests, or need for services (ii) discharged their functions (iii) co-operated with each other (iv) co-operated with other services including the local education authorities and the local housing authorities; in respect of the three persons named above during the period referred to above and thereafter.
4. To reach conclusions as to the circumstances leading to Victoria Climbié's death and to make recommendations to the Secretary of State for Health and to the Secretary of State for the Home Department as to how such an event may, as far as possible, be avoided in the future.
5. To deliver a report of the Inquiry to the Secretary of State for Health and to the Secretary.

At the extreme end are the terms of reference provided to James Baker for inquiry into the explosion at the BP Texas City refinery. There were over 880 words which could be distilled down to "examine the processes used". In the case of Texas City the terms of reference were very prescriptive as to what needed to be examined.

An examination of the terms of reference given to the inquiries referred to in the previous chapter reveals a pattern, a mental model (see Table 4.3), for setting the requirement.

Table 4.3   Consolidated Terms of Reference

	Pattern of Activity	Actual Wording From Terms of Reference
1.	The action to be taken	Assess, inquire into, investigate, identify, examine, explain, establish, review and evaluate
2.	The target of the action	The events, the facts and circumstances, the underlying causes, where responsibility lies, the process, the performance, the response, the adequacy, the impacts, the arrangements, the extent, the decisions, the effectiveness
3.	The way the inquiry is to be conducted	What, why, how Conducted in accordance with
4.	What is to be achieved	Identify and correct threats (deficiencies/areas of vulnerability) to the safe operation Consider general experience derived, draw lessons How can we avoid such tragedy in the future, options for guarding against (such failures)
5.	Further action to be taken	Reach a judgment, conclusions, make recommendations, advise on
6.	The stakeholders to be engaged	Ensure that the views of ... are taken into account
7.	Public disclosure	Oversee full public disclosure, establishing an archive, manage the process of public disclosure
8.	The need to report	Deliver, submit, produce a report

While each part may not be specifically stated with every set of terms of reference, they are often implied, or just taken for granted. My proposition here is that leaving such things to implication and perception must be seen as a vulnerability as it may create a potential failure in cross-understanding between those involved within the process.

The PASC[29] also concludes (1) that great care needs to be taken when drawing up terms of reference so that they do not impede a full investigation, (2) that they enjoy wide support, and (3) that the chair needs to be consulted during their preparation. However, no matter how much care is taken, they will need to be interpreted by the inquiry team. To give one example, in paragraphs 9 to 11 of his report, Lord Hutton elaborates on his interpretation of his (see Table 4.4).

Table 4.4   Lord Hutton's Interpretation of his Terms of Reference

9. ... In my opinion these terms of reference required me to consider the circumstances preceding and leading up to the death of Dr Kelly insofar as (1) they might have had an effect on his state of mind and influenced his actions preceding and leading up to his death or (2) they might have influenced the actions of others which affected Dr Kelly preceding and leading up to his death. There has been a great deal of controversy and debate whether the intelligence in relation to weapons of mass destruction set out in the dossier published by the Government on 24 September 2002 was of sufficient strength and reliability to justify the Government in deciding that Iraq under Saddam Hussein posed such a threat to the safety and interests of the United Kingdom that military action should be taken against that country. This controversy and debate has continued because of the failure, up to the time of writing this report, to find weapons of mass destruction in Iraq. I gave careful consideration to the view expressed by a number of public figures and commentators that my terms of reference required or, at least, entitled me to consider this issue. However I concluded that a question of such wide import, which would involve the consideration of a wide range of evidence, is not one which falls within my terms of reference. The major controversy which arose following Mr Andrew Gilligan's broadcasts on the BBC Today programme on 29 May 2003 and which closely involved Dr Kelly arose from the allegations in the broadcasts (1) that the Government probably knew, before it decided to put it in its dossier of 24 September 2002, that the statement was wrong that the Iraqi military were able to deploy weapons of mass destruction within 45 minutes of a decision to do so and (2) that 10 Downing Street ordered the dossier to be sexed up. It was these allegations attacking the integrity of the Government which drew Dr Kelly into the controversy about the broadcasts and which I consider I should examine under my terms of reference. The issue whether, if approved by the Joint Intelligence Committee and believed by the Government to be reliable, the intelligence contained in the dossier was nevertheless unreliable is a separate issue which I consider does not fall within my terms of reference. There has also been debate as to the definition of the term "weapons of mass destruction" (WMD) and as to the distinction between battlefield WMD and strategic WMD. Mr Gilligan's broadcasts on 29 May related to the claim in the dossier that chemical and biological weapons were deployable within 45 minutes and did not refer to the distinction between battlefield weapons, such as artillery and rockets, and strategic weapons, such as long range missiles, and a consideration of this issue does not fall within my terms of reference relating to the circumstances surrounding the death of Dr Kelly.

10. I further consider that one of my primary duties in carrying out my terms of reference is, after hearing the evidence of many witnesses, to state in considerable detail the relevant facts surrounding Dr Kelly's death and also, insofar as I can determine them, the motives and reasons operating in the minds of those who took various decisions and carried out various actions which affected Dr Kelly.

11. In order to enable the public to be as fully informed as possible I have also decided, rather than set out a summary of the evidence, to set out in this report many parts of the transcript of the evidence so that the public can read what the witnesses said and can understand why I have come to the conclusions which I state.

12. Whilst I stated at the preliminary sitting on 1 August that I did not sit to decide between conflicting cases advanced by interested parties who had opposing arguments to present, it has been inevitable in the course of the Inquiry that attention has focussed on the decisions and conduct of individual persons, and therefore I think it is right that I should express my opinion on the propriety or reasonableness of some of those decisions and actions.

As we can see from Lord Hutton's analysis of his task, he has already made a number of judgements even before he starts his inquiry which would affect his product. This is both understandable and unavoidable, however it is already dividing his audience into those who will see his work an analytical triumph or just another "white wash" or cover-up.

This bias may be set at the very start of the inquiry process. Let us take as an example the Hillsborough Independent Panel that reported in 2012. One of the panel's terms of reference was to "consult with the Hillsborough families to ensure that the views of those most affected by the tragedy are taken into account". Along with the other terms which required the panel to oversee full public disclosure, manage the disclosure, establish an archive and then report, the panel could not help but have their inquiry perspective lean towards the view of the families of those who died and who had been instrumental in calling for the inquiry, as their views of what had happened did not reconcile with what had been published up to this point. So now we have two parts of the story, the Taylor reports which were viewed by many as being biased in favour of the establishment view of what had happened and the report of the "Independent Panel" which might be seen as giving a balancing view, that being the perspective of the families of the deceased. From the perspective of a risk manager trying to learn from this case, I now have to balance these two perspectives and can only wonder whether those who set up the inquiry had hoped that the Independent Panel would have established the definitive unbiased truth or whether this could only be done through an analysis of everything that had been published on the subject.

Another examination of where bias may have been built in at an early stage is in the of reference given to Haddon-Cave by the then Secretary of State for Defence. In distinct contrast to the practice of the AAIB and the other accident investigation boards, his terms of reference required him to assess "where responsibility lies"[30] and this he does. In his report he "specifically names, and criticise(s), key organisations and individuals who bear a share of responsibility". He goes on to acknowledge that his criteria for naming individuals was that, in his view, their conduct fell well below the standards which might reasonably have been expected of them. When contrasted to the judgement by Dame Janet Smith of the police action in respect of the Shipman Inquiry, Haddon-Cave's selection of those to be named appears somewhat arbitrary. While he was clear in his criticism, he makes no attempt to put their actions into context or to explain why he did not select others within the chain of command, up to and including the Chancellor of the Exchequer and the Prime Minster, both of whom would have exerted direct and indirect pressure on those named. Contrasted to the work of Snook, Haddon-Cave's analysis into this aspect of the events left as many questions as it answered on the organisational aspects of the causes. While his analysis made reference to the work of Rasmussen, he made no use of his analytical tool[31] the purpose of which is to address this very issue. In his defence, one has to question whether the format of his terms of reference caused him to skew his work to finding someone to blame.

The problem with the multiple functions of inquiries is that each of the other functions competes with the need to learn and therefore makes learning more difficult. This issue might be coupled with criticism that some inquiry reports are so technical (as in specific changes to formal processes, infrastructure, machinery, technology or method) and so specific to the case in hand that while they might have prevented the accident that happened, they do little to teach others unless they meet exactly the same situation in the future. Only in hindsight might the lessons be seen to have a wider application. An example of this can be seen in the Select Committee report[32] where they contrast the 1983 Franks Review (after the Falklands Conflict) and the Butler Report (2004) and note the similarities such as (1) the limitations on intelligence sources, (2) the intelligence assessment machinery and (3) the relationship between the different agencies. A reading of the Bichard report (2004), missed by the Select Committee, provides interesting parallels in quite a different context. This shows how lessons learnt in one area might be missed by another, despite their relevance.

When looking to learn from inquiries we therefore have to be conscious of the potential audience, whether directly or indirectly involved. Therefore we now need to consider who is calling for the inquiry, who sets them up and why, and who benefits; this will determine some of the fundamental forces that shape the way the inquiry is conducted and therefore, as a result, what is learnt and by whom.

WHAT AUDIENCE IS BEING ADDRESSED?

It is clear that the purpose of inquiries is not always simply to find the causes of an event, but also to learn lessons with the hope that such events in the future may be prevented. There can be seen to be three potential macro constituencies that may need to be addressed and satisfied by any report. These constituencies may be labelled as political, judicial and learning.

Inquiries can be seen to have a political dimension. This might be seen as one group seeking to gain an advantage over others. Here the aim of calling for an inquiry, or the desired outcome of the finding, may be to reinforce their position or weaken the position of those who oppose them. Even the Commons Select Committee suggest that "it is more cynically alleged that inquiries may involve kicking an issue into the long grass, blaming predecessors in government, making a gesture, or simply buckling to public pressure to do something."[33] In their own report on inquiries they admit that their research has a political purpose. They say: "Our research has therefore revealed a long-term diminution in Parliament's role in the process of public inquiries. We regard this as a serious development, and one which needs to be addressed urgently".[34] This political dimension can be seen to manifest itself by the criticism from some parties that the report is a "whitewash" or a cover-up and thereby indicating that the report did not enhance the position they had taken or the view that they held. While this dimension has lessons to teach us about the contradictory views held and the conflicts within organisations, they are less likely to offer direct lessons that help to prevent future unwanted occurrences.

The second dimension that can be identified is that of judicial. This can be seen in the outcome desired ("redress against perpetrators") or in the process used. While some parties to an inquiry may call for "justice", to others this justice might seem arbitrary. For example, justice for passengers might conflict with justice for the crews. Justice for grieving families might conflict with justice for those having to make decisions under great pressure and with partial information. While society may need to allocate blame (more about this later) and it has rules for doing so (enshrined in the judicial system), the *local rationality* on which these are based may not necessarily be to the benefit of society overall (also addressed in more detail later). The processes used for the inquiries which are of interest here are judicial in nature whether they are judge led or not. By looking at what they concentrate on, we can see what they are concerned with, and their underlying mental model.

One of the key barriers to learning from this dimension would be the judicial preference for rules and certainty. To those not intimately involved in the law and its application, we are faced by a complex set of rules that seem to be applied in an unfathomable and therefore arbitrary manner. It seems that laws and regulations from one domain are flexed and adapted to circumstances for which we are totally unprepared. Case law builds and the mysteries are withheld from those who would benefit from knowing. I have used the word "withheld" as I am referring to what Diane Vaughan called *structural secrecy* where "rigid hierarchies can further inhibit the flow of information". I use the word withheld because (1) findings are not generally accessible to the public, even if those who are interested know what to look for, (2) findings are often not written in a manner that can be easily understood by those outside the legal system, and (3) many of those who are aware of a particular issue do not have the resources to use the legal system to clarify the issue. In other words, the bureaucratic structure holds the lessons "secret".

The second issue is the unintended consequences of the way the law is applied. As an example I would refer back to Chapter 2 where a senior executive in a shipping company noted that while training records were essential to improving the skills and standards of their crews, should something go wrong, these same records were used against the organisation. Therefore, on balance, the consequences for his organisation may be reduced if he and his board did less to prevent the occurrence than they were able to do.

The third barrier to learning might be the perception of *verbatim compliance*. The judicial system is seen to place high reliance on the application of rules, or to outsiders, the interpretation of the rules. However, as the academic literature on *verbatim compliance* indicates, rules have their place only within a specific context. Regulation also has its place but neither rules nor regulations are panaceas. Diane Vaughan and Charles Perrow discuss[35] the advantages and disadvantage of various regulatory models and the only conclusion that can be drawn is that there is no ideal model; they all have significant weaknesses and therefore any recommendation that seems to offer regulation as a panacea should be approached with caution. Goddard and Eccles point out a further disadvantage of regulation. They show that some may either abrogate responsibility for judgement to the regulator or see that unless it is forbidden "then it cannot be irresponsible ... to adopt it".[36] This finding is supported by my own research, detailed in Chapter 2. The appliance of rules and regulations in the wrong context can also lead to unwanted occurrences. This contrast of perspectives can be seen when comparing judicial reviews, which frequently comment on where rules are broken, with the work by Roe and Schulman on the *high reliability organisation,* which puts value on people using rules flexibly in order to deliver a safer and reliable product. If couched in terms of "more rules" or "more regulation", or advocating a specific model of regulation without recognising the inherent weaknesses in the model proposed, lessons learnt in this judicial context might be ignored by those who see themselves as practical and pragmatic.

The final dimension of inquiry reports is the one that focuses on learning lessons. However, such lessons have two audiences. The first is the parties directly involved in the events which are the focus of inquiry. The second is society in general. It is understandable that the inquiry focuses on the events that are at the heart of the inquiry. They examine that event and decide how it might have been prevented. This focus on the prevention of the events that have already occurred may place barriers between the lessons learnt and external parties. The lesson may therefore be lost to others.

In summary, the analytical perspective, whether it is political, judicial or learning, may create barriers which prevent the communication of valuable lessons to others. If we are to learn from the past, those conducting the inquiries need to be aware of these issues and address them in their reports.

POLITICS, BLAME, ACCIDENT PREVENTION

As suggested earlier, there is a tension between society's need to allocate blame and the desire to learn from such events in order to avoid them in the future. This tension can be seen in the statement on the setting up of the Haddon-Cave Inquiry to the House of Commons on 13 December, 2007, the Secretary of State for Defence said:

> *In order to encourage openness, evidence given during the course of the review will not be used in disciplinary proceedings against the individual who gave it unless there is evidence of gross misconduct.*[37]

On the surface this may appear to be a fair position to take. However, without being clear about what constitutes gross misconduct, those who were the subject of the inquiry would, quite understandably, become defensive in the way they answered any questions. Even where gross misconduct is not found, those subject to the inquiry will be only too aware of how it may affect their career, their future and their view of themselves. Justice for the victims can again be seen to be at odds with justice for those involved. For this reason the accident investigation boards (as opposed to those conducting inquiries) see their purpose as finding out what happened and why, and they try to avoid the thorny subject of responsibility.

Charles Perrow divides victims into four categories.[38] These are the operator, others who are voluntarily involved, those who are involved involuntarily and what Perrow labelled "intergenerational". In the case of a plane crash, these might respectively be seen as the crew, the passengers, victims on the ground and the families of those involved. As suggested earlier when discussing Turner's view of context, what is now considered to be an accident has changed in the recent past. We also see a difference in which victims receive the most detailed consideration. Whereas the main consideration used to be given to those directly involved in the occurrence, now society sees fit to give the same if not more consideration to the families of those killed or injured as they once did to those killed or injured themselves. This change can be seen in both the change in emphasis within the coroner court system, the terms of reference for the Hillsborough Independent Panel and the cases brought against the Ministry of Defence by the families of deceased servicemen.

These aggrieved families now have the presence and the desire to pursue their cases, their lawyers find creative ways to help them with consequences never foreseen and the media uses these cases to sell newspapers. In Andrew Marr's book on his "trade",[39] he makes it quite clear the media is like all other business, which is being in the business of selling its product in order to survive and the use blame to sensationalise story in order to attract public interest. Therefore while the media plays an important role as a catalyst to the inquiry and learning process, their input is quite arbitrary as their interest waxes and wanes. For this reason I will not consider their role further. Lessons for the future management of risk and jeopardy can be hidden in complicated case law, inaccessible to those for whom it might have implications. These cases change the context, so critical to successful risk management, in unforeseen ways.

We can see this process at work within the Coroner system. While the formal role of Coroner was established in 1194, "the Coroners Act of 1887 made significant changes here, repealing much of the earlier legislation. Coroners then became more concerned with determining the circumstances and the actual medical causes of sudden, violent and unnatural deaths for the benefit of the community as a whole".[40] By 2005 the emphasis had changed from the whole community to a recommendation by Dame Janet Smith that, "The (Coroner's) report should be primarily for the benefit of the family of the deceased person"[41] and should explore the question "why". While from the *local rationality* of the Smith Inquiry these recommendations were logical and expedient, there was scant consideration of their unintended consequences. The rationale is set out and it shows an instance of mission creep, where the original purpose expands to fit a perceived need. What the Smith Inquiry does not do is to question whether the Coroner has the complete competencies (*seat of understanding*) necessary to undertake the expanded task which she now recommends; this might be seen as being consistent with her recognition of separate judicial and medical expertise required by the job. The question becomes whether a person is capable of undertaking the task of determining "why" something has happened without a full understanding of the subject matter of the relevant knowledge. If they do, can their determination be anything other than a simplistic interpretation of the true complexities involved? If this is the case, can their recommendations be taken at face value as being safe to implement and being without unintended consequences?

We can also take as an example the case of the UK Ministry of Defence (MOD) and its use of Snatch Landrovers. On 18 October, 2012, to quote the *Daily Mail*:

> *Judges at the Court of Appeal in London ruled that the families could sue the Government for negligence – saying the Ministry of Defence had a duty of care over its personnel even when they were on the battlefield. The decision opens the door for civil action which could leave defence chiefs with a multi-million pound bill for damages. A senior MP warned the ruling would have far-reaching consequences for generals making decisions on the battlefield.*
>
> *Following a hearing in London in June Lord Neuberger, Lord Justice Moses and Lord Justice Rimer ruled in favour of the families, who argued the MoD had failed to provide armoured vehicles or equipment which could have saved lives.*[42]

Of course, to quote the same article, the families' lawyer argues:

> *We maintain that the MoD's position has been morally and legally indefensible, as they owe a duty of care to those who fight on behalf of this country.*

If we were to backdate this ruling to early 1944, we would be faced with an interesting parallel. The Allied tank, the Sherman, was no match against the German Tiger tank. In the end, to compensate for having weaker armour and guns the Allies developed tactics to outmanoeuvre and destroy their German enemies. This was achieved at a high price in men and material. If asked, would the Courts have ruled that the Allied High Command was negligent in its duty of care for asking its soldiers to face such an uneven contest?

Should the Normandy invasion have been delayed until the Allies had a better tank? What lessons do we learn from this example? In risk management terms what does this teach us about what is acceptable (therefore not negligent), in terms of timeframe, between the emergence of a threat and a counter being deployed and then in what circumstances must the capability be deployed?

But, of course, the case is not as straightforward as it might seem to be as portrayed in the press. The actual findings of the court,[43] as far as I could understand them, are more nuanced. What might be seen by the public as being ridiculous can be seen as being logical and rational when viewed from the perspective of an appeal court judge. What is seen by outsiders as an issue of restrictions on the military to conduct operations is seen by the court as an issue of jurisdiction and the need to determine when or what might be included under the term combat immunity. These differing perspectives make cross-understanding between the disciplines difficult to achieve and therefore lessons more difficult to learn.

The case also raises the issue of when government politics and the politics of blame interact. The Court of Appeal[44] referred to when, what was known as Crown immunity, was removed from the MOD and the provisions made at the time (see Table 4.5).

Table 4.5   Crown Immunity Provision

53. It is significant to recall that the effect of Section 10 may be revived by order made by the Secretary of State under Section 2 of the 1987 Act, but not unless:-
"it appears to him expedient to do so-
a) by reason of any imminent national danger or of any great emergency that has arisen; or
b) for the purposes of any warlike operations in any part of the world outside the United Kingdom or of any other operations which are or are to be carried out in connection with the warlike activity of any persons in any such part of the world."
The Section allows for orders to be applied to particular circumstances and persons (s.2(3)), and no order made can have retrospective effect (s.2(4)).
54. These provisions show that Parliament cannot have thought that the imposition of liability in negligence was detrimental to the troops, and the absence of any application for an order shows that the Secretary of State did not think it necessary, in order to protect his ministry or the high command, to abrogate the laws of tort when conflict in Iraq was imminent. It is difficult to see why, in those circumstances, the courts should be expected to know better.

Here we see two issues. The first is risk transfer and the second is the utilisation of hindsight. In the case of risk transfer, the failure by one department within the MOD to revive the provision of the act might be seen to place greater stress and jeopardy on others within the department now exposed to possible jeopardy. The second issue is hindsight referred to in the final sentence. While the circumstances had changed and while judges are prepared to use knowledge gained in hindsight to criticise others, they do not seem to think it appropriate to use the same knowledge gained in hindsight to remedy errors. The judgement can be seen to have made no provision for this omission just being an oversight.

Finally we see here the view that it might be possible to provide a neat separation and precise definition of those actions within the MOD that fall into two groups, those inside and those outside when "active operations" start and when they finish. It seems that judges are prepared to criticise those who find themselves ensnared by the unexpected interactions of complex systems, but they themselves still seem to take a reductionist perspective by judging those associated with unwanted outcomes without consideration of the full extent of possible unexpected interactions. This shows us that, to quote Professor James Reason, "The law has yet to adopt a systems view of human error."[45]

The quest for justice sets the context for a particular way of viewing the world, a particular limited rationality. We see a desire to allocate responsibility which is aligned to the need to allocate blame. Dan Gardner asserts, "The instinct for blame and punishment is often a critical component in our reaction to risk."[46] This raises a question about why humans have the need to allocate blame. Gardner goes on to say that, "The absence of outrage is the reason that natural risks feel so much less threatening than man-made dangers." So we now see outrage and the need to blame as drivers within this type of activity. Studies have identified what has been referred to as the grief cycle. This is a five-stage process consisting of denial, anger, bargaining, depression and acceptance. Intertwined with these stages comes guilt (often referred to as *survivor guilt*) and the need to find someone else to blame in order to assuage that feeling of guilt. Society also seems to feel the need to allocate blame and punishment. For example and in contrast to Snook's analysis of the Iraq friendly fire case, according to Professor Scraton who provided the families' perspective in the case of Hillsborough, Mr Justice Hooper "expressed concern that 'no individual has been personally held to account in a criminal court'. He then quoted Jack Shaw: 'I share the anger that no one has suffered punishment or has been disciplined for what happened at Hillsborough.'"[47]

What is "blame"? The simple dictionary definition of blame is "assign responsibility for a fault". However it is more than that. To blame is more the act of censuring, condemning or making moral judgements about those deemed to be at fault. Professor Reason tries to explain, in layman's terms, the pathology of blame.[48] He lists seven factors that help us distance ourselves from any guilt. They are:

- The need to *point an accusing finger* at a guilty party and to endorse our own feeling of righteousness.

- By attributing base personal characteristics of carelessness, stupidity, incompetence, recklessness or thoughtlessness. This is referred to as the *fundamental attribution error*.

- How western culture places great value on being in control of our own destiny,[49] "people want to live in a world of certain knowledge, not in a world that is hard to understand and predict and where accidents and errors reign".[50] This is referred to as the *illusion of free will*.[51] This is linked to our desire to minimise our perception of uncertainty. The *illusion of free will* can be seen to be linked to *the illusion of certainty*.[52] This illusion is the fundamental tendency of human minds to create certainty and this illusion can be created and exploited as political and economic tools. Therefore we want to believe that, having free will, highly trained professional (such as doctors and pilots) can decide not to make mistakes.

- Another mechanism used to provide distance is the belief that only bad things happen to bad people or that only bad people do bad things. Based on this is the illusion that, because I am not a bad person bad thing will not happen to me. This is referred to as the *just world hypothesis*.

- There is also a universal tendency to perceive past events as more foreseeable and more avoidable than they may have been. Therefore we can again distance ourselves because we have the illusion that we would have seen the warning sign whereas those involved did not. This builds on the *fundamental attribution error* and multiplies the *outrage*. This is referred to as *hindsight bias*.

- This distancing is further reinforced by the tendency to see those directly involved as the primary cause (referred to as the *principle of least effort*). Reason also reports the tendency to limit the search for unsafe acts or errors. The first act encountered, which is often those directly involved, suffices for the purpose of the investigation; this has been referred to as the *principle of administrative convenience*.

Gabe Mythen[53] points to how blame is used as a political tool. In this context it signifies distrust based on "otherness" (that is of outsiders, another "tribe" or those who are just different). We can see this in the way immigrants can be blamed for the woes of their adopted nation.

On paper this might be seen as providing a logical and rational way for blame to be attributed. However, there is a myriad of work that shows when we are stressed or grieving we are unlikely to be rational. Therefore if we were to try to place ourselves in the place of the "agent" (the person deemed to be responsible), we would find this hard to do as we would be likely to add all the knowledge we gained in hindsight as well as creating an unfeasible proposition of how we would have stopped *the unwanted* outcome.

From the body of literature that examines legal decision making, we find work, such as that by Feigenson and Park, which looks at how emotions affect the allocation of blame. They say:

> *Angry people blame more because the cognitive structure of the anger they experience ("disapproving of someone else's blameworthy action and being displeased about the related event") makes salient the role of dispositional factors of other people (as opposed to situational factors) as causes of harm, which in turn engenders blame. Thus, emotion influences blaming judgments indirectly.*[54]

Thus, it is these feelings of outrage and guilt that drive the need to blame. In turn, these emotions affect subsequent judgements made. Feigenson and Park conclude:

> *The research on debiasing (or correction) indicates that in order to purge judgments of unwanted bias, the decision maker must be (i) aware of the unwanted influence; (ii) motivated to correct the bias; (iii) aware of the magnitude and direction of the bias; and (iv) able to adjust the response appropriately.*[55]

If we return to the Haddon-Cave report[56] into the crash of an RAF Nimrod aircraft over Afghanistan, we see he states:

> In this Report, I specifically name, and criticise, key organisations and individuals who bear a share of responsibility for the loss of XV230. I name individuals whose conduct, in my view, fell well below the standards which might reasonably have been expected of them at the time, given their rank, roles and responsibilities, such that, in my view, they should be held personally to account ... but with due regard to the requirements of fairness and the Salmon principles.[57]

We see here that the courts who arbitrate on responsibility and liability that fall out of unwanted events have a completely different frame of reference to those involved in the day-to-day management or governance of these potential issues. The court evaluates actions of individuals on the basis of written rules (the law) as opposed to the context of the actions. We see this in the comments of Dame Janet Smith where she recommends that, "Case examiners should be advised that they should not take mitigation into account when making their decisions."[58] Practitioners often see the ruling of the courts as utopian and impossible to adhere to in a practical context. When in the future another practitioner falls foul of the same law, and therefore provides another example of a "failure to learn", the courts do not seem to ask themselves whether they may have had a part to play in this failure.

FAIRNESS

Horvath provides a summary of the literature on blame from a psychological perspective. He lays out[59] the level of responsibility (Table 4.6 – Quoting Heider) that might lead to blame being attributed to an individual or a group and he also looks at fairness.

Horvath makes reference to "Fairness Theory", and role played by the constructs of "could", "should" or "would". He explains this as follows:

> When a negative event is experienced, a victim asks whether the causal agent involved could have done anything differently. The victim might also ask whether the agent "should" have acted differently on the basis of social roles or moral rules. Finally, the victim asks whether the victim "would" have done anything differently had the victim been in the agent's place.[60]

Table 4.6   Heider's Responsibility Attributes

Level	Description
Association	An individual is responsible for the outcome if the individual is associated with the outcome.
Causal Responsibility	An individual is responsible for the outcome if the individual caused the outcome.
Foreseeability	An individual is responsible for the outcome if the individual could have anticipated that the outcome would occur.
Intentionality	An individual is responsible for the outcome if the individual intended for the outcome to occur.
Justifiability	An individual is not responsible for the outcome if the individual's intentional actions were justified by the situation.

While this might be seen as a type of *substitution test,* one major caveat needs to be noted. In this case the victim will be vested in guilt avoidance and is therefore unlikely to avoid the use of hindsight to supplement what he or she would have known or how they might have acted.

An alternative view of fairness was produced by the 1966 Royal Commission on Tribunals of Inquiry (known as the Salmon Commission). Salmon produced "six cardinal principles" (see Table 4.7) which it thought addressed the issue of fairness and therefore ought to govern the conduct of Inquiry proceedings.

Table 4.7   Salmon Fairness Principles

1. Before any person becomes involved in an inquiry, the Tribunal must be satisfied that there are circumstances which affect him and which the Tribunal proposes to investigate.

2. Before any person who is involved in an inquiry is called as a witness he should be informed of any allegations which are made against him and the substance of the evidence in support of them.

3. (a) He should be given an adequate opportunity of preparing his case and of being assisted by legal advisers.

   (b) His legal expenses should normally be met out of public funds.

4. He should have the opportunity of being examined by his own solicitor or counsel and of stating his case in public at the inquiry.

5. Any material witnesses he wishes called at the inquiry should, if reasonably practicable, be heard.

6. He should have the opportunity of testing by cross-examination conducted by his own solicitor or counsel any evidence which may affect him.[61]

While the Select Committee proposed and the Government accepted that these rules should be reformulated, the revised rules changed little in principle. Here the principles of fairness can be seen to have a clear judicial perspective. They are not concerned about whether the outcome is fair, they are about fair process which is built on the expectation (with the implied mental model) that fair process will lead to a fair outcome. The idea of fair process is seen to equate to having legal representation at the inquiry. Case law and its seemingly endless process of appeals provides us with evidence that would suggest that this proposition is still open to debate!

So what is fair? We can see the conflicting interests play out in practice. The warehouse fire at the premises of Wealmoor (Atherstone) Ltd, which resulted in the tragic death of four fire-fighters, provides us with our example. The deaths led to a police investigation that cost the taxpayers of Warwickshire nearly £5 million. The investigation led to the prosecution of three senior fire-fighters for gross negligence (of which they were acquitted) rather than prosecution of anyone for setting the fire. Warwickshire County Council was fined £30,000 for breaches of health and safety regulations (a failure to keep proper records): the judge decided to limit the fine because he "didn't want the public purse to suffer any more than it needed to."[62] No one seemed happy with the final outcome. The wife of one victim said "I get very angry when people talk about how much the investigation and the trial has cost … Four men lost their lives, what does it matter how much it cost to investigate their deaths? They're entitled to justice."[63] On the other hand, the Chief Fire Officer for Warwickshire led criticism of the decision to prosecute and said (the three officers) were "treated like common criminals". The Fire Brigades Union said "it was absurd that the arsonists who started the fire had not faced trial while fire officers had". The police officer who led the injury said that he thought it was the "right thing" to do in order to provide "answers for their families and loved ones".[64] He justified the investigation because "three men were charged and brought to trial"; he also said, "Where there is a loss of life, nobody is above investigation."[65] (This is similar in sentiment to the comment made by Dame Janet Smith where she said, "Doctors should not be treated any differently from others whose errors lead to death.")[66] The quest for fairness is complicated and perhaps it may not be possible to be totally fair to all the parties involved. However, this case does raise some important questions about the relationship between investigation and prosecution, and the various local rationalities at play in this case. We can see both here and elsewhere how those conducting inquiries seem to feel compelled to link the two rather than seeing them as separate activities. In terms of local rationale, we need to question whether this is possible for the police or elsewhere for judges conducting inquiries despite their remit to do so.

UNDERSTANDING CAUSALITY

In common with the various accident investigation boards, the MOD guide (JSP832) emphasises that "the purpose of a service inquiry is to establish the facts of a particular matter (this term encompasses accidents, incidents, occurrences or events which may require investigation) and to make recommendations in order to prevent recurrence". Paragraph 5.8 goes on to state "that service inquiries are not to explicitly attribute blame or legal (criminal or civil) liability" as do the various accident investigation boards. The inquiry is directed to look at "facts of a particular matter" or causes.

Here we enter another linguistic tangle. Let us contrast the Joint Service Publication (JSP) with EU Reg996 (2010) and work by Professor Reason. The EU regulation defines "causes" as meaning "actions, omissions, events, conditions, or a combination thereof, which led to the accident or incident", this is really not very helpful as we need to understand what was in their mind when they used the words "which led to". The regulation does go on to say "the identification of causes does not imply the assignment of fault or the determination of administrative, civil or criminal liability", which suggests that, in their mind, being the cause does not automatically put the person at fault.

The JSP is more specific, it talks of "causal" and "contributory" factors. It says:

> 5.7 The panel should determine those factors which may have caused or contributed to causing the matter under investigation. Causal factors may be those that, in the opinion of the panel, if removed would have stopped the accident from occurring. Contributory factors may be those that, in the opinion of the panel, if removed would not have prevented the accident from happening but may have affected its outcome. Such factors will inform the inquiry's recommendations.

Professor Reason talks of *cause* and *conditions* set in a legal context. He quotes others when he says:

> These factors [conditions] ... are those which are present alike both in the case where such accidents occur and in the normal cases where they do not; and it is this consideration that leads us to reject them as the cause of the accident, even though it is true that without them the accident would not have occurred ... To cite factors that are present in

the case of disaster and normal functioning would explain nothing ...
Such factors do not "make the difference" between disaster and normal
functioning.

... Accidents happen because:

- *Universals: the ever-present tension between production and*
  protection create
- *Conditions: latent factors that collectively produce defensive*
  weaknesses that
- *Causes: permit the change conjunctions of local triggers and active*
  failures to breach all the barriers and safeguards.[67]

There is a final factor that needs to be considered here and that is the difference between complicated and complex causation. Nicolas Taleb, amongst others, reminds us of the difference. In essence, in complicated systems, such as electro-mechanical devices (in a plane for example), the interactions are predictable. In complex systems, such as between electro-mechanical devices, software and human operators, the interactions, "the interdependencies are severe ... causing complications and series of cascading side effects".[68] In his book *Drift into Failure* Professor Sidney Dekker explains why this differentiation is important. He says, "Complexity means that a huge number of interacting and diverse parts give rise to outcomes that are really hard, if not impossible, to foresee"[69] which opens up the possibility that "accidents could be produced without any part failing, or without anything external interfering, but rather as a result of normally functioning components interacting in unforeseen ways".[70] He concludes that the ethical consequences of taking a complexity and systems view of failure is that, and we see echoes of Scott Snook here, they have no answer to who is accountable for drift into failure.[71] From a learning and a mitigation point of view, it is very important not to confuse the two, for to do so, might, in itself have severe unintended consequences. Therefore the gross simplifications of complex systems, which are appropriate to the judicial system, may suggest dangerous solutions in the more complex world outside the court room.

Within these documents we see two mental models of causation which are not immediately compatible. This may not be helpful but it is useful. This raises two important issues. The first is the allocation of responsibility between what James Reasons has described as the sharp and blunt ends of business and the second is the scope of change required to address universal issues.

In 1997 James Reason described what he calls the positional paradox where most of the blame mostly falls on "the personal shortcomings of those at the sharp end"[72] who have to deal with the system as they find it rather than those, at the blunt end, who design and set up systems that have inbuilt mechanisms of failure. Francis in his report on the Mid Staffordshire NHS Foundation Trust says, "It would be easy to offer criticism of individuals in relation to the failure to investigate more intrusively, but the fault lay in the inadequacy of the systems in place to pursue a potentially serious concern effectively."[73] This must raise the question, who designed and approved the systems and should responsibility lie there? Reason sees this issue as being one of fairness, as do others working in this field, which is why academic research has adopted a more systemic view of these problems. The fallacy of immediacy is nicely illustrated by Nicholas Taleb when he says, "It would be unintelligent to attribute the collapse of a fragile bridge to the last truck that crossed it" and how symptom can often be confused with cause. This can be contrasted with the judicial focus on "immediacy" of the cause as can be illustrated by Phil Scraton's report on the private prosecution of Superintendents Duckenfield and Murray after Hillsborough. Alun Jones (the QC for the families) argued in court that while "the ground was 'old, shabby, badly arranged, with confusing and unhelpful signposting [and] there were not enough turnstiles'. There existed a police 'culture' ... which influenced the way in which matches were policed". Yet the "primary and immediate cause of death" lay with the defendants' own failures.[74] By these comments, and also overlooking other issues such as the safety certificate being out of date and the effect of the "find your own level" policy, the QC therefore sees that, in terms of the law, only the very last act, the most immediate one, is the one that really matters. If this is the liability that consistently takes precedence, it would bring into question the need for any comprehensive safety/risk management system. Organisations would only have to ensure they were not the most immediate factor to any potential disaster. Safety systems, regulations and oversight bodies could be seen to have no responsibility and therefore no real role to play. The question of where the responsibly might lie between the sharp and blunt ends is one that does seem to divide the academic and the judicial worlds. There are even some who see the desire to allocate blame to the blunt end as being an overtly political issue; if this is the case society as a whole will never benefit from such inquiries.

The other issue is the scope and effort required to remedy a universal issue as opposed to a cause. While a cause may be fixed by a revised procedure or additional specific training, universal issues tend to require long-term cultural adjustment where the action required is both harder to identify and resolve.

These issues do make us ask questions about the relevance of the immediacy of any cause (whether this is by time, proximity or impact) and therefore the scope of the challenge we are taking on to change it. While changing things that are direct causes may be difficult, trying to change *universals* will present an even greater challenge.

INDIVIDUAL BIAS

All decisions are biased; some more so than others. The more we think that our decisions are not biased, the more danger there is that they will be. Being aware of how we think, of the mental models we use, the ingrained assumptions and the world view we have, can help to militate against this potential bias. In addition to understanding how we think, we need to be aware of the common biases that enter into the decision-making process; some of the most common are listed in Table 4.8. In order to judge whether the recommendations are fit for our purpose, we need to consider how they may be biased. For example, how much of the judgement was based on what was known after the event rather than it being based on what was known and perceived at the time.

Table 4.8   Common Forms of Bias

Bias	Explanation
Anchoring (or Adjustment)	Predictions are unduly influenced by initial information which is given more weight in the forecasting process.
Attribution (of Success and Failure)	Success is attributed to one's skills but failure to bad luck, or someone else's error. This inhibits learning as it does not allow recognition of one's mistakes.
Availability Bias	Reliance upon specific events easily recalled from memory, to the exclusion of other pertinent information. The ease with which an occurrence can be brought to mind will affect the perception of risk. (The more emotional and the more vivid the easier they are to bring to mind.)
Confirmation (Search for Supportive Evidence) (Confirmation Error/Trap Platonic Confirmation)	Willingness to gather facts which lead towards certain conclusions and to disregard other facts which threaten them: you look for evidence to confirm your hypothesis; find evidence that supports the hypothesis; ignore fallacy (negative empiricism – "I know what is not").
Control Bias	People are more likely to accept risk if they are in control.
Conservatism Bias	Failure to change (or changing slowly) one's own mind in light of new information/evidence.

Bias	Explanation
Framing (Failure of Invariance)	The way the issue is stated will affect the decision made. Inconsistent choice from the same facts depending on how the issue is "framed".

Group Polarisation (Groupthink) Culture	When people share belief they become:
	
	    more convinced they are right;
	
	    more extreme in their beliefs.
	
	People go with the consensus despite the evidence.
	
	Evaluating risks as a group makes them feel less risky than evaluating them individually.

Hindsight Bias	Things appear to be more predictable after the fact. Events look less random than they are. Backward/forward processing of history (easier to see causality in hindsight). "It was so obvious" (when the results are known) or, in US culture, the "Monday morning quarterback".
Illusory Correlations	Belief that patterns are evident and/or two variables are causally related when they are not.
Inconsistency Bias	Inability to apply the same decision criteria in similar situations.
Recency Bias	The most recent events dominate those in the less recent past, which are downgraded or ignored.
Regression Effects	Persistent increases (in some phenomenon) might be due to random reasons which, if true, would (raise) the chance of a (subsequent) decrease. Alternatively, persistent decreases might (raise) the chances of (subsequent) increases.
Selective Perception	People tend to see problems in terms of their own background and experience.
Survivor Bias	History is written by those who win; "Accumulated Advantage" (AA).
Optimism, Wishful Thinking	People's preferences for future outcomes affect their forecasts of such outcomes.
Underestimating Uncertainty	Excessive optimism, illusory correlation and the need to reduce anxiety result in underestimating future uncertainty.
Von Restorff Effect	Bias in favour of remembering the unusual (and therefore giving it undue weight) but the easier something is to recall then the more common it is thought to be (Example Rule); even if you know a fact is incorrect the strength of the memory is more important than the accuracy when you make a judgment call. (Feelings supersede/trump rationality (numbers).)

HINDSIGHT BIAS

At this point I would like to focus on one type of bias and that is hindsight. While this problem is well recognised, this does not prevent it. Professor Brian Toft acknowledges this problem; the final recommendation[75] in his report stated:

> *when evaluating the results of someone else's mistake perhaps it would be useful if society as a whole would reflect upon the observation made by Turner and Pidgeon (1997:135) in that:*

> *"..if we are looking back upon a decision which has been taken, as most decisions, in the absence of complete information, it is important that we should not assess the actions of decision-makers too harshly in the light of the knowledge which hindsight gives us."*

This view is reinforced by others. The US Presidential Commission into the 9/11 attacks said, "As we turn to the events of September 11, we are mindful of the unfair perspective afforded by hindsight."[76] Lord Laming notes that, "Those who sit in judgement often do so with the great benefit of hindsight."[77] Lord Donaldson adds that, "With hindsight it is easy to see a disaster waiting to happen. We need to develop the capability to achieve the much more difficult – to spot one coming."[78] All but two of the inquiry reports reviewed acknowledged the issue of, or use of, hindsight. This usage falls into one of four categories.

First is the single acknowledgement of hindsight as a form of immunisation. The Columbia Inquiry in 2003, the Haddon-Cave in 2009 and the FSA report into the Royal Bank of Scotland (RBS) in 2011 all acknowledge the issue of *hindsight bias*. The Norwegian 22 July Commission added that, "It is naive to believe that one can avoid all hindsight." This acknowledgement of the problem does not however mean that the report team does not fall prey to this form of bias. However, how reports handle this issue is also informative. One way of handling hindsight is to acknowledge what has been deduced through its use. The FSA report into RBS provides a very good example of this approach; on over 30 occasions it states clearly that it was the use of hindsight that enabled them to see and appreciate what had been happening. A second example of how to handle hindsight is from the Columbia Investigation report; its states that, "Rather than view the foam decision only in hindsight, the Board tried to see the foam incidents as NASA engineers and managers saw them as they made their decisions."[79] Here we see the inquiry team wrestling with what they know with hindsight and what the participants might have known at the time such as when they say, "But that characterization is only possible in hindsight. It is not how NASA personnel perceived the risks as they were being assessed, one launch at a time."[80]

The second use of hindsight is to enable investigators to understand better the event due to additional information not available at the time. The Smith report into the Shipman case provides two examples; in the first the author says, "With hindsight, it is clear that those episodes were a product of his pethidine abuse" and in the second she says, "With the benefit of hindsight, one can see that this willingness to make home visits created many opportunities for killing."[81] While this is a wholly legitimate use of hindsight it would be a mistake to assume that what is known in hindsight could or should have been known to those participating in foresight. To make assertions such as "it was a matter of foresight and common sense"[82] should be fully justified within the report if the report is not to lose some of its credibility.

Leading on from the previous usage of hindsight, where knowing the results helps people understand what happened, it's third use is to enhance the lessons to be learnt. The report into the loss of the Columbia spacecraft stated that "we also know – in hindsight – that detection of the dangers posed by foam was impeded by 'blind-spots' in NASA's safety culture".[83] This implies that the blind-spot was discovered in hindsight rather than being obvious to those involved at the time.

Finally, inquiry teams ask participants to re-evaluate their action in hindsight. The value of this approach has to be questioned. It comes across as a form of passive aggressive behaviour that is trying to induce the witness to make some self-incriminating remark. As everyone is capable of improving their evaluation of their own acts as well as the acts of others in hindsight, witnesses may find themselves in a double blind. To follow the line of questioning presented by the inquiry may lead the witness away from what they were thinking at the time and the accurate depiction of the situation as they saw it at the time. However, to reject the premise would be to deny one possible counterfactual construct. While this adversarial methodology may be accepted for other judicial purposes its use to solicit why something occurred may be of less value.[84]

The US Presidential Commission on Deepwater Horizon does however provide a clear example of where the panel was able to separate the knowledge they had through hindsight and what may have been known by those involved at the time and how it might have been interpreted. In the section on the immediate causes[85] the Commission provide, in detail, the data that should have been available to the drilling team, they explained the ambiguous nature of the data, the reasons why the data may not have been available and a possible explanation of why the crew did not act in the manner that might have been expected. In the end, when the Commission came to their conclusion, whether you agree with them or not, they did provide a rich understanding of what might have happened.

Hindsight has an important role to play during inquiries. It can help the inquiry team not only to discover but also explain what happened. It would however be a mistake to assume what is clear in hindsight was clear to those involved in the events. It would be a mistake to assume that data that is clear in hindsight was anything other than part of a blizzard of white noise at the time. We can use the example of a lottery ticket to illustrate this point; when we look at a lottery ticket we know that the answer is in front of us, we have all the data necessary to make the correct choice. All we have to do is to choose the right numbers but what are the odds of that happening? It would also be wrong to assume that because someone has warned that something might occur that it would have been easy for those involved to differentiate those *crying wolf* from *Cassandra* (those who choose the correct outcome).

SELF-AWARENESS

The final part in having a clear analytical perspective is the issue of self-awareness. In Chapters 2 and 3 we see the part played by destructive forces such as arrogance and hubris. Therefore when formulating recommendations those doing so need to be aware of what they know and what they do not know, of their own strengths and weakness.

Sir Michael Bichard announced at the end of his inquiry on the Soham murders on 30 March 2004 that he would reconvene after a period of time to assess the implementation of his recommendations. He told the PASC:

> *I have introduced … [a six-month review]. I have written to those involved and I am waiting for their response, simply because I have seen too many inquiries with excellent recommendations not followed up, and I did not want that to happen.*[86]

At the stage that he first announced this review his recommendations would not have been accepted. The PASC states:

> *An inquiry is asked to make recommendations to the Minister who commissioned it. When the Minister receives these recommendations, it will be for him to determine how they should be addressed.*[87]

The Haddon-Cave report provides us some examples where the report author seemed to have overreached. Four of his recommendations were rejected: see Table 4.9.[88] You may note that the abbreviations in this example are not explained by the document's author and so their transparency to the general public has to be questioned.

Table 4.9   Rejected Haddon-Cave Recommendations

Haddon-Cave's Recommendations	MOD Response
"RTSAs shall be folded into the MAA as a distinct regulatory function with Service specialists employed to provide appropriate input on Service-specific environmental requirements." (Recommendation 21.A.4)	The RTSA model proposed by Mr Haddon-Cave does not offer sufficient agility or sufficient governance, and his proposition that AOAs should be able to issue, unilaterally, Operational Emergency Clearances (OECs) would represent a lower level of safety assurance than is in place today. We have, therefore, decided to leave the initial authorisation of a Release to Service, and its subsequent in-service management, with the single-Service Assistant Chiefs of Staff, within the Services but separate from the day-to-day management of flying operations. Before an initial Release to Service is issued, however, it will in future be fully assured by the MAA. Any adjustments, including OECs, will be monitored by the independent MAA, and the RTS will be periodically re-issued following extensive audit. This refinement to the Haddon-Cave model will deliver the intent of his recommendation, while retaining operational agility and improving on both current, and is (sic) proposed, governance arrangements.
"Safety Cases should be re-named 'Risk Cases' in order to focus attention on the fact that they are about managing risk." (Recommendation 22.2)	We believe that name changes will add confusion; the intent will be achieved without the name change.
"A single professional body should be formed for Safety Experts to set professional and ethical standards, accredit members and disseminate best practice." (Recommendation 28.4)	The Department wishes to align itself to the maximum extent with civilian and expert bodies. Rather than create a separate safety body for the MOD, we propose to continue to work with existing safety bodies including the Institution of Occupational Safety and Health and other professional engineering bodies, such as the IET, IMechE, RAeS. These bodies all have specialist groups dealing with safety and have ethical and professional standards.

Table 4.9   Continued

Haddon-Cave's Recommendations	MOD Response
"The Orwellian-named DE&S 'Director General Change' and 'Director Business Change' should be re-named, respectively, 'Director General Stability' and 'Director Business Stability'." (Recommendation 28.8)	DE&S has a two-star post entitled Director Change to oversee the implementation of its four year business improvement programme. We believe a post title must indicate clearly and succinctly the purpose of the role, and business improvement frequently requires changes. We accept entirely Mr Haddon-Cave's view that "change for change's sake" should be avoided, and that stability is beneficial once the required results are achieved, but will be retaining current post titles.

It is relatively easy for an investigator to recommend name changes on the basis of their own dislikes and preferences. However, to recommend such action might be seen both as arrogant and to lack understanding about what underlies the original words used as well as the effort required to produce these unnecessary changes. The other two recommendations were rejected as not being fit for purpose, again indicating a lack of understanding by the inquiry team. In addition to the four rejected recommendations, the MOD accepted 18 recommendations "in principle"; this stance might raise the suspicion that the recommendations were only accepted in principle rather than having any intention to act. The Select Committee report points to where it may be more difficult to reject recommendations outright. In his evidence to the Committee, Graham Mather claimed:

> Sometimes the inquiry does not have the expertise to redesign the system that it is inquiring into, and very often they try to do that. You are sometimes stuck with recommendations which, as a manager or a policy-maker, you know would not work, but, at the same time, you want to take on board the inquiry's findings.[89]

The reactions of the public or political opponents may induce an organisation to accept recommendations "in principle" but then fudge the issue, obfuscate or impose delay. In the 18 recommendations made by Haddon-Cave that the MOD "accepted in principle" we can see words in the response[90] that enable the recipient not to have to reject the recommendation but also not to embrace them wholeheartedly either. As an outsider, how is one to read these responses; what are we to learn from this exchange? In Table 4.10 I make comment on four of the lessons that I have taken away from reading these recommendations.

Table 4.10   Recommendations Accepted in Principle

Recommendation	MOD Response
21.A.1 – A Military Airworthiness Authority shall be established.	The response said: "…save for an adjustment relating to the Release to Service Authority described previously."
21.A.13 – The MAA shall put in place appropriate arrangements which permit Duty Holders in the AOAs to go beyond the bounds of the RTS to meet specific operational requirements…	The response said: "The operational agility that Mr Haddon-Cave was seeking to enable is delivered through the refined RTSA arrangements."
Comment	The author's proscriptive solutions may have made them more difficult to implement than was necessary. This suggests that where recommendations are not *specific technical* recommendations, these should focus on what change should be achieved rather than proscribing the "how".
21.A.9 – The MAA shall be given appropriate financial, manpower and estate resources which shall be ring-fenced.	The response said: "The MAA will be allocated appropriate resources to fulfil its function … "
22.3 – "Risk Cases" should henceforth be drawn up and maintained in-house …	Having earlier rejected the renaming of "safety cases" to "risk cases", the response said: "the MOD will still rely upon industry to provide the initial design safety case."
Comment	The author seems to have an unrealistic mental model of how government departments work and the context of the time. This goes to credibility and makes me want to question his other recommendations in much greater detail.
24.1 – Careful consideration is given to … weaknesses [in the area of personnel within Airworthiness] and a New Personnel Strategy formulated.	The response said: "Also need to be coherent with wider departmental personnel strategy."
25.1 – Careful consideration should be given to the … problems and the formulation of a New Industry Strategy which addresses them.	The response said: "As part of the Defence Acquisition Reform Programme, work is being put in hand next year to re-examine our relationship with industry as a whole."
28.7 – "Officers" terms on appointment should no longer include "change objectives".	This recommendation looks to remove the construct of Standing and Change objectives which are widely embedded in HR systems throughout government and commerce. The response said: "Staff will be reminded of the need to."
Comment	One of the debates within the PASC paper is the need to understand a system before recommending changes. These three recommendations would seem to lack an appreciation for the wider system and the role it plays in delivery of the MOD's outputs. The unintended consequence of these recommendations may have been to further *sub-optimise* the performance of the MOD overall.
28.1 – The excessive use of acronyms should be discouraged.	The response said: "Joint Service Publication 101 already discourages use of acronyms."

Table 4.10   Continued

Recommendation	MOD Response
28.2 – The ubiquitous use of PowerPoint should be discouraged.	The response said: "PowerPoint can be a very useful briefing and recording tool ... its use should not be ubiquitous."
Comment	These recommendations look at cultural issues that go far beyond that of safety within the organisation and are deeply embedded issues. Here we also may be seeing "that which is espoused being different from what was actually practised" within the organisation. From a learning perspective, we seem to have an author who is "throwing one out there" (or in this case two) and an organisation would have no real idea how this basic issue of "clear communications within a complex cultural environment" can be tackled.

Even where recommendations are accepted, one can see tension over what has been learnt and what is new. Two examples from Haddon-Cave are:

> Recommendation 28.5: "There should be regular articles in in-house magazines and websites drawing attention to, and discussing, safety and airworthiness issues and best practice." This received the response, "The MOD already has a number of specialist safety publications and we will look to making these more widely accessible. We will also encourage greater coverage of safety and airworthiness issues in wider publications." Such recommendations that appear to lack an understanding of the strengths as well as the weaknesses in the current system can only do harm to the credibility of the report's author.

> Recommendations aimed at fostering a New Safety Culture (page 576). The response said: "We accept that Mr Haddon-Cave's model of Safety Culture is one to which the MOD should aspire. Significant organisational and cultural barriers still prevent, however, full acceptance of such a culture, and further work will be required to determine the full extent of these barriers." Here Haddon-Cave might be seen to be "hoist by his own petard". Any organisation that has tried to carry out such a culture change will realise that it is a major undertaking. In paragraph 13.80 he criticised the then Chief of Defence Logistics for not conducting an overall impact assessment. Haddon-Cave does not seem either to have conducted such an analysis of his recommended change, present his analysis for external scrutiny or required the MOD to conduct such an analysis before planning any implementation.

Such polite responses as those provided by the MOD to Haddon-Cave might be seen to hold questions about the quality of the original recommendations and raise questions as to whether there may be benefit to be gained from having detailed discussions with the other stakeholders prior to the production of recommendations as suggested by the Commons Select Committee.

Testing Recommendations

There are some tests that can already be applied to any set of recommendations. The purpose of these tests is to help with cross-understanding (therefore developing and maintaining trust between the communities) between those with a judicial perspective and others who approach this work as academics or practitioners. I bring six issues to the fore here. The first is to test whether the recommendations address a cause or a universal issue, the second addresses the *substitution test*, the third is the *reverse fallacy*, the fourth is viability of multi-skilling, the fifth is unintended consequences and the final one is the use of peer review.

TESTING FOR UNIVERSALS

The first test that should be applied concerns the identification of what Reason has labelled *universals* as described above. If we accept Reason's model then the first two factors (*universals* and *conditions* are ubiquitous) and therefore changing them will need a far more fundamental change than the action required to prevent *causes*.

A first step would be for inquiries to start to differentiate between these three categories (or any other categorisation that they think to be appropriate) so that issues such as *production pressure, cost cutting, poor leadership* and *poor communications*, which are universal, are not confused with causes. Those more familiar with the underlying body of academic work would also be looking out for phenomena such as *fantasy documents, the liability of newness, unruly technology, bystander syndrome, normalisation of deviance* and *practical drift*, to name but a few of the over 200 previously identified by research. Each may have had a role to play and could well be identified if those inquiring knew where to look.

Therefore, in order to fully understand any recommendation, we need to understand the findings. In order to fully understand the findings we need to understand the mental model used to construct the findings. Understanding the mental model would help others to see the cause and effects paths envisaged and therefore why a particular intervention might or might not work. For example, poor communications[91] or communications failure[92] is often cited as a problem and this leads to recommendations that communications need to be improved.[93] We need to question whether such recommendations are either helpful or useful.

Besides general statements that actions should be taken to promote effective communication or that cultures should be changed to encourage open communication, many recommendations propose new methods of communications, communication systems, improved training and enhancements of procedure. Some even propose that a specific communication takes place. However none of these recommendations can ensure effective future communications, yet this limitation is never reflected by the inquiry. The recommendations do not seem to take into account the extensive body of work done (such as on the limitation of language[94] or that individuals perceive the same events in very different ways) that highlights the difficulties in ensuring effective communications.

SUBSTITUTION TEST

While a "wholly just culture is almost certainly an unattainable ideal"[95] it should remain an aspirational goal. James Reason[96] lays out the basic dilemma which is that while "it would be quite unacceptable to punish all errors and unsafe acts ... it would be equally unacceptable to give a blanket immunity (as) accidents can happen as the result of the unreasonably reckless, negligent and even malevolent behaviour of particular individuals. The difficulty lies in discriminating" between these two. Reason then goes on to describe Neil Johnston's *substitution test*:

> *When faced with accident or serious incident in which the unsafe acts of a particular person were implicated, we should perform the following mental test. Substitute the individual concerned for someone else coming from the same domain of activity and possessing comparable qualifications and experience. Then ask the following question: "In the light of how events unfolded and were perceived by those involved in real time, is it likely that the new individual would have behaved any differently?" If the answer is probably not then ... "apportioning blame has no material role to play, other than to secure systemic deficiencies*

and to blame one of the victims". A useful addition to the substitution test is to ask of the individual's peers: "given the circumstances that prevailed at the time, could you be sure that you would not have committed the same or similar type of unsafe act?"[97]

Here we see a need to discriminate between the failing of an individual and the failing of a system. I will use the example of the Columbia tragedy to illustrate this point further. The NASA space shuttles were very complex craft (with millions of parts) which were operated at the edge of the scientific and engineering knowledge. This limit was recognised in an acceptance of over 5,000 individual hazards of which over 4,000 were categorised as "Criticality 1/1R"[98] (this meant that the consequence of failure would be "loss of crew, vehicle, and mission",[99] some having redundancy others not). Vaughan also points out that these items had different probability of failure and so would have been perceived to have a different level of risk. Therefore within the mind of the chair of the Mission Management Team (Linda Ham) there would have been a mental model which ranked these concerns and therefore it would have been this list that drove the way she prioritised her time. "More's Law" suggests that an individual's responsibilities will exceed both their authority and capacity. This was one of the interesting aspects that I thought was missing from the inquiry report. The report concentrated on what happened and what the leadership failed to do. It did not explore which issues occupied their time and how they used their available capacity to discriminate between what they were doing and what they should have been doing. By using the *substitution test* I would have been interested to explore whether this was just a *normal accident* where More's Law played a contributory part and why they failed to see and appreciate what turned out to be (in hindsight) the most critical issues on the flight?

Consciously or not, Dame Janet Smith makes the point well:

The hearing of this stage of the Inquiry has been a painful experience for many of those involved. For those who faced criticism, it must have been a very anxious time. Those few who have been found responsible must live with that responsibility for the rest of their lives. I must and do feel sympathy for them, even though their predicament was of their own making. It was a misfortune for CS Sykes, DI Smith and Dr Banks that they were ever caught up in the consequences of Shipman's criminality. There must be many others who would also have failed if put in the position in which these men found themselves.[100]

The *substitution test* provides a way of testing whether the issue was caused by a specific individual or is more systemic; it may help to differentiate between an individual being at fault or whether that individual was just unfortunate to be in the wrong place at the wrong time and the tragedy just happening on their watch. The *substitution test* can be seen to be related to the legal *Reasonable Man* test (discussed later) but differences are quite significant. Where the former looks at the prevailing circumstances as seen from the perspective of someone with the appropriate *seat of understanding* (asking questions such as: What skills levels did they have? What did they know? What did they not know? What else did they have on their plate at the same time?), the latter looks at it from the perspective of what a reasonable person might expect them to know, whether it is with a *reasonable man's seat of understanding* or not.

THE REVERSE FALLACY

The next test that I would suggest is, what I have called, the *reverse fallacy* test. The *reverse fallacy* can be seen when an action or omission is seen as being significant in the context of one particular tragedy, and so a recommendation is made that it is universally inappropriate. An example of this can be found in criticism of what has been referred to as the "can-do" culture; that is the desire and drive by practitioners to overcome obstacles in order to achieve a goal.

There is a clear conflict between the findings of some inquiries and the findings of academic studies. A number of inquiries have criticised the can-do attitude of the organisation involved. Haddon-Cave[101] "see(s) 12 uncanny, and worrying, parallels" between the loss of Nimrod XV230 and loss of the Space Shuttle Columbia. One of these is the can-do attitude within each organisation. He equates can-do with make-do but leaves the subject rather in the air at this point. His clear premise, for he has nothing positive to say about it, is that a can-do culture is bad for safety, the implication being that it should be replaced.

These comments need to be set against the academic work done by Roe and Schulman on *high reliability organisations*[102] or Andre de Waal into *high performance organisations* (not to confuse the two). Dr de Waal defines *high performance organisations* as:

> An organisation that achieves financial and non-financial results that are exceedingly better than those of its peer group over a period of time of 5 years by focusing in a disciplined way on what really matters to the organisation.

Over ten years of research de Waal has identified five factors and 35 characteristics that define *high performance organisations*. One of these factors is that the organisations have high-quality employees and one of the essential characteristics is labelled "resilience". Dr de Waal uses the word resilience to embrace the idea of a can-do attitude and sees this as being essential to becoming a *high performance organisation*.

We therefore have a clear conflict between what we learn from inquiries, a can-do attitude of employees is negative, and what we learn from academia, a can-do attitude of employees is positive. The experience of many organisations is that a can-do attitude of employees has significant benefit to effectiveness. Therefore, if managers were aware of both sides of the argument, they would, on balance, be likely to promote a can-do culture within their organisation.

Care needs to be taken when asserting that anything is universally good or universally bad. A question often worth asking is, "What alternative course of action was open given the data available?" For example, I refer to Diane Vaughan's highly acclaimed book on the Challenger tragedy. Vaughan describes the advantages and the disasters of "management by exception" as part of the NASA flight safety reviews. She concludes that "the disadvantage was that many anomalies were not regularly reviewed by top administrators".[103] The implication of her statement was that they should have been. However Vaughan did not discuss the consequences if they had been; the potential paralysis of the system as the top administrators discuss the 1,000s of technical issues which were likely to be beyond their *seat of understanding*. In such circumstances, authors should consider asking the question, "What was the alternative?" in order to test whether their proposition possibly contained a *reverse fallacy*.

Just because it is wrong in one instance does not mean that it may be beneficial in another. Therefore, to avoid the potential loss of credibility, those writing inquiry reports need to check their findings and recommendations for potential *reverse fallacies*.

VIABILITY OF MULTI-SKILLING

Many roles demand a lot from their holders; again I refer to More's Law. These roles have multiple facets to them all of which require the application of quite different skills and knowledge. Management is seen as, "A dynamic and complex problem where goals have to be set within the available resources and priorities established so that risk can be ameliorated. There are few areas as dynamic and as complex as matching the available human resource to the organisation's business strategy in order to maximise functional flexibility."[104]

We see a tendency for organisations to try to tackle their problems by using existing resources. We see a key facet of a resilient organisation as having the right resource readily available. However, for most organisations it is a case of working with what they have. As we see from the most popular type of recommendation, which is for new resources and capabilities, organisations are not always successful at doing this. My previous research into our ability to multi-skill was based on operational experience and this demonstrated to me the importance of mindset when undertaking tasks. I saw soldiers injured because, while having the skills, they adopted the wrong mindset for the task in hand (it should be noted that this was in the early 1990s long before I had ever heard of such concepts as mindset). The question became one of how quickly a person with the right skill and knowledge could flip from one task to another and adopt the appropriate mindset. This thinking required them to develop a way to analyse the role required of a post holder, the skills and knowledge for each role, the regularity and frequency with which each skill-set was used and refreshed, and the performance expected from them. I later conducted academic research into this subject and developed the model in Figure 4.1 which shows the types of issues that need to be considered if such switches are not just to be taken for granted. While such issues may not need to be considered for minor changes, the question becomes one of when they do need to be considered.

The question becomes, when do we need to be aware of our ability to do so? Here we need to bear in mind Millar's work on the "magical Number 7 plus or minus two", and the idea of "stickiness". Stickiness is the issue of how quickly people can clear their mind of one issue to make space for another. I would ask you to think of the occasions you have become obsessed with one idea and then been unable to take another on-board; this is a stickiness issue.

If we are to learn from tragedies, we need to recognise the limits that humans have and the complexity involved in many management roles. We need to be aware of our ability to switch between the roles given to us and we need to be realistic about what is achieved.

We might take as an example a senior policeman who is asked to handle his budgets in the morning and crowd control in the afternoon. We have to question what needs to happen and what he needs to know to do each to the standard required; we need to question how much we are actually relying on the *Union Carbide Factor*.

Figure 4.1   Skills Functional Risk Management Tool

The Baker report into the Texas City tragedy provides a second point for debate. Baker states:

> *Browne's passion and commitment for climate change is particularly apparent. In hindsight, the Panel believes that if Browne had demonstrated comparable leadership on and commitment to process safety, that leadership and commitment would likely have resulted in a higher level of process safety performance in BP's U.S. refineries.*[105]

This statement raises the question as to how many other critical functions was the CEO of BP required to oversee and, given the finite hours available to him, how thinly could he spread his leadership across these tasks and still remain effective. When more leadership is demanded in a report there never seems to be a corresponding debate about which other areas should receive less leadership. The viability of the multiple roles of such executives was again not discussed.

Formal consideration of the viability of the multiple coexisting skill-sets necessary to fulfil many management roles is a complex task. It needs consideration of aptitude, basic training and experience; it needs consideration of culture, procedures, protocols and checklists; it needs consideration of additional and advanced training and finally it needs consideration of familiarity with the specific tasks including any refresher training available. While this is possible the question is whether it is practicable to do so and, if so, in what circumstances should it be done? Without such consideration can the findings of an inquiry be fair?

UNINTENDED CONSEQUENCES

At several points already the issue of unintended consequences has surfaced. One example which might be considered is the Bichard Report that followed the murder of two ten-year-old girls at Soham in Cambridgeshire. The Bichard Inquiry became a major driver for child protection as he made recommendations that, "New arrangements should be introduced requiring those who wish to work with children, or vulnerable adults, to be registered."[106] The new arrangements that have been put in place have, according to reports in the media, had unintended consequences. The bureaucratic arrangements have led to wasteful and timewasting multiple checks on single individuals, created difficulties for small organisations who rely on volunteers and been intrusive into arrangements between family members and friends. There can be no doubt that the intentions behind the recommendation are worthy; however, society needs to determine what is meant by (what is its mental model of) the idea "every child matters". While we must look to protect every child from harm, we also need to be aware of the opportunities lost to other children by these arrangements. Where does this responsibility lie?

Who should be responsible for ensuring that recommendations do not induce unintended consequences? Is it the person making the recommendations, is it the person accepting the recommendations, or is it the people implementing the recommendations? If the responsibility does lie with those implementing the recommendations, is there a responsibility on those making the recommendation to word them in such a way as to not restrict how the objective is to be achieved? All actions and activity are vulnerable to prompting unintended consequences; what we now see is a need for those involved in inquiries to be alert to and guard against this possibility.

PEER REVIEW

One lesson comes through from the academic literature on unwanted events, from academic practice and from life experience in general. This is that everybody is fallible. Therefore, if everyone is so fallible then those conducting inquiries are also likely to be fallible! If this is the case then inquiries need to incorporate quality control measures. This might take the form of peer review.

In Rita Donaghy's 2009 report, *Inquiry into the Underlying Causes of Construction Fatal Accidents*, great play is made of the peer review of this work by a team of academics. While the use of peer reviews may offer an addition to good practice, two important issues are raised by its use in this case. The first is whether it actually was an independent peer review and the second was the expertise (*seat of understanding*) of those conducting the peer review.

Peer review in the academic world is seen as being independent and aspires to be an unbiased evaluation of a piece of work. In the case of the Donaghy report those involved in what was offered as a peer review were actually active in the inquiry offering their specialist knowledge and judgement to the report team. Therefore, to label this work as peer review may suggest more independence of review than was warranted. The lesson that emerges here is that it should be considered to be good for an inquiry report to be subjected to peer review before it is published if the lessons learnt are to have greater authority. The practice for setting up the peer review mechanism needs to be examined in order to determine who arranges the peer review (the panel chair or the person who initiated the inquiry), the terms of reference for the peer review and the perspective and *seat of understanding* of those conducting the peer review in order to provide balance with those who conducted the inquiry. This leads me into my second point which is that of specialist knowledge.

As you can see from the literature reviewed in Chapter 2, there is not a single academic and professional discipline that embraces all aspects relating to unwanted occurrences. In the case of the Donaghy report, the specialisms employed were Safety Science (safety management and regulation and therefore prone to use the *dot* paradigm), a lawyer specialising in Socio-Legal Studies, and someone with particular interests in employee representation and consultation on health and safety, the politics of health and safety at work. All of these are highly relevant disciplines. However, again going back to Chapter 2 we see that it is not what you do well that will catch you out, it is the area that is overlooked (the gap) that will. The question therefore for those setting up inquiry teams or using peer review to enhance the credibility of the findings and recommendations of the report, is, "What perspective is being omitted and how will this affect the shape of our findings and recommendations?"

One option within the UK is that such oversight might be conducted by the appropriate Select Committee or some other governance body (assuming that they have sufficient expertise to do so). This body would then ensure that the recommendations are well based and will be effective before committing resources. In many ways such peer review should be considered in the same light as other pre-legislative scrutiny; both have as part of their goals the desire to prevent unintended consequences.[107] Therefore, all the arguments in favour of pre-legislative scrutiny might also be used in support of a peer review process for inquiry reports. This raises the perennial problem of who polices the police, who regulates the regulator, where does this supervision stop?

HOW MANY RECOMMENDATIONS IS ENOUGH?

In the sample of inquiries analysed for this book we see a wide range (the smallest number being ten and the largest being 162) in the number of recommendations made. This makes the average number of recommendations produced 56. This raises the question as to whether there is an ideal number. In 2013 Robert Francis QC produced his report on the Mid Staffordshire NHS Foundation Trust Public Inquiry[108] that contained 290 recommendations. There may be a temptation to make changes for change's sake[109] or to consider that there should be a correlation between the importance of the subject matter and the thoroughness of the report but, I would suggest, this temptation should be avoided. An analysis of the Francis recommendations would seem to reveal that, as the narrative unfolded and deficiencies were found, recommendations were made. At the end all these recommendations were simply collated and presented in the report. This leads to examples such as Recommendation 237 "There needs to be effective teamwork between all the different disciplines and services..." and Recommendation 263 "It must be recognised to be the professional duty of all healthcare professionals to collaborate ...". The inquiry team seem to have made little attempt to consider how to produce their recommendations in such a way as to help them be implemented most effectively. Anyone who has worked within a large bureaucracy will recognise that when recommendations are made in any review or audit, the tendency is for them to be acted upon as separate items. This report requires 290 separate processes to be put in train.

The Francis report provides an example of a job half done. Within the 290 deficiencies a number of key themes emerge such as issues of openness, accountability, process and training. They range for macro issues such as changing the whole culture of the NHS to micro issues such as hand sterilisation. It can be seen that many of the recommendations are related and need to be tackled in a coordinated manner. In this way they could be grouped without any of the detail being lost. It would therefore have been possible to distil the list of recommendations to between 50 and 100 thereby making the task of implementing them easier and more effective.

Inquiry teams need to test their list of recommendations for their practicality of implementation. By setting themselves a nominal target of say 50, they would be forced to examine which recommendations should be grouped under the same work streams where each provides criteria for judging success rather than being a recommendation in their own right. The final list of recommendations should be distilled further in order to articulate the principles which lie behind the recommendations. In the case of the Francis Report there were five: (1) the production of fundamental standards, (2) the promotion of openness, transparency and candour, (3) strengthen nursing, (4) strengthen leadership, and finally (5) making more usable, comparable practical information available as quickly as possible. This would also help those implementing the recommendations to test their actions against the original intent. Without such a distillation, the authors of such reports remain vulnerable to the criticism that I remember so well from school, "Answer the question, do not just tell me all you know about the subject"; in this case the question is, "How do we improve the system so this will not happen again?"

Following Through

One of the mantras for *performance management* is that "what don't get measured don't get managed". In this we see the need to monitor and audit to ensure that lessons identified by the inquiry are learnt by the organisation. As within the work of Campbell,[110] we see in the ESReDA guidelines and the House of Commons PASC HC51-I paper the need to follow through any recommendations and to ensure that they are properly enacted.

The PASC see "preventing recurrence through learning lessons is a key success criterion for inquiries."[111] They say that their evidence:

> *suggested that there was a need for an audit system for ensuring that relevant recommendations had been implemented ... potential recommendations should be tested out prior to finalising reports to ensure they were feasible and workable ... inquiry is asked to make recommendations to the Minister who commissioned it. When the Minister receives these recommendations, it will be for him to determine how they should be addressed.*[112]

However, the majority of the section on "Learning lessons" focuses on (1) the procedural mechanisms required to ensure that recommendations are followed up, (2) the timeframe within which this should be done and (3) whether and how recommendations should be tested before they are made. They heard from Lord Laming that, "Parliament would see a role in taking forward the issues, not just on the floor of the House, but in select committees and the like." They conclude that inquiries should be expected and enabled to test out potential recommendations. As Sir Ian Kennedy said, "If you are going to make any recommendations ... then you must have some understanding of the system."[113] They also conclude that any follow up should occur within two years of the end of the inquiry although Sir Brian Bender suggested that one route "could be through a select committee saying, 'let us look at this three or five years on and have a short inquiry, investigation, into whether not only has the Government done what it said it would do, but whether it has changed the world'". However, nowhere in their discussion is there any debate as to what is required to ensure a recommendation is successfully converted into effective action. This would seem to present a significant gap within their understanding of the debate.

From the work of the Select Committee and the ESReDA guidelines, I would summarise the new guidelines on "follow-through" as:

- Those with responsibility for the activities affected by the recommendations should take them into account.

- They should conduct a risk assessment as to whether the recommendation should be enacted based on whether it will achieve its aim, whether it is practicable and whether it is free from potential unintended consequences.

- They should formally accept or reject each recommendation based on their risk assessment.

- They should record their responses to each recommendation.

- Where recommendations are accepted, an action plan should be devised including the allocation of resources, timelines and priorities.

- Timelines should be realistic and geared to practical implementation rather than political imperative.

- Actions should be followed through with an appropriate *performance management* regime and tracked through to their completion.

- Appropriate governance arrangements should be put in place to oversee the progress achieved.

- Steps should be taken to preserve the "lessons learned" as part of the corporate memory.

- Steps should be taken to ensure lessons are learnt across the industry sector and more broadly where appropriate.

As in many idealised systems, there are practical difficulties in implementing these steps. In particular the process by which recommendations are tested for practicality and unintended consequences and how to devise systems within which lessons are not lost. These issues need to be addressed directly.

There is another aspect of learning that is equally important and yet is also often overlooked. This is what is referred to as *double-loop* learning. This is where the system evaluates itself to see whether the analytical and learning processes might be improved. I see little evidence to suggest that this has been incorporated into the inquiry process; I address this subject again in the next chapter.

Summary

In the previous chapter I examined what inquiry reports report. In this chapter I examined how the quality of the recommendations might be tested. Borrowing ideas from *performance management* literature, I explored *what good looks like* in this case and adopted the test of whether a recommendation or body of recommendations are "adequate or inadequate-to-purpose".

In discussing whether a recommendation could be considered to be adequate, I focused on two issues. The first was whether the recommendation met its purpose and the second was to look at some of the tests that might be applied.

To answer the first question I looked at the purpose of inquiries; the structure of their terms of reference; who their audience was; the ideas of politics, blame, prevention and fairness; our understanding of causality and finally issues of bias.

To answer the second question, I suggested some of the tests that might be applied to recommendations in order to examine their adequacy. The first test suggested was to determine whether the recommendation was aimed at addressing a cause or a *universal* issue. The second test was for a *substitution test*, the third was a *reverse fallacy*, and the fourth asked whether we expect too much from individuals. The penultimate test suggested was to test the recommendation for unintended consequences and finally the idea of peer review was raised.

One of the mantras for *performance management* is that "what gets measured gets managed". As in any such learning or *performance management* system, there is a need to monitor and audit progress not only to ensure the target organisation learns but also to ensure that the analytical system learns. In the case of these top level inquiries we see very little of this later learning.

In the next chapter I return to the issue of formulating recommendations and examine what might be learnt that could improve future practice.

Endnotes

1   http://www.archive2.official-documents.co.uk/document/cm64/6481/6481.pdf, accessed 3 December 2012 (see para.10).
2   Boin and Schulman (2008), page 1059.
3   Reason (1997), page 193.
4   Smith (2005), Report 2, page 138.
5   Micheli (2012).
6   Turner (1976b), page 380.
7   "Boy drowned as police support officers 'stood by'" http://www.guardian.co.uk/uk/2007/sep/21/1, accessed 5 November 2010.

8   "Cliff hero resigns in safety row", http://news.bbc.co.uk/1/hi/england/tees/7183017.stm, accessed 6 November 2010.
9   *Scotsman* Newspaper Report dated 13 March 2010: http://news.scotsman.com/news/Firefighters-told-to-39use-common.6149249.jp, accessed 5 November 2010.
10   http://www.bbc.co.uk/news/uk-11629992, accessed 5 November 2010.
11   Lovell and Kluger (1994).
12   http://www.bbc.co.uk/news/magazine-20097554, accessed 28 October 2012.
13   Turner (1976b), page 380.
14   Perrow (1999, first published in 1984).
15   Colligan and Murphy (1979), page 85.
16   Sagan (1993).
17   Vaughan (1996).
18   Vaughan (1997), page 85.
19   http://www.aaib.gov.uk/home/index.cfm, accessed 29 October 2012.
20   http://www.maib.gov.uk/about_us/index.cfm, accessed 29 October 2012.
21   http://www.raib.gov.uk/home/index.cfm, accessed 29 October 2012.
22   http://www.hse.gov.uk/strategy/strategy09.pdf, accessed 29 October 2012.
23   http://www.hse.gov.uk/pubns/hse41.pdf, accessed 29 October 2012.
24   http://www.hse.gov.uk/enforce/enforcementguide/investigation/index.htm, accessed 29 October 2012.
25   HC 51-I (2005), page 7.
26   HC 51-I (2005), page 8.
27   HC 51-I (2005), page 45.
28   HC 51-I (2005), page 9.
29   HC 51-I 2005, page 33 and 34.
30   Haddon-Cave (2009), page 6, para.1.8.
31   Rasmussen (1997), page 185.
32   HC51-I, page 49, para.138.
33   HC51-I, page 9, para.11.
34   HC 51-I, page 13, para.22.
35   See Vaughan (1996) and Perrow (2007).
36   Goddard and Eccles (2012), page 146.
37   Haddon-Cave (2009), page 6.
38   Perrow (1999), page 67.
39   Marr (2004).
40   http://www.coronersociety.org.uk/wfBriefHistory.aspx, accessed 18 November 2012.
41   Smith (2005), Report 3, Recommendation 24.
42   http://www.dailymail.co.uk/news/article-2220232/Army-families-win-right-sue-Government-soldiers-deaths-mobile-coffins.html#ixzz2B35UGl74, accessed 2 November 2012.
43   Neutral Citation Number: [2012] EWCA Civ 1365 dated 19 October 2012.
44   Neutral Citation Number: [2012] EWCA Civ 1365 dated 19 October 2012. Paras 53 and 54.
45   Reason (2008), page 92.
46   Gardener (2008), page 81.
47   Scraton (2009), loc 4494.
48   Reason (2008), pages 74–77.
49   Slovic (2000), pages 110–111.
50   Gigerenzer (2003), page 244.
51   Reason (1997), page 127.
52   Gigerenzer, (2003), pages 9–22.
53   Mythen (2004), page 170.
54   Feigenson and Park (2006), page 150.
55   Feigenson and Park (2006), page 156.
56   Haddon-Cave (2009), page 8.
57   See http://nimrod-review.org.uk/linkedfiles/nimrod_review/procedure.pdf, accessed 16 June 10.

58   Smith (2005), Report 5, Recommendation 62.
59   Horvath (2001), page 12.
60   Horvath (2001), page 29.
61   PAC HC 51-I, 2005, page 98.
62   http://www.bbc.co.uk/news/uk-england-coventry-warwickshire-20637819, accessed 10 December 2012.
63   http://www.bbc.co.uk/news/uk-england-coventry-warwickshire-20629538, accessed 10 December 2012.
64   http://www.bbc.co.uk/news/uk-england-coventry-warwickshire-18251348, accessed 10 December 2012.
65   http://www.bbc.co.uk/news/uk-england-coventry-warwickshire-18263983, accessed 10 December 2012.
66   Smith (2005), Report 3, Recommendation 34, page 30.
67   Reason (2008), page 137–138.
68   Taleb (2012), page 56.
69   Dekker (2011), loc 206–207.
70   Dekker (2011), loc 1301–1302.
71   Dekker (2011), loc 3349.
72   Reason (1997), page 113.
73   Francis (2013), page 55, para.1.62.
74   Scraton (1999), 2009 e-book loc 4606–4608.
75   Toft (2001), page 48.
76   Presidential Commission (2002) – 9/11 attack, para.9.2.
77   Laming (2003), para.1.14.
78   Donaldson (2000), page 43.
79   CAIB, page 196, para.8.2.
80   CAIB, page 197.
81   Smith (2005), Report 1, para.1.18 amd 13.22 respectively.
82   Haddon-Cave (2009), page 272, para, 11.39.
83   CAIB, page 184, para.7.4.
84   HoC, HC-52-I, page 20, para.41.
85   US Presidential Commission (2011), page 115–122.
86   PASC HC51-I (2005), page 50, para.140.
87   PASC HC51-I (2005), page 50.
88   www.parliament.uk/deposits/depositedpapers/2009/DEP2009-3174.doc, accessed 4 November 2012.
89   PASC HC51-I page 50, para.139.
90   www.parliament.uk/deposits/depositedpapers/2009/DEP2009-3174.doc, accessed 4 November 2012.
91   Ladbrooke Grove Report (2001), Shipman Report 5 (2005), Donaghy (2009), Montara Report (2010), Hillsborough (2012), Norway's 22 July Commission (2012).
92   Donaldson (2000), CAIB (2003), Shipman Report 5 (2005), Deaths in Custody (2012).
93   Taylor (1990), Cullen (2001), Donaghy (2009), RAIB report into Greyrigg crash, Walker (2009), Montara Report (2010), BEA (2012) AF447, Norway's 22 July Commission (2012), HIP (2012).
94   Woolgar (1980).
95   Reason (1997), page 205.
96   Reason (1997), page 205–213.
97   Reason (1997), page 208.
98   Dunbar and Garud in Starbuck and Farjoun (2005), page 209.
99   Vaughan (1996), page 133.
100   Smith (2005), The Shipman Inquiry, Report 2, para.16.31 (http://www.shipman-inquiry.org.uk/sr_page.asp?ID=103), accessed 17 October 2012.
101   Haddon-Cave (2009), page 447.
102   Roe and Schulman (2008), page 137.

103   Vaughan (1996), page 259.
104   Lauder (1997).
105   Baker (2007), page 67.
106   Bichard (2004), Recommendation 19, page 15.
107   http://www.publications.parliament.uk/pa/cm200506/cmselect/cmmodern/1097/109705.
       htm, accessed 22 December 2012.
108   Francis (2013).
109   Taleb (2012), page 118.
110   Campbell (1998).
111   PASC HC51-I (2005), page 49, para.137.
112   PASC HC51-I (2005), page 49, para.139 and 140.
113   PASC HC51-I (2005), page 54, para.152.

5

Making Recommendations

So far in the book we have looked at what is known about why unwanted occurrences may occur and how this might coalesce in a mental model. We have also examined what inquiries examine and we have drawn this together into a second mental model quite different from the first. In these two models we may start to see potential difficulties in cross-understanding between the communities that use each. We have also looked at some criteria that might be used to test the quality or adequacy of any recommendations produced.

In this chapter we go further in looking at the formulation of recommendations. We look in greater detail at the importance of who decides what the recommendation might be, the expertise required and the composition of an inquiry panel. We will then look at what we might learn about this subject from both the literature and the practices. Finally, as a result of these reviews, I will suggest guidelines for future practice.

My starting point for this chapter is the premise that (1) inquiries have a very important role to play in helping our society to function in a way we would all like, (2) all humans are fallible, have their limitations and make mistakes, and so (3) a guiding principle should be that those conducting inquiries should "first, do no harm". This is that they should not make matters worse and they should do everything in their powers to avoid generating further unintended harmful consequences.

Who Decides?

Miles' Law states that, "Where you stand depends on where you sit." The importance of this can be seen in the jockeying for the composition of the inquiry team whenever there is a call for an inquiry. All parties to inquiries have a predisposition and therefore a political position on the issues to be discussed. The jockeying can be interpreted as at least "accepting that if we cannot get someone who is inclined to your perspective, as a minimum, we should avoid getting someone who is inclined towards the other side's views". So those people setting up the inquiry look for someone of stature and integrity who is seen to be impartial. However, Miles' Law reminds us that unbiased and impartial may be another fiction with which, we as a society, are likely to delude ourselves. Everyone has their own bias and *seat of understanding* which combine and form a perspective. We have already looked at perspectives and various forms of bias. I will now discuss why *seat of understanding* is important and therefore why integrity and impartiality may not be enough. To this end I look at the role of expertise and independence, the necessity for having an appropriate *seat of understanding*, and finally, the composition of a panel.

EXPERTISE

Stature and integrity may not be enough when conducting an inquiry. The expertise of those with judicial training is explained in the Select Committee's paper but is this enough? Both Diane Vaughan and Scott Snook discuss the issue of the expertise required to appreciate the implication of the data they see. In his summary of the lessons learnt from his case study, Snook asked the question, "Do you have any DUKES that might be 'pigs looking at watches'?";[1] this was his colourful way of asking whether the command element of an organisation (the DUKES) understand the data in front of them (unlike a pig looking at watch). This issue links back to the issue of Failure to Appreciate discussed in Chapter 2. This leads directly to two further issues. The first is from where inquiries receive the relevant expert advice and the second is whether they understand (I would say appreciate) what they are seeing and hearing.

Trusting the wrong people

The danger of taking advice from the wrong people is clear from the Columbia case and the relationship between Linda Ham (the Mission Management Team Chair) and Calvin Schomburg (a Johnson Space Center engineer). The Columbia report states:

> *Shuttle Program managers regarded Schomburg as an expert on the Thermal Protection System. His message downplays the possibility that foam damaged the Thermal Protection System. However, the Board notes that Schomburg was not an expert on Reinforced Carbon-Carbon (RCC), which initial debris analysis indicated the foam may*

have struck. Because neither Schomburg nor Shuttle management
rigorously differentiated between tiles and RCC panels, the bounds of
Schomburg's expertise were never properly qualified or questioned.[2]

In hindsight the investigation board could see that Schomburg was not the
right person from whom advice should have been taken. The report goes on:

> *Ralph Roe, Lambert Austin, and Linda Ham referred to conversations*
> *with Calvin Schomburg, whom they referred to as a Thermal Protection*
> *System "expert." They indicated that Schomburg had advised that any*
> *tile damage should be considered a turnaround maintenance concern*
> *and not a safety-of-flight issue, and that imagery of Columbia's left*
> *wing was not necessary. There was no discussion of potential RCC*
> *damage.*[3]

This case provides interesting lessons about the role played in such events by
the inclination to ask people we know because they are more accessible than the
right people, to assume the boundaries of competence being wider than they
are and finally the role played by being disinclined to declare or being aware
of one's own limits. Here we might reflect back on the Donaghy report and the
expert advice she used; this is not to question their undoubted expertise but it
is to ask whether it was the right expertise for the question that she was trying
to address.

When we look at inquiries we have to question whether we see the same
mistake as made by Linda Ham in her selection of Calvin Schomburg as her
advisor. When inquiry chairs select the experts that they want to give advice,
how do they select the experts if they do not appreciate the subtle differences
between the available expertise? If they select experts who are well known
or even those highly respected for their expertise, this is no guarantee that
the person has the actual expertise needed for their case. This provides an
additional reason for inquiries to justify in their report the expertise they call.

Limits of experts

This issue of competence may not only be relevant to those co-opted into
conducting inquiries but also to professional investigators. One example is
provided by Roed-Larsen and Stoop who have said:

> *Investigators, confident with operational experiences gained in their domain, may lack the necessary expertise to use scientific methods in their work or do not have the necessary competences to participate in ... interdisciplinary investigations after a major event.*[4]

Dien and colleagues highlight another issue and that is either where analysts are in a "wrong" position within an organisation to address the whole scope of the issue, whether it may not be in their self-interest to do so or where they have difficulties gaining access to relevant organisational data. Dien also accepts that these analysts might also have difficulties making sense of the data available to them. They go further and say that, "Some corrective measures are out of the sphere of competence and responsibilities of persons in charge of drafting corrective measures, and of persons in charge of decision-making regarding their implementation."[5]

Credibility of experts

In response to the ESReDA paper, Dechy and his colleagues emphasise the need for those making recommendations to engage with those having a deep understanding of the organisation if the full value of the learning process is to be extracted. They say:

> *Once the AI (accident investigation) is completed and often before that, it is necessary to communicate to the stakeholders ... in order to initiate and facilitate the learning process ... We wanted to pay attention to the stage of the recommendations design (after analysis, findings and lessons learned stages) that requires specific knowledge of the organisational network (actors, stakes, and political dimensions) and behaviour of the sociotechnical system.*[6]

If we go back to the Adams Model in Chapter 1, we see what is referred to as *virtual data,* which is where we do not really understand an issue and therefore where we have to rely on the advice of someone else who we believe knows what they are talking about. Therefore if those with "a deep understanding of the organisation" are to learn from those making recommendations, the latter group must have credibility. In the case of the Haddon-Cave report, we can see his use of names such as James Reason and Jens Rasmussen to add credibility to his report (much as I have done in this book). This attempt at fostering credibility can have unintended consequences. In the case of the Haddon-Cave report the first issue is that I do not recognise some of the interpretation given to the academic work cited. The second issue is that with a wave of a pen he looks to change Reason's *Informed Culture* to an *Engaged Culture*.[7] Haddon-Cave acknowledges Reason's treatise embraces the idea of acting, so I have to ask, why change the name? His reasoning is that, to him the term *engaged culture* "correctly emphasises the responsibility of an organisation actively to manage safety"; but does it? How am I expected to interpret this word? I know what Reason means because I can find an explanation in his book.[8] But what does Haddon-Cave mean? If I check my dictionary the word does not mean what he says it does. If I check my academic literature, where I find six references to *engaged culture* relating to "candor and a willingness to challenge",[9] I find no other reference to *engaged culture* relating to Haddon-Cave's use of this term and I can also find no work on this subject by Lt Col (Dr) Dillinger whom he quotes. The issue here is one of cross-understanding; changing aspects of what is understood on this subject adds ambiguity and therefore can be seen to hinder, rather than help, wider learning. This leads me to question the validity of the recommendations because, as virtual data, I will only trust the recommendations if I trust the source. By seeming to overreach their level of expertise, authors of these reports can damage their own credibility.

The lesson here is, for both those who are the subject of inquiries and those who conduct them, the need to be careful when offering or accepting expert advice. The acceptance of virtual data requires trust. This trust depends on the sources of advice used, determining the limits of the expertise of those giving the advice and being able to evaluate both the advice and the source from within one's own perspective and *seat of understanding*.

Part of the issue of credibility depends on the expertise of those conducting the inquiry and their perceived independence. Expertise in itself may not be enough; the relevance of the expertise is also important.

SEAT OF UNDERSTANDING

I introduced the construct of *seat of understanding* in Chapter 2 and explained that it meant having the training, knowledge, experience and current data required to make the appropriate judgements. There is an argument that those who conduct inquiries do not need to be expert in the subject, all they need is to be highly analytical and have good judgement. In the academic world some even argue that there are advantages to having no prior knowledge of their subject as prior knowledge would lead to personal bias. Using the lessons we have learnt earlier, I would suggest that this proposition is false for, according to work by Karl Weick and others, expertise enables you to *see what is not there* that should be, as well as what is there (whether it should be or not). One example of a failure in the current model is the various Hillsborough inquiries which have shown that judge-led inquiries can fail to produce accurate findings. First there was the Taylor report, then in 1997 a report by Lord Justice Stuart-Smith and finally in 2012 the weaknesses in this process were exposed by the report of the Hillsborough Independent Panel.

The question then becomes one about what expertise is required to extract valuable lessons from an unwanted occurrence and to make recommendations that are valid for the purpose of teaching those lessons to others. What *seat of understanding* is it necessary for those conducting inquiries to have in order for them to "see the invisible"?[10] An example of this phenomenon can be seen in the case of Hillsborough when, "An off-duty police officer ... (said): 'By 2.45 to 3 p.m., the crowd wasn't moving. No movement in the crowd. Usually there's a swaying motion backwards and forwards. There was none at all ... I knew I was looking at something that was extremely dangerous.'"[11] He had not seen what he would have expected to have seen. This type of understanding can only come from experience. Another example, at the opposite end of the spectrum, is provided by Professor Anthony Redmond when he described the need to train doctors specifically to prepare them to take part in disaster relief work. He explained that without the understanding provided by the training, doctors new to such situations saw chaos for they did not recognise or use the coordination mechanisms that were in place.[12]

Dame Janet Smith opens the doors to this discussion. Recommendation 4 of her Report 3 states, "The Coroner Service requires medical, legal and investigative expertise."[13] However she immediately goes on to question the *viability of this multi-skilling* by saying in Recommendation 5 and 6:

> *Many of the functions currently carried out by coroners (who, in the main, have a legal qualification only) require the exercise of medical judgement. Some of those functions (and others which I am recommending) require legal expertise. In the future, those functions should be carried out respectively by a medical coroner and a judicial coroner. Both the medical and judicial coroners should be independent office-holders under the Crown.*

The Coroner Service should have a corps of trained investigators, who would be the mainstays of the new system. The Coroner's investigator would replace the Coroner's officer but have a greatly enhanced role. More routine functions, at present performed by Coroner's officers, would be performed instead by administrative staff.

These recommendations suggest that Dame Janet Smith recognises that it may not be possible for one person to have all the knowledge and skills required and so a multi-disciplined team of *requisite variety* is required where individual expertise is combined in order to provide the required capability. Peer review may be used as a way of providing the *requisite variety*. This is a lesson that might also be applied to the make-up of an inquiry team. As part of their report, the panel should be required to explain why the make-up of the team was *adequate-to-purpose* or where gaps may have existed.

INDEPENDENCE

Independence is seen to be important when judging the impartiality of an inquiry team. However the first question this should raise is "independent of whom?" In terms of independence, Lord Heseltine gave us a more jaundiced view of the process, suggesting that if you have to have an inquiry, "Reach your conclusion and then choose your chairman and set up the inquiry." However Lord Howe stated to the same committee, "I think that governments need to be protected from the temptation to rig the inquiry."[14] The primary concern is therefore that inquiries are seen to be independent of the politicians who set them up.

For similar reasons, the issue of independence is also raised in relation to regulatory bodies. As we have discussed earlier, both Vaughan and Perrow have debated the advantages and disadvantages of the various regulatory models and they note that independence brings disadvantages as well as advantages. Dechy et al. offer the warning that a board with too much independence could propose unrealistic recommendations.[15]

While independence might be seen as an idea, it may be unobtainable in reality. Social, political, professional and other pressures are at work sometimes overtly and at other times more subtly. "Openness" is offered as the alternative to independence but again there are questions about what is meant by openness. One of the versions of openness is that those conducting the inquiry make a full declaration of interests as part of the report. Another version of openness is that the inquiry process should be open to public scrutiny. Lord Hutton said, "I wished the inquiry to be in public, that I wanted the public to hear every word that was spoken and to see every document that was put in evidence … My intention always was that the transcript could be published, that the media could publish every word."[16] However one also has to question whether this version of openness might become another version of "hiding in plain sight" where the important detail is obscured by the quantity of data released. In addition one has to question how many people would fully understand all the nuances of what had been revealed. This form of openness however also works against the promotion of openness of witnesses. Such public scrutiny may cause witnesses to be guarded in what they say, thereby making an accurate summation of the events more difficult to obtain. This can be seen in the frustration of the families of the fire-fighters killed in 2007 at the Atherstone fire when they asked, "If their crews were so confident in their abilities and of the decisions made on that fateful night, why then did those firefighters not have the courage to tell it like it was when questioned by police or taking the witness stand? ... Why would they not want to tell the truth and why would the defendants not want to give their accounts?"[17] Was the answer to this understandable question as simple as they did not want to put themselves in jeopardy by potentially saying something that might be misconstrued? Because of the nature of the inquiry, it was not in the fire-fighters' interest to be open in that forum.

Openness, like many other aspects, is not a single clear-cut issue. One solution does not fit all circumstances. Taking a risk management perspective, maybe the discussion should focus on *the unwanted* occurrence to be avoided (such as cover-ups, government pressure or political interference) rather than trying to specify a single approach that might not achieve the intended result. In the future, inquiries could be required to canvas stakeholder concerns and then state how each of these issues was addressed.

COMPOSITION OF INQUIRY PANELS

It is clear that an inquiry needs to have both credibility and to be authoritative if the lessons learnt are to be adopted. If the findings are not to be challenged, the inquiry team needs to be seen as being knowledgeable, impartial and as having integrity. As societal expectations change and as we learn more about the strengths and weaknesses of our inquiry process, we may need to look again at the composition of inquiry panels.

The Public Administration Select Committee's report[18] debates the structure of inquiry panels. They examine the advantages and disadvantages of a single judge or a panel, and the advantages and disadvantages of judge led and non-judge led panels. As we have debated earlier, inquiries can be used to satisfy a number of different purposes. However, as my focus is on why we seem to fail to learn, I will examine the issue of inquiry composition from the perspective of its effect on learning outcomes. I therefore need to join these two issues based on the ideas of *requisite variety* and the *viability of multi-skilling*.

The law of *requisite variety* suggests that it takes complexity to understand and manage complexity. One of the principles of *high reliability organisations* is a *reluctance to simplify*. If we combine this with the question of whether multi-skilling is viable (again debated earlier in the book), we come to the point whether one person can have the knowledge, skills and multiple perspectives necessary to really understand complex issues. Judges may argue[19] that they have to deal with complex issues every day and so are well equipped to do so. I would contend that they are judging issues within a single context (the law) and employing a single perspective (a judgely one). Mr Justice Beatson argued to the Select Committee that the skills that judges have are "strongest where the task of the inquiry is solely to find facts". Professor Jowell argued that judges operate in the context of "guidance of principle derived from similar previous cases. Political controversies, however narrowly confined, normally involve a wider set of relevant issues ... and a different set of principles to those found in the law reports" and Sir Michael Bichard commented that while he saw some advantage in using judges in some cases, "If you are talking about learning and improving for the future, I am not sure a judge is the best person to do that".[20] Judges, in common with everyone else, have their strengths and their weaknesses. Therefore, where complex cases require us to learn then the *requisite variety* needs to be employed to distil and communicate these lessons. This requires a team of people, a panel. According to the Select Committee, the use of prominent people or judges, in itself, does not immediately give credibility (see Table 5.1).

Table 5.1   Judges and Credibility

39 ... Since 1990, out of the 31 notable inquiries ... 65.5% have been chaired by a serving or retired judge. The Salmon Commission (1966) recommended ... that the chairman of any tribunal should be a person holding high judicial office. This would, he believed, give assurance that the inquiry was being conducted impartially, efficiently and judicially, and ensure that findings continued to achieve the same measure of public confidence and acceptance that they had in the past.

40. The use of senior judges was supported by the Council on Tribunals in 1996. It commented "... In addition to their legal expertise, judges, by their experience, are well equipped to assess evidence, and their independence and impartiality will command public confidence". A similar view was expressed by Lord Woolf, the Lord Chief Justice, who considered that "the fact that an inquiry is conducted by a judge or with a judicial chairman enhances the confidence of the public as to the impartiality and thoroughness of the inquiry". The Government also supports the use of judges to chair inquiries, "...The judiciary also has a long tradition of independence from politics, and judges are widely accepted to be free from any party political bias".[21]

This may be as it appears from the perspective of the judiciary or politicians, however one does not need to look hard to find cases where a legal judgement is seen by the press and the public as being out of touch with reality and therefore to have little credibility. The Select Committee does warn of the potential damage that might be done to the judiciary if their findings and recommendations presented in inquiry reports are greeted with derision and ridiculed. Lord Norton, who is sceptical about the use of judges as chairpersons, believed that a panel of at least three people would allow for someone with a legal background to be appointed. In the end the committee recommended the use of panels in politically sensitive cases and "where judges are seen as the most appropriate chair, they should be appointed as part of a panel or be assisted by experts".[22]

Lord Laming "appointed four people who had experience that I do not have".[23] Dame Janet Smith also raises the idea of having a balanced inquiry team in the context of the Coroners[24] and General Medical Council.[25] This raises the question of the balance required. In the current composition of inquiry panels we can see the contribution of those with a legal perspective and those with a highly specialised academic background. When Bonar Law set up the first inquiry under the 1921 Act, he asked for:

> *A Committee consisting of a judge … There ought also to be a well-known business man … and the third member …should be a good public accountant.*

A lot has changed since 1921. Again we have to ask as to the expertise required by a panel if it is to get to the heart of the problem at hand and to produce practical and realistic recommendations. What does a balanced inquiry team now look like? As well as the judge or senior lawyer (whose role might be to ask the penetrating questions and facilitate or arbitrate between competing views) we have to decide what knowledge and skills are necessary in order to understand what happened and why, but also what knowledge and skills are required in order to produce practical and realistic recommendations. We see Rita Donaghy used experts centred on understanding the causes of accidents and the law. Maybe now we should be asking, "What was missed?" Which other discipline examined in Chapter 2[a] might also have been used? When recommendations are produced, what additional expertise (such as *performance management*, operational management, change management or organisational psychology) might have been sought? Within each discipline, which school of thought should be followed? For example, within change management there are those who think that if the organisation changes its routines, cultural change will follow. Others reject this proposition. While this may appear to be a very academic argument, it creates very practical problems. Each approach entails a specific mental model of what change is required and how that change will change other aspects of the organisation. Each has hidden assumptions with possible unintended consequences. It will not be possible to create a perfect team, however the panel needs to be aware of their gaps and explain the potential limitations of their work. These limitations will have an effect on the credibility of the resulting recommendations and therefore whether the lessons learnt will be taken up by others.

When we now look at inquiry reports we should be looking at those who conduct the inquiry to determine whether we find them credible before we take note of what they say. When we evaluate advice we should first look to see whether we trust the intention of those giving the advice and then look to see whether we trust their expertise in this matter. Therefore, I suggest that before we accept lessons learnt from a particular occurrence, we should go through the same process. For example I have chosen four inquiry teams and outlined their expertise in Table 5.2. The reports used are the Columbia Accident Investigation Board, The Woolf Report into ethical business conduct within BAe Systems plc, the report of the Hillsborough Independent Panel and the report from the Norwegian 22 July Commission into the attacks on the Government Complex and Utøya Island. It should be noted that not all inquiries state clearly the name and experience of their panel members and therefore it is not always possible to conduct this analysis. In these latter cases the findings of the inquiry are less likely to have weight with unrelated third parties and therefore lessons they may have to offer are more likely to be lost.

---

a   Project management, operational risk management (encompassing *enterprise risk management*), accident investigation and prevention, crisis management, resilience engineering, *high reliability organisations*, and that which relates to *normal accident theory*.

Table 5.2   Inquiry Panel Make-up

CAIB (US – 2003)	Woolf Report (UK – 2008)	HIP (UK – 2012)	22/7 Commission (Nor – 2012)
Retired four star Admiral	Former Lord Chief Justice of England and Wales	Bishop of Liverpool	Lawyer and partner at the law firm
Naval, 2 star Commander, Naval Safety Center, Virginia 2x Air Force General Air Force 1 star General	Former Chairman of the Board of Directors and Chief Executive Officer of the Coca-Cola Company, currently a director of Wal-Mart Stores, Inc.	Lawyers who work together to make a contribution to the protection of civil liberties	Commissioner of Police
Ph.D. degrees in Physics from the Massachusetts Institute of Technology (MIT). He is an expert in aircraft wake vortex behavior and has conducted safety analyses on air traffic control procedures, aircraft certification	Former Group Finance Director and then member of the Defence Management Board and chaired the Defence Audit Committee at the Ministry of Defence, Director of the Institute of Business Ethics	Expert in the field of access to information, and is a member of the Advisory Council on National Records and Archives	Researcher at the Faculty of Law
Director of the NASA Ames Research Center	Began career with the British Treasury, later Chairman of Morgan Stanley International	Television executive producer, factual producer of Jimmy McGovern's Hillsborough drama documentary	Former chief of police
Director, Space Policy Institute, Elliott School of International Affairs, The George Washington University, Washington, DC		Medical consultant and health administrator	Head of the Norwegian Intelligence Service
Professor of Physics and Applied Physics, Nobel Laureate in Physics		Retired Deputy Chief Constable and law graduate	Retired as CEO of NSB (Norwegian State Railways) and businessman
Professor of Physics, and first American female astronaut in space		Professor of Criminology, and author of book of the tragedy	Chief County Medical Officer
Retired Chairman and Chief Executive Officer, McDermott International		Well-known name in TV news – brought up in Liverpool	Writer and historian

CAIB (US – 2003)	Woolf Report (UK – 2008)	HIP (UK – 2012)	22/7 Commission (Nor – 2012)
Director, Office of Accident Investigation, Federal Aviation Administration		Distinguished Senior Research Fellow and archivist	Police Chief Inspector with operational experience
Professor of Aeronautics and Astronautics and Engineering Systems			Degree in political science. A researcher, specialising in terrorism and terrorist acts
			Head of Department at an upper secondary school

The first point about Table 5.2 is to look at the words that I have used to describe each person. While I have extracted the words from the reports, and I had no intention of editorialising, some may see bias within the descriptions given. Therefore it can be seen that there is a need to manage the perception of bias even at this early stage. For the recommendations to have credibility, the inquiry team must have credibility. For the inquiry team to have credibility they must show that they have *requisite variety* to provide the *seat of understanding* necessary to see the invisible factors that were at play at the time that the events occurred. For the report to be seen as balanced, those without a necessary expertise must demonstrate sufficient cross-understanding to appreciate what was happening, and those with a particular expertise must demonstrate that they are aware of when their expertise is applicable to a situation and when it is not, and finally, those with practical experience of the subject in hand have to show that they are open-minded enough to be able to see what might be at fault within their existing culture but on the other hand had not fallen prey to their own version of Stockholm syndrome. In this case the term Stockholm syndrome might be applied to situations where blame is easier to apply rather than explaining how those engaged at the time might have seen and appreciated what was going on (sense-making) and therefore why they might have acted in the way that they did; for without this understanding unreliable lessons may be learnt. Readers may like to review how much credibility they might give to the findings of the inquiries based on their evaluation of the *seat of understanding* and management of bias amongst the inquiry team.

The quality of the findings and recommendations, and therefore the lessons learnt, starts with an assessment of those conducting the inquiry. If those conducting an inquiry see that organisations have failed to learn from the past, they need to ask whether the same thing might happen to the lessons they have found and whether their team had the right combination of skill and expertise, whether they had the *seat of understanding* necessary to be credible to those outside the immediate circle of those affected by the inquiry. If lessons are not to be lost, inquiry reports need to be clear about their *seat of understanding* and expertise of those making the judgements.

As we have already seen, inquiries are required to examine very complex issues which may be beyond the *seat of understanding* of any one individual (much as some may like to think that it is not!). If neither panels nor peer review are used to provide the *requisite variety* or to validate the findings and recommendations of a particular inquiry, then the chair needs to enhance the credibility of their work by acknowledging any potential weakness in their understanding, analysis or findings.

What Might we Learn from Others?

So what advice has been given to those constructing recommendations? The answer is, surprisingly little. If we look at the evolution of recommendations over the last 50 years, we can however see practice develop and de facto standards emerge. In this next section I will describe both paths before concluding by offering a standard for practice based on this review.

LESSONS FROM LITERATURE

In 1998 Campbell[26] examined this subject from the perspective of the evaluation of training programmes. In this context, knowledge is transferred into action through a three-stage process. Stage 1 is to prepare both the recommendations and an action plan, stage 2 is to formulate the recommendations and stage 3 is to draw up a plan for corrective action. Here we see again a system at work. In our context a boundary within the system emerges; this boundary is a limit on responsibilities between those responsible for constructing the recommendations and those with responsibilities for implementing the recommendations. As we now know from Chapter 2, boundaries are often a cause of system failures and so this one may also have its part to play in the failure to take the correct remedial action following a recommendation.

For stage 1 of this process Campbell recommends that:

Once the information and data have been analyzed and interpreted,
the findings can be reported. Concluding statements summarize the
findings, focusing on the important points. The conclusions are then
used to formulate recommendations. When listed, the sequential
procedure is:

1. *Interpret the data and report the findings.*
2. *Draw conclusions.*
3. *Formulate recommendations based on the conclusions.*

For stage 2 Campbell offers "no hard and fast rules" but suggests that "all
the conclusions and recommendations must be consistent with one another
and with the findings". Campbell does however offer three questions to help
analyse conclusions and recommendations. These are:

- *Is there evidence to support them?*
- *Are they compatible with the evaluation purpose and objective(s)?*
- *Are they logical?*

Campbell also remarks that:

Better than any individual formulating a recommendation is a
cooperative effort by all stakeholders. The practice of providing
opportunities for involvement is just as important at this stage as it
was during the planning. In any case, the purpose is to recommend
refinements or changes where there is reasonably high agreement that
they are needed.

While we see the point Campbell is making, that all the stakeholders need
to be engaged, we can also see the difficultly this might create. Such close
cooperation between the inquiry team and those being inquired into may leave
the inquiry vulnerable to accusations of bias in favour of the "establishment".
So we have a choice, impartial but impractical recommendations or less
"impartial" recommendations (because of the loss of their utopian flavour) that
are more implementable; as we see again, every choice has advantages and
disadvantages, society will need to choose.

Finally, Campbell sees the need to draw up a plan of action, "where there is
reasonably high agreement that they are needed". He warns:

Training may "fail" because of improper or unclear objectives; changes in requirements, personnel, equipment, etc.; or lack of job preparation emphasis, e.g. inappropriate content and instructional methodology. In addition, a host of factors may inhibit or even prevent the application of the skills on the job. Therefore, it is critical to develop a plan of action to correct deficiencies identified through the course/program evaluation. Furthermore, changes may be undertaken to reduce the time required for trainees to attain proficiency or to retain training effectiveness while lowering costs.

The importance of the action plan cannot be overemphasised. Refinements or changes are achieved only through action. It is not enough to identify a problem and recommend solutions. Training personnel must develop detailed action items to ensure that the needed refinements or changes are made.

Action plans specify what is to be done and when. They also identify the individual(s) responsible for taking action. Suffice it to say, someone in the training organisation should monitor the activities to ensure that they are carried out as planned, changes to the courses/programmes are consistent with the evaluation recommendations, and the expected benefits actually occur.

I quote Campbell at length on this last point because it outlines what a complex and fraught task it is to turn knowing into the appropriate action. We can only guess at the number of steps required to turn a recommendation into an action within establishments such as a department of state or a multinational organisation.

While others[27] have said something similar, the first extensive guidelines that I could find did not come from academia but were produced in 2008 by the UK Ministry of Defence; this is referred to as JSP832, "Guide to Service Inquiries".[28] In this document there is guidance as to the production of recommendations (at paragraphs 5.9 and 5.10 – see Table 5.3).

Table 5.3 Ministry of Defence Guidelines

5.9 The panel should make any appropriate recommendations that it considers will prevent recurrence of such an accident or incident in the future. The recommendations should be based on and cross referred to the findings and must relate to the TORs of the inquiry.
5.10 The standard format for the presentation of recommendations should feature:
a. A list of the causal factors that led to the incident occurring.
b. Against each causal factor mentioned in a. above, any measures that, in the opinion of the inquiry, should be taken to prevent this arising in future.
c. A list of the contributory factors that contributed to the outcome of the incident.
d. Against each contributory factor, any measures that, in the opinion of the inquiry, could be taken to mitigate the risk of that factor arising in future.
e. Any other recommendations for improvement in procedures, which may not have contributed directly to the matter under investigation but have been identified by the panel during the course of the inquiry.

In 2009 an European Safety Reliability and Data Association (ESReDA) Working Group[29] added more detail (see Table 5.4).

Table 5.4 ESReDA Guidelines

6.2 Turning findings into recommendations
Recommendations should flow directly from the analysis and findings and contain applicable corrective action(s). Corrective actions (safety measures) may be categorized according to:
• Their position with regard to the risky phenomenon: from preventing the occurrence of the hazard (via detection, monitoring and preventive measures) to reducing the vulnerability (via protection and emergency response measures) for those people, systems or environments at risk;
• Their position with regard to the socio-technical level: re-engineering the process, redesigning the human-machine interface, reorganizing the work on the shop-floor and at the management level(s), redesigning organisational and power relationships, changing regulations and procedures.
As mentioned previously regarding the socio-technical system view, the definition of different types of recommendations requires various types of expertise (Rasmussen 1997).
Turning findings into recommendations can be interpreted simply as analysing the learning experiences of those involved and transforming them into meaningful recommendations. During this process it is important to bear in mind the following:
• Making meaningful recommendations requires a thorough understanding of the system;
• Once accident causes have been identified, it is helpful to refer to a model of the system in order to develop recommendations;
• It is essential to involve and communicate with appropriate stakeholders (those controlling the risks in the system) whilst developing recommendations. This process (of discussing options) leads to more credible recommendations and greater understanding of what needs to be done by the stakeholders;

- When findings are complete and the time has come to move to recommendations, they should be formulated to address the following goals to:

  - Prevent such accidents/events from happening again;

  - Mitigate the consequences should such an event happen again in the future;

  - Address knowledge deficiencies revealed during the investigation;

  - Identify weaknesses in the processes (human, technical or managerial) with special focus on the interfaces (human-technical, human-managerial, technical managerial), as these potentially could be the weaker parts of the processes within the system;

  - Focus on strengthening these weaknesses;

  - Propose special processes as an early-warning system to quickly address potential breakdowns within critical processes with a potential to trigger cascading effects;

  - It may be appropriate to include a reasonable time limit for responding to a recommendation if this is not already mandatory by regulation or law. This may be seen as a way to indicate the investigator's ranking of priorities, however skill and caution is needed if this technique is used. It must be remembered that recommendations are just that – good proposals or ideas based on the evidence provided during the investigation. They are not mandatory, except in the instances when a safety authority turns them into directives of what must be done.

Please note that some independent investigation safety boards have developed a specific team and set of procedures to deal with recommendations; Indeed, the process is not as simple as it might appear.

In general, two principal strategies are available for drafting recommendations:

- Coping with deviations from a normative level of performance [Rule-based] based on optimal operating conditions, and restoring the situation and/or system state to what it was before the disruptive event. This strategy deals with "resilience", i.e. the ability of a system to return to its normative level of performance following an overload. In this scenario, the system will be brought back into the original set of operating parameters;

- Coping with deficiencies in the system's design and operation. Safety enhancement can be achieved by timely adaptation of the system characteristics and primary working processes. The system will adapt its operating parameters to enable changes in the operating environment.

6.3 Applying the recommendations

Essentially, recommendations are statements of the lessons drawn from the investigation by the investigators. Learning the lessons means taking some actions and implementing some changes. The role of those with authority to implement the recommendations can be considered against the following guidelines:

- It is for those with responsibility for the activities affected by the recommendations to take them into account and follow-through with appropriate action;

- In determining their response (to either accept or reject) the recommendations, the responsible party should consider all information relevant to manage and/or control the risk(s) involved;

- Responses to recommendations should be recorded: any rejected recommendations should be supported by a justification or rationale; any accepted recommendations should be accompanied by an action plan;

- Actions taken in response to recommendations should be tracked through to their completion;

- Formal steps should be taken to preserve the "lessons learned" in the corporate memory (such as a database of recommendations and actions, a record of why changes are made to systems, etc.). Similarly, steps should be taken to ensure lessons are learnt across the industry sector and that its memory is also preserved;

- Lessons must not rest only with individuals but with systems' change and mechanisms to ensure the lessons are not lost;

- A key challenge is in the proactive use of databases of lessons and/or recommendations. Only through the continual use of these databases to challenge safety management systems and develop refinements, will the full potential of the investigative process be realised. The goal is a "living memory" that constantly informs of actions to be taken rather than a dormant listing residing in a rarely used "black box."

6.4 Codes of good practice

The following codes of good practice should be respected and practised:

- Recommendations need to be clear and unambiguous;

- The accident investigation report needs to clearly set out the reasoning applied, based on evidence of what happened, and forming the basis of the recommendations;

- Consultation with system owners (i.e. involved parties) on draft recommendations before publication leads to more practicable recommendations and a better likelihood of a more positive response;

- The integrity and credibility of investigators is crucial to securing acceptability of their findings. This is mainly achieved by professional reputation based on actual behaviour. Codes of conduct covering such matters can be especially helpful, though, at the start of an investigation to provide assurance to stakeholders in the absence of knowledge about the individual investigator(s).

The MOD and ESReDA guidelines provide a point from which to start looking at what has evolved in practice.

LESSONS FROM PRACTICE

Inquiry reports themselves provide us with examples of practices that make learning easier. It is clear that examples of good practice are being recognised by those producing inquiry reports as their format can be seen to evolve, and as they evolve, they become easier to digest and to use as the basis for learning lessons. While the Sheen report into the Zeebrugge tragedy was seen as being thorough and insightful, and it had a significant impact on the development of practices that followed, it is not the easiest document to read and digest. The Common's Select Committee made nine recommendations on good practice[30] (see Table 5.5). It should be noted that the government response, while accepting these recommendations, contained a number of caveats and they saw no need to set them out specifically as good practice.[31] Following their response the government published their guidance in Standard Notes published in the House of Commons' Library[32] and in statutory instruments.[33] These are not the most obvious places where one might look for such lessons.

Table 5.5   Public Administration Select Committee Suggested Good Practice

> - Adopt panels as the preferable form as they ensure expertise, provide public reassurance and reinforce independence;
> - Have terms of reference which enjoy the widest possible consensus and are subject to a period of appropriate deliberation and discussion;
> - Have a presumption of openness;
> - Set budget limits, publish costs and explain overruns; set time limits in the original announcement and justify extensions publicly;
> - Build in procedural lessons – learning and evaluation of the inquiry process;
> - Have rigorous, perhaps parliamentary, audit of recommendations and lessons;
> - Test emerging findings and proposals for feasibility and practicality;
> - Ensure fairness but minimise the use of Counsel for the parties; and
> - Ensure access to papers and people by legal/subpoena powers or other informal assurance systems.

I would also highlight two additional features found in the report that seem to make the lessons learnt easier to adsorb. The first is how they fit into the report overall and the second is the way they are worded.

While no one report can be offered as an exemplar, a number of practices have been identified that help communicate the lessons learnt. When producing a report designed to focus on the lessons learnt, consideration needs to be given to how the document will be read as this is likely to affect whether it will be read by people other than those who have to. Amongst the features that might affect this are:

- **An Executive Summary**. Long and complicated reports, such as Haddon-Cave (2009) and Leveson (2012) have used executive summaries to help their audience assimilate the key messages. If executive summaries are used, consideration should be given to using this device to lead the audience into the main body of the report rather than the summary being just seen as delivering the key messages.

- **A Clear Purpose**. Many, but not all, reports start with a clear statement of the purpose and aims of the inquiry. In some reports these are lost in annexes at the back. Setting a clear aim and purpose helps the audience to establish a framework of expectations that is so important to learning. This enables readers to set their expectations for what will be included and excluded from the debate and where the boundaries lie.

- **Peer review**. While reports, such as Borthwick (2010), may recommend peer review for others, few use them for their own work. One exception is the Donaghy report (2009) which included what she considered to be a peer review of her process. As stated in the previous chapter, other inquiries should consider the use of peer review in order to enhance their credibility.

The second issue is the wording of recommendations. The examples used in this section have been chosen at random in order to illustrate clearly the point that I am trying to make. As remarked on earlier in the book, I am not reviewing the appropriateness of the recommendations in the context of their particular inquiry. I am however commenting on how they communicate to others outside their direct audience who are trying to learn from their experience and findings. The aim of this section is to provide those producing or critiquing recommendations with an alternative perspective of how certain constructs appear to someone who is trying to learn from them.

Recommendations need to be worded to ensure that they are not ambiguous either in intent or as to the act required. I can illustrate my point. One of the major criticisms in the Laming Report (2003) of the agencies involved in the death of a child was the failure of them working in a coordinated manner. However he only made one recommendation that refers to "joint working" – see Table 5.6.

Table 5.6   Laming 2003 Recommendation 14

The National Agency for Children and Families should require each of the training bodies covering the services provided by doctors, nurses, teachers, police officers, officers working in housing departments, and social workers to demonstrate that effective joint working between each of these professional groups features in their national training programmes. (paragraph 17.114)

In paragraph 17.112 Lord Laming states, "Each training body should be required to promote training specifically designed to bring together staff from different agencies on topics where joint working is essential." This statement seems to reinforce that the goal of such training is to enhance the effectiveness of joint working. This essential element becomes obscured by the wording of the recommendation which also fails to refer to the paragraph that holds the key reason (para.17.112). The wording of the recommendation only requires that joint working "features" in the training rather than being an essential goal and therefore its intent becomes ambiguous and may easily be lost.

The Anderson Report (2002) into an outbreak of Foot and Mouth disease within the UK provides a couple of examples of rather ambiguously worded recommendations – see Table 5.7.

Table 5.7   Anderson (2002) Recommendations 50 and 75

Recommendation 50: The Government should make explicit the extent to which the wider effects of disease control strategies have been identified, measured and taken into account in policy decisions.
Recommendation 75: Farm assurance schemes should take account of animal health and welfare, biosecurity, food safety and environmental issues.

The precise requirement or way to judge the extent to which something has been "taken into account" either in policy decisions or other areas, or the effect that this might have, is somewhat vague as a directive. While these recommendations might make sense within the context of the report, neither their high-level intent, the action required nor how success will be judged is immediately apparent, and these things are therefore very difficult to see. The value of such recommendations has to be questioned.

Comparison of recommendations shows that having expressed the intent in a positive manner may have beneficial effects. To illustrate this point I would contrast two recommendations, one from Dame Janet Smith's fifth report into the Shipman case and the US Commission into Deepwater Horizon – see Table 5.8.

Table 5.8   Smith v. US Commission

Smith – Recommendation 6 Private grievance complaints should be dealt with by appropriately trained PCT staff. The objectives in dealing with such complaints should be the satisfaction of the patient and, where possible, restoration of the relationship of trust and confidence between doctor and patient.
US Commission – Recommendation B2 The Department of the Interior should reduce risk to the environment from OCS oil and gas activities by strengthening science and interagency consultations in the OCS oil and gas decision-making process.

On initial analysis these two recommendations seem to contain the same type of information; however the second one seems clearer than the first. In order to understand this perceived difference, I then examined the words used and the structure given to the data. The first issue that struck me was the difference in the action words. The first recommendation used transformational wording ("dealt with") rather than the outcome wording ("reduce risk") and so I was more comfortable with the espoused goal. The second issue that I noted was that the responsibility for who was to take action was clear from the start in the second recommendation but was only ever an assumption in the second (I assume this is an action for each Primary Care Trust (PCT)). The third issue noted was the structure of each recommendation. The first is rather passive in tone and the second is more active and direct. From these two examples we are able to see that passive and reflective recommendations, while appearing more thoughtful, may be hard to understand and action.

Finally I have selected two examples (see Table 5.9 and Table 5.10) from Dame Janet Smith's inquiries into the activities of Harold Shipman. I use these examples to illustrate where we see recommendations having complex interaction with the target system.

Table 5.9   Smith (2005) Report 4 Recommendation 18

> GPs who keep a stock of Schedule 2 controlled drugs should be required (as now) to keep a CDR and to observe existing safe custody requirements. They should be permitted to keep the CDR in electronic form. The CDR should provide for the keeping of a running stock balance for each drug stocked. Each GP who is either a principal in or employed by a practice that keeps controlled drugs for practice use should be under a legal obligation to comply with the terms of a standard operating procedure (SOP) devised or approved either by the PCT with which the practice contracts or, if and when a controlled drugs inspectorate is set up, by that body. The SOP should specify, among other things, the frequency with which the stock must be checked. Adherence to such SOPs should be mandatory and should be subject to regular inspection. Any doctor working as a locum should be under an obligation either to comply with the practice SOP or to make his/her personal arrangements to provide Schedule 2 drugs and to accept responsibility for keeping the necessary CDR. I suggest that the Healthcare Commission (or, if it comes into being, the controlled drugs inspectorate) should be responsible for approving SOPs for GPs in private practice and for ensuring compliance. Advice as to compliance and best practice should be issued nationally and should also be available from PCT officers in the course of the annual clinical governance visit or review. (Chapter Six and paragraphs 14.119–14.133)

The eighteenth recommendation in Dame Janet Smith's fourth report (the control of drugs) is set out in Table 5.9. In this case I determined that the primary purpose of this recommendation was a new electronic controlled drugs register (Capability [3]). This was seen to be a "legal obligation", maybe requiring the law to be changed (Political [3]), some specific instruction about the process to be adopted (Technical [1]), the allocation of responsibility (Bureaucracy [2]), and there was an issue of compliance (Bureaucracy [3]). Finally this course of action would be overseen by an "annual clinical governance visit or review" (Performance Management [1]).

Table 5.10   Smith (2005) Report 5 Recommendation 75

The November 2004 Rules should be amended so as to provide that the arrangements for the obtaining and consideration of performance assessments and for the management and supervision of doctors who are the subject of voluntary undertakings relating to performance should be directed by a medically qualified case examiner, who should fulfil the functions previously carried out by a performance case co-ordinator. If a case is to be closed on the basis of a performance assessment, the decision should be taken by two case examiners, one medically qualified and one lay, and, if they disagree, by an IC panel. (Chapter 25 and paragraph 27.248)

The second example (Table 5.10) is also taken from the reports produced by Dame Janet Smith. In this case the primary purpose of the recommendations was seen to be an amendment to rules (Political [2]) concerning arrangements (Bureaucracy [1]) for the appraisal of individuals (Performance Management [3]). These appraisals concerned the competency of individuals (Standards [2]) and the allocation of roles and responsibilities (Bureaucracy [2]).

The wordings of these recommendations do therefore provide us with some insight as to how the author sees the various building blocks are related.

SUMMARY

Here we can start to see clear differences between the perspectives of someone focused on learning and those within the judicial system. The judicial model differs considerably from my own as a practitioner, which is rooted in years of trying to foresee *the unwanted* and preventing it from happening. At this point I need to acknowledge that my mental model is likely to differ from the views of other people working in this area. Even within this limit group of people cross-understanding is likely to be an issue. In this book I only use my own mental model as a contrast to the generic judicial model developed as a result of this discussion. The important point is the distance between the two which makes cross-understanding difficult and learning even more so.

Is this important? To answer this question we need to go back to the Challenger tragedy to see how different perspectives, different paradigms, may have had an extraordinary part to play in what happened to that spacecraft. In her analysis of the Challenger disaster, Vaughan provides an example of how changing from a positive to a negative paradigm can have a significant effect on the outcome of a discussion. She describes[35] the moment when the paradigm of discourse flipped; the paradigm changed from one where the question was "prove the Shuttle is safe to fly" to one of "prove the Shuttle is unsafe to fly".

This can be seen as a change from proving a positive proposition, to proving a negative one. While the effect of this change (the accident) has been discussed at length, the significance of the flip on the course of the debate has received far less attention. This flip can be seen as the result of a clash, in this instance, between a "safety first" paradigm and a "scientific" paradigm where data drives decisions. Up to this point the two paradigms had worked in tandem: the flip caused them to clash: those involved had to instinctively choose one to resolve that clash; they chose science: there was no data to support "no go": the decision was made. The point is, perspective is important; it can be the difference between life and death.

Revised Recommendation Guidelines

In our quest to improve the quality of inquiry recommendations, we are now ready to summarise what we have discovered so far. We can see that not only should all recommendations be justifiable, but also clear as to the action required and well structured. We might also question the value of recommendations that just comment or admonish for they do not add to our learning. It is important that recommendations are fully justified if society is to invest the time and effort necessary to adopt them. For recommendations to be justified they must:

- Contain applicable corrective action or indicate deficiencies in knowledge (in this latter case further research may be recommended).

- Be based on reasoning that flows directly from and is cross-referenced to the findings.

- Show a clear design strategy (rather than being just a list of individual actions) which explains how the future will be improved rather than just explaining the past.

- Show a thorough understanding of the system (preferably referring to a model of the system) and show how the recommendation will not encourage further sub-optimisation of the system or other unintended consequences.

- Derive from the integrity and credibility (expertise) of investigators: this goes back to the Adams Model where, if we cannot see, feel, touch or measure, we have to trust the person or people giving the advice.

- Be peer reviewed; to learn we have to trust, we therefore need to see that an opinion is not only fully justified but has also been fully tested.

- Involve and communicate with the appropriate stakeholders; again we see tension between the need and desire to learn and any political or judicial goals that the inquiry may attract. It is clear that learning and enacting lessons can only be enhanced by engagement with the other relevant stakeholders.

- Articulate (1) the perspective adopted, (2) any conflicts of interests and (3) sources of bias or any other analytical limitations. As has already been said, trust in those giving advice is a very important factor as to whether the advice will be heeded. Whatever can be done to build that trust would be worthwhile.

Recommendations need to address all the important deficiencies revealed during the investigation. They need to encompass:

- **Causal factors**: against each causal factor measures should be recommended to prevent them reoccurring.

- **Universals, conditions and other contributory factors**: against each factor should be considered and measures taken to mitigate them.

- **Risky phenomena:**
  - preventing the occurrence of the hazard (detection, monitoring and preventive measures);
  - reducing (mitigating) vulnerabilities (via protection, deflection and emergency response measures);
  - **Improvement of procedures**: the re-engineering of processes with a special focus on the interfaces and early-warning systems.

- **Deficiencies in knowledge or skills.**

However, this list may not be complete. It is important therefore that there is a clear understanding of the boundaries being used and how it is envisaged that the system operates within these defined boundaries. We also need to understand what "start/stop" rules the inquiry has adopted and why. If we refer back to Figure 3.1 – Basic Mental Model, we see one list of different aspects of any system that may need evaluating. While inquiries may not adopt this model, if they wish to gain and maintain the trust of their wider audience, they should produce one of their own to explain their underlying thinking.

Finally, I suggest that recommendations also need to be structured so that they:

- Are self-contained (as many people will only read the recommendations); that is, they can be understood as a stand-alone statement when extracted from the context of the report. They are clear and unambiguous about:
  - the action required, and how success should be judged;
  - who is responsible;
  - how the system will affect and be affected by the changes;
  - the relationships and interaction between recommendations;
  - the risks involved in taking these actions.

- Differentiate between Macro, Mezzo and Micro recommendations.

- Rank priorities.

- Set realistic time limits for response and "follow-through" which indicate that they appreciate the size of the task involved.

There are two final checks that need to be made. The first looks at the potential for learning and the second embraces Perrow's warning about *normal accidents*.

Throughout the inquiry process there is an emphasis on learning. It is natural that the main focus of the learning will be on those directly involved both as individuals and as a sector of society. However, it is rare for the same accident to happen twice. Some may be a variation on a theme, the same but different, but identical accidents are unusual. The question then becomes one of how widely lessons can be generalised to other people and other areas of activity. While applicability may be easy to see in hindsight, the application in foresight is much more difficult. If those conducting inquiries condemn practitioners for any perceived *failure of foresight*, they should be prepared to recommend how the lesson learnt may be applied more generally.

Perrow's warning that complex and closely coupled systems may interact in unexpected ways should make those producing the reports search for any hidden dangers in what they recommend. Even with all the tests previously applied, the danger of unintended consequences will be ever present. Report authors need to have the humility to recognise that they are vulnerable to this error of judgement, to heed Perrow's warning and check, check and check again.

Once the recommendations have been formulated, authors then need to decide how they are integrated into the structure of the document. Inquiry reports come in many different formats and use many different structures. Over the years a growing consensus has emerged that has helped to make it easier for important lessons to be extracted from these documents. In general there are two approaches adopted. The first is to use a time-based narrative which explains how the events unfolded and then to draw conclusions and make recommendations. This approach has the advantage of logic and flow, however the danger is that the lessons learnt become lost in the body of the text. The second approach is to base the structure of the documents around the recommendations and lessons learnt and then structure the document around the arguments that support this advice. Here again we see a tension between two cultures, one which focuses on what happened and why, which then draws lessons, and one that is focused on learning and disseminating the lessons which are justified by an explanation of the what and the why. While the choice of structure will be a personal preference and either format will cover both aspects, whichever one is chosen will slant the report towards making an explanation easier to understand or making the lessons easier to learn. Those conducting the inquiries should be aware of the choices they make and explain them to their audiences.

The inquiry report from New Zealand on the Pike River Coal Mine tragedy provides our example. At the beginning of the report (on page 12) the author provides a "Snapshot". In this we learn:

> *The mine was new and the owner ... had not completed the systems and infrastructure necessary to safely produce coal ... Pike's ventilation and methane drainage systems ... (and) extracting coal by hydro mining, (was) a method known to produce large quantities of methane. There*

were numerous warnings ... In the last 48 days before the explosion
there were 21 reports of methane levels reaching explosive volumes ...
The warnings were not heeded. The drive for coal production before the
mine was ready created the circumstances within which the tragedy
occurred ... The company was continuing to borrow to keep operations
going ... the company's original prediction that it would produce more
than a million tonnes of coal a year by 2008 had proved illusory.[36]

From these words I can see potential (1) *liability of newness*, (2) *production pressure*, (3) *amoral calculation*, (4) *fantasy plans*, (5) *communication failure*, and (6) *normalisation of deviance*. I also have questions over whether it was too early in the life of the organisation for *safety drift* to be a factor and whether those setting up the enterprise had the necessary *seat of understanding*. From a *risk governance* perspective my interest is the "cause of the cause" and so which of the potential factors that I have identified will turn out to be *universal* or *conditions* rather than *causes*. I am interested in what induced the organisation to fail to heed warnings or why competent and diligent people thought, at that moment, that their act or reluctance to act was appropriate. In order to find answers to my questions I am faced with reading through the details of a report that is nearly 450 pages long. I would question how many people have time to conduct such a review and so would expect these lessons to be lost to a much wider audience who may have benefited from any new insight that this report might have provided.

Parliament looked to provide guidance in 2005, which seems never to have been delivered. In his report published in 2013, Francis commented, "It may come as a surprise for some to appreciate that there is no effective established template for the setting up or administration of a public inquiry and, therefore, the team has had to start from scratch."[37] It might be tempting to compare this timeframe with the timeframe which those who were the subject of Francis's work had failed to act. While the Cabinet Office has an advisory role with Departments and inquiry teams,[38] the focus of this work is the legal framework rather than the process or the promotion learning. While individual departments are expected to learn from their own inquiries, there is no mechanism for these lessons to be spread between departments. Those practitioners more directly involved in the learning process have produced guidelines but a question remains as to whether those conducting inquires have learnt about or from this work.

Summary

In this chapter we have looked at the formulation of recommendations in order to find ways that their quality may be assured. The first thing recognised was that the quality of the recommendations would depend on the quality and expertise of those producing the recommendations. We also saw that expertise in itself is not enough. It is important that the expertise is relevant and those involved need to have an appropriate *seat of understanding* if they are to *see what is not there* as well as what is. We saw the *requisite variety* of skills required to grasp such complexity. We also saw that even if the inquiry team had the appropriate expertise, if they were not seen to be independent then they would not have the credibility required for their recommendations to receive the attention that may be due to them.

Endnotes

1   Snook (2000), page 239.
2   CAIB (2003), page 149.
3   CAIB (2003), page 151.
4   Roed-Larsen and Stoop (2012).
5   Dien et al. (2012), page 1406.
6   Dechy et al. (2012), page 1387.
7   Haddon-Cave (2009), page 572, para.27.11.
8   Reason (1997), pages 191–221.
9   Nadler (2004), Building Better Boards, HBR, 82.5, Page 102.
10   Klien (1998).
11   Scraton (1999), e-book Loc 4717–4719.
12   BBC Radio 4 Today Programme, 26 December 2012 – 0752 am.
13   Smith (2005), Report 3, page 25.
14   PASC HC51-I, page 30, para.70 and 72.
15   Dechy et al. (2012), page 1388.
16   PASC HC51-I, page 37.
17   http://www.bbc.co.uk/news/uk-england-coventry-warwickshire-18278559,   accessed   11 December 2012.
18   PASC HC51-1 (2005), pages 27–29.
19   For example see Lord Huttons comments at page 28: "Judges are used to trying very grave issues on their own."
20   PASC HC51-1 (2005), pages 21.
21   PASC HC51-1 (2005), pages 19.
22   PASC HC51-1 (2005), pages 30.
23   PASC HC51-1 (2005), pages 29.
24   Smith (2005), Report 3, page 193, para.8.48.
25   Smith (2005), Report 5, page 64, para.106.
26   Campbell (1998).
27   Law et al. (2003), pages 420–421.
28   JSP832 (2008).
29   ESReDA (2009).
30   PASC HC51-I page 59, para.116.

31   Cm6481 2005, page 21.
32   SN/PC/02599 (2011) and SN/PC/06410 (2012).
33   SI 2006 No.1838 The Inquiry Rules.
34   Bichard (2004), page 12, para.78.
35   Vaughan (1996), page 249.
36   Panckhurst (2012), page 12.
37   Francis (2013), page 21, para.52.
38   Email from Cabinet office dated 7 January 2013.

6

Do We Learn?

Towards Learning

So what have we learnt? In this final chapter I look to draw together the threads of this discussion and reflect on what we might learn about the conduct of inquiries if we examine them through the lens of accident prevention or risk management. One of the fundamental premises must be the adage "First do no harm". In this sense, the recommendations of an inquiry should not make the situation worse or create a whole new set of issues and problems by the proposed changes. The Commons Select Committee set out to enhance our learning from inquiries. Dame Janet Smith also sees the role of the Coroner service as being to "ensure that the knowledge gained from death investigation is applied for the prevention of avoidable death and injury in the future"[1] But how do they and others envisage this learning will happen?

Inquiries often find fault where an organisation fails to articulate their processes clearly, yet those departments that set up such inquiries do not set out detailed standards or procedures to which an inquiry must conform or comply. The production of guidance on such issues as record keeping, the formulation of recommendations, the report production standards, and the level of compliance required should be published and be regularly reviewed.[2]

The aim here is to equip a wider audience to learn the most from the experience of others (*free lessons*) – not how useful they are to those directly concerned with the issue (which would be expected). At this point it is also important to note that we have identified three approaches to inquiries. The first is political, the second is judicial and the third is learning: we have seen that both the political and judicial approaches may have detrimental effects on learning and therefore, for the purposes of this chapter, the assumption is made that those involved have a genuine desire to learn and that the learning approach should not be undermined by political or judicial considerations.

TWO SIDES OF THE SAME COIN

At the beginning of the book I felt the need to state that I see benefit and jeopardy as being indivisibly related; that I see *performance management* and risk management also as being indivisibly related. The fact that I have to articulate this belief says something about how this may not be a common orthodoxy. Much of management literature and practice articulates how benefits can be pursued yet they seem to give little consideration to the jeopardy that lurks close by. I take as an example the book *Cranfield on Corporate Sustainability;*[3] this is an anthology that pulls together 12 articles that explore ideas on being a sustainable organisation. If you scan both the context and the index you will find no reference to *risk* or *risk management*. This raises the question as to how you might have a mental model of sustainability without considering risks, failures or the other hazards that might jeopardise the future of the organisation. Contained within the book are references to unintended consequences, "don'ts", safety and risk management, however these are all seen as incidental to the main thrust of the argument. The only time I have seen an argument against balance was in an article by Tom Peters which suggested that if you wanted excellence you had to focus specifically on the task at which you want to excel. I would therefore suggest that if *the unwanted* is to be avoided, we have to focus on preventing it. But do we?

One of the findings of the Service inquiry into the flooding of HMS Endurance (16 December 2008) concerns the protagonists' attitude towards risk management. The inquiry found that:

> Risk management within the Marine Engineering Department onboard
> ENDURANCE is not instinctive, and is seen as a non dynamic activity,
> conducted by the one departmental Risk Assessor ... many interviewees
> were of the opinion that risk management can only be a formal process
> which focuses on the protection of personnel rather than equipment
> or the platform ... (and) were of the opinion that risk management is
> limited to those who have attended the course.[4]

The report recommended that the appropriate authority "develops a programme to ensure risk management is more instinctive, inclusive at all levels and include a better understanding of cumulative risk".[5] The Endurance inquiry suggests that risk management is often seen as a specialist subject. This leads to the idea that "if we have a risk management function then we have it covered". I would suggest that this is inadequate and, if we are to learn from the past and from the mistakes of others, we have to study how this might be done and teach it as part of general management training. A brief survey of Business Studies courses (both at Bachelors and Masters levels) reveals that risk management is not considered to be a core subject; if it is covered, this is often done as part of the project management module. I would suggest that, if we are to increase our chances of avoiding such unwanted events in the future, we need to give wider consideration to this subject on all business studies courses or, if this is considered to be too much, at least remind people to ponder the unintended consequences of the actions or the options reviewed.

LEARNING ORGANISATIONS

While we see a clear desire to "learn lessons" (over three million hits were found on Google), while we see many risk-related academic disciplines all seeking to learn from the experience of others and while we see studies of how organisations learn, a search of academic studies into how effectively we learn reveals none. It is clear that we do learn, based on measures such as deaths per passenger miles, we see that air travel has become safer over the last 50 years. What is more difficult to ascertain is where we learn most effectively and where we do not learn at all; whether technical recommendations have a high probability of having the desired effect and whether the more abstract ones, such as suggesting the need for better leadership or a cultural change, have a very low probability of being effectively implemented (and why). What is also difficult to ascertain is whether our ability to improve is starting to plateau; in the case of the report on Air France flight 447 we see where measures taken to mitigate one source of failure creates others. This issue is becoming more common.

Academics give us concepts such as *organisational learning*[6] to help guide us. We are told that there are five key areas of *organisational learning*. These are:

1. Personal mastery (expertise and *seat of understanding*).

2. Mental models (the need to challenge the mental models that members of organisations bring with them).

3. Team learning (a commitment to team learning).

4.   Shared vision of the future (cross-understanding).

5.   Systems thinking which ties everything together.

However, knowing a few of the terms does not equate to being a learning organisation. We saw in the MOD's reply to the Haddon-Cave recommendation on learning the same sort of top-level understanding where we questioned whether this would actually lead to effective learning or just the production of a suitable corporate veneer.

To learn we have to have a common language as a prerequisite to developing the cross-understanding necessary to learn lessons. The common language starts with the actual national language used and it includes the technical language that structures the conversation. We see both of these issues illustrated in the Norwegian 22 July Commission report. In terms of national language, only the recommendations were published in English. Few non-Norwegians have either the time or the resources to translate the rest of the report. In terms of technical language, the fact this report only translated the recommendations into English emphasises these as being the most important aspect of the report and being seen as the greater source of learning. This limit in common language meant that the full value of the recommendations could not be understood by all those who might be interested, other lessons available within the main text and findings would also be missed and therefore, much of the learning available would be overlooked even by those most interested in such lessons.

In Chapter 2 we discussed how in order to prevent *failure of foresight* we need to see, appreciate and act. We can now see how this triptych also needs to be applied to *organisational learning*. We can see how *distancing through differencing* might prevent one from seeing the lessons available and how failure to appreciate the value of *isomorphic learning* may prevent organisations from acting. However for effective learning to take place we need to be able to monitor and measure success. For this to happen, reports need to be much clearer about *what good looks like* and start to define this in clear and measurable terms.

In his evidence to the Commons Select Committee, Sir John Gieve (Permanent Secretary at the Home Office) stated that "the pressure for [public inquiries] is increasing all the time, and there is a risk that we overdo it and go over a lot of events which are very similar where there are not a lot of new lessons to be learned".[7] Does he have a point? The answer to this question again depends on the perspective taken and it depends on for whom the lessons are new.

EXAMPLE OF LESSONS LEARNT

Let us look at two examples; the first is the report into the 2001 outbreak of Foot and Mouth Disease by Dr Iain Anderson and the second is the 2012 report into the coal mine tragedy that occurred at Pike River mine in New Zealand.

In the report by Dr Anderson we see an example of where a report's author attempts to extract lessons learnt in addition to providing recommendations. It has to be said that his inquiry was set up specifically to learn lessons. The lessons are detailed in Table 6.1. While these lessons may be new to those involved in this particular set of events, these same lessons will reveal nothing new when read by someone who is familiar with crisis management literature and practices. What we do not know is whether Dr Anderson felt that he was revealing something that was universally new or not.

Table 6.1   Anderson's Lessons to be Learnt

- **Maintain vigilance** through international, national and local surveillance and reconnaissance.
- **Be prepared** with comprehensive contingency plans, building mutual trust and confidence through training and practice.
- **React with speed and certainty** to an emergency or escalating crisis by applying well-rehearsed crisis management procedures.
- **Explain policies, plans and practices** by communicating with all interested parties comprehensively, clearly and consistently in a transparent and open way.
- **Respect local knowledge** and delegate decisions wherever possible, without losing sight of the national strategy.
- **Apply risk assessment and cost benefit analysis** within an appropriate economic model.
- **Use data and information management systems** that conform to recognised good practice in support of intelligence gathering and decision making.
- **Have a legislative framework** that gives government the powers needed to respond effectively to the emerging needs of a crisis.
- **Base policy decisions on best available science** and ensure that the processes for providing scientific advice are widely understood and trusted. These lessons should be incorporated into a national strategy designed to:
  - **Keep out infectious agents** of exotic disease.
  - **Reduce livestock vulnerability** by reforms in industry practice.
  - **Minimise the impact** of any outbreak.

The report on the Pike River tragedy by the Honourable Graham Panckhurst also revealed no new fundamental understanding. What it did reveal was a failure to use what had already been learnt elsewhere. What it also revealed was that "New Zealand has a poor health and safety record compared with other advanced countries". This was despite this being the "12th commission of inquiry into coal mining disasters in New Zealand. This suggests that as a country we fail to learn from the past". Despite the knowledge needed to prevent this tragedy being available it had, in this case like many others, been overlooked.

By the employment of what is referred to as *double loop learning,* we start to see a need to ask a different question. While we will always want to know what happened in a specific case, we start to see that the debate should have moved on in the decade between these two reports. In Chapter 2 I have outlined what we do know. What a detailed examination of over 20 inquiry reports showed is that both those conducting these inquiries and the people who are the subjects of the inquiries seem to have only a cursory acquaintance with this knowledge. The questions that I now find most interesting are (1) "Why do we not know?" and (2) "What causes the causes?"

INQUIRIES INTO INQUIRIES

In 2012, as a result the Hillsborough Independent Panel report and questions over the thoroughness of the Waterhouse Inquiry into allegations of child abuse, we saw calls for inquiries into the conduct of previous inquiries. Let us take the tragedy at Hillsborough as our example. Immediately after the tragedy in 1989 there were the reports by Lord Justice Taylor.[8] This was followed by Coroner's inquiries and court cases. However, nearly a decade after the tragedy and after much judicial activity, many felt that the truth had not yet been revealed. In 1997 the Blair Government asked Lord Justice Stuart-Smith[9] to re-examine the events but he failed to find anything new. The then Home Secretary (Jack Straw) assured the families that the judge had been thorough and impartial.[10] Many were still not satisfied. In 2010 yet another Home Secretary set up yet another inquiry but this time it was chaired by a bishop; this became known as the Hillsborough Independent Panel. This panel brought a fresh perspective to the subject and did pose some important questions both about what happened on the day and the way the subsequent inquiries were handled. However, despite the years of examination and debate some issues central to learning from this experience remain unresolved. Let us look at some of these issues.

The first issue is the dynamics of crowd behaviour and factors (such as the consumption of mind-altering substances) that may affect it. Everyone accepts that alcohol had been taken, what is not agreed is the effect that this had and therefore the significance of this factor.[11] Both reports take a clear and opposing position but neither is very helpful from a learning perspective. Could the truth lie somewhere in between? I think there is agreement that it would be unfair to suggest that those who died or were injured were responsible for what happened to them. However being in a crowd is, by its very nature, inherently dangerous and the study of crowd dynamics is a very specialist subject. (This does not mean that people should fear of death or injury when congregating in very large groups.) In none of the reports is this subject pursued and so no lessons are learnt about crowd dynamics outside of specialist groups and those who read the specialist publications. What is important for the future prevention is the question, "What was different in this case?" The Hillsborough Independent Panel (HIP) seems to dismiss the issue of alcohol because the marker used (80mg/100ml) was not justified when discussing the issue of alcohol and those attending a leisure event.[12] What is not discussed is any possible *butterfly effect*. Throughout the study of disasters we see how minor issues can lead to catastrophic effects (for example how one defective nut can cause an aircraft to crash). The question that this raises is how might even a small amount of alcohol consumed by a small number of people affect the dynamics of a crowd? This leads to questions about who has this information and who needs to have it if we are to ensure future foresight on these issues.

There is a second issue on crowd dynamics and this is, what in this instance was different in the crowd dynamics that caused the initial crush outside the gates to occur? What were the warning signs that told those with responsibility that, this time, the crowd flow would not follow the usual pattern? What do we need to teach those who are given responsibility so that they can recognise the difference between a safe (*normal chaos*) and an emerging unsafe state (*abnormal chaos*) so that they have time to take the appropriate action? Without the benefit of hindsight, what made the football match different from all the others that had taken place at that venue?

Coupled to the issue of warning signs is the issue of distraction. There is a question over whether those responsible for controlling the crowd, as it approached the Lepping Lane turnstiles, might have been distracted at the critical moments. For example when, according to the Taylor report,[13] a single fan had tried to push the police officer in charge of that end off the position he had taken to obtain a clearer view of the situation. The HIP on the other hand make no reference to this incident but were quite clear that "the view that this was caused by fighting, brutality or riotous behaviour is not supported by the statements of others present nor by the CCTV footage".[14] However what is seen as "riot" by one person may be seen as "panic" by another. By the time the critical decisions needed to be made the situation was confused and confusing. There is the potential that those who are close enough to see what was happening might find themselves distracted from a wider appreciation of the situation and just have to react to immediate events in their vicinity. The question for me is, "What distractions did those people face that may have inhibited them from seeing and appreciating that wider action needed to be taken? Where should they have placed themselves in order to have a clear first-hand experience of what was happening but also to avoid becoming involved to the detriment of their role?"

The police's actions were criticised as "a case of slow-motion negligence".[15] However, from a disaster recovery perspective, we need to consider what *recovery window* was available to those in charge on this occasion. The idea of *recovery window*[16] is discussed within the anthology that examines the 2003 Columbia disaster; the *recovery window* is a period between a threat emerging and the accident occurring. It is the period within which those responsible have to see, appreciate and act appropriately. In the case of the Hillsborough tragedy we need to consider the point at which "normal" became "abnormal" and the time after which deaths could not be prevented (in this case the first death). "Supt Marshall considered that the police lost control of the crowd outside the stadium at approximately 2.44pm."[17] Because there is no evidence present in the various reports to the contrary, I am assuming that, while the police may have had concerns before this point, such concerns would also be part of the pattern seen as normal and it was only at this point that police realised that the situation was past the normal. The gates were opened at 2.47pm[18] and "supporters were being crushed to death by 1459 hours".[19] Given that there must be a margin of error over the timings given, the *recovery window* in this case was at best 15 minutes but more likely to have been around ten minutes (I speculate that death became inevitable minutes before the first death occurred). It should be noted that in the case of Deep Water Horizon the *recovery window* was six to eight minutes[20] and in the case of Air France flight 447 it was about four and half minutes.[21] By listing what needed to have been done correctly within the *recovery window* we might start to see the enormity of the task we ask of others. From a judicial perspective we may classify any failure to ensure that necessary actions are carried out correctly within this window as negligence. From a *normal accident* perspective we might consider that only by good luck would things not have gone wrong. By choice, we would try to avoid having a system this complicated that needed to work perfectly in order to avoid tragic consequences.

Throughout the investigation into the Hillsborough tragedy there are questions over police competence and the decision by South Yorkshire Police to replace the experienced match commander, Chief Superintendent Brian Mole, with Chief Superintendent David Duckenfield just weeks before the match. In his book *Hillsborough – The Truth*, Professor Scraton calls this "the most important question".[22] The HIP found that, "None of the documents disclosed to the Panel indicated the rationale behind this decision."[23] In the same way there is no evidence presented to suggest that the change was anything other than a routine rotation of personnel. The timing of the change may have been, in anything other than *hindsight*, unfortunate rather than anything else. It should be noted however that elsewhere in the HIP it says, "Following a controversial but serious incident, unrelated to his duties as Match Commander, C/Supt Mole was relieved of his duties just three weeks before the Semi-Final and moved to another location."[24] (This raises the question as to how they came to this conclusion if "none of the documents disclosed" this. It can only be presumed that the evidence behind this statement was presented in another form. Considering the body of his work, I assume this was from Professor Scraton who was a member of the Panel. In his book he attributes the changes to what he calls the Ranmoor Incident.[25]) What we therefore have are two related issues. These are the timings of the change of personnel and *liability of newness* that this would bring.

Liability of newness is inevitable that at the start of any new appointment and enhancing expertise is often the point of giving people new roles. The question is then one of timing; deciding when the change should take place. Any such changes in management create a *zone of vulnerability* (a time when the system is more vulnerable to failures). In the case of the Hillsborough tragedy the *zone of vulnerability*, created by the *liability of newness* was also coupled with a question over the overall *viability of multi-skilling* amongst senior police officers. Obscured in the routines of policing are a multitude of skills required in a multiple of contexts. Each officer will have his or her own strengths and their own weaknesses, however their roles do not differentiate these and so, occasionally (consistent with Perrow's *Union Carbide Factor*) one is caught out and found to be wanting in a particular circumstance. They fail to find the necessary expertise which enables them to *see what is not there*. Therefore, from the perspective of learning, the question revolves around the criteria used to determine the date for the handover between the two men and how realistic it might be for an organisation to identify and guard against such vulnerabilities.

We see from before that the mental model that exists in a person's head is critical to what they see and how they appreciate what they see. There is therefore a question over the mental model that those in charge had of the situation which faced them. The HIP report stated that, "From the documents disclosed to the Panel, it is apparent that the collective policing mindset prioritised crowd control over crowd safety."[26] If we accept that this was the case, from a learning perspective we have to ask not whether this was right in view of the outcome but was it understandable in the context of the time. There is also an alternative interpretation and this is that the mental model that existed at the time was that crowd safety was an issue of control for "public safety and public order are just other sides of the same coin" to quote Alun Jones (the Hillsborough families' QC).[27]

We are likely to draw false lessons if we view and judge the event from our current perspective; how can we tell how our view and social mores will be judged by those 20 years hence? The question in respect of learning is how anyone can judge whether the mental model that they have of the situation they face is the appropriate one. From a learning perspective we would need to go back and examine why the police (both locally and nationally) had built up the mental model that they had, examine what had changed and whether those changes should have been significant enough to have changed the collective mental model (an even more tortuous process than changing an individual's mental model). This same mental process leads the Ministry of Defence to be accused of preparing for the last war rather than the next. In many ways we all do this, which is why sometimes we are faced by situations that we just do not recognise, which in turn leads to us having a *cosmological episode*.

Typical of inquiries is that they distil the events down to what they see as being the root cause. In the case of the Hillsborough tragedy what we learn is that as one gate was opened another should have been closed. The HIP noted that the Taylor report had "directed severe criticism towards senior officers" and had labelled this omission "a blunder of the first magnitude".[28] In hindsight and after months of deliberation, it has been judged by some that this would have prevented the tragedy. However what is not clear, either from Taylor or from those who used the label he created, was the mental model he would have expected the police commander to have or from where he would have expected that commander to have derived that mental model. The question

I have from a learning perspective is whether such an expectation is realistic. To judge this issue we would need to understand the mental model required by those responsible in order to take what, in the end, would turn out to be the appropriate act. To do this we would need to consider the number of similar interactions of which they would need to have been aware for only in hindsight could it be distilled down to the two that in this case mattered. One has to question whether this would have been feasible. In addition we can see that the mental model would have two significant constraints put upon it by policy decisions taken prior to the event. The first was to allow the fans to "find their own level"[29] and "there was no contingency plan to delay kick-off".[30] By continuing to build this picture we can again start to see the complexity of the picture the commander faced. To compound his problems we have recognised the *liability of newness* he places on the system, an imperfect picture he faces and the weaknesses in the communications systems. From studies of *high reliability organisations* we have been made aware of this fine line between situational awareness and a failure of comprehension (*losing the bubble*) as a prelude to a *cosmological episode*; the lesson from *high reliability organisations* is that the possibility of the loss of situational awareness is normal and the system needs to be able to cope with it and to continue to function effectively. From a judicial perspective, such an event, such a failure by a professional, is more likely to be labelled negligence. Here we can see a distinctive difference between the judicial and learning perspective.

The final and most glaring question that is again raised by reading the report of the Independent Panel is, "Why do organisations feel the need to 'cover-up' what they did or did not do?" The superficial answer to this question is that they fear blame, liability or public opprobrium. Within the literature and practice there is an on-going debate about whether it is possible to examine objectively the circumstances surrounding events if the parties to the discussion are, as a result of the debate, going to be placing themselves in jeopardy of judicial sanctions. A clear example of this concern was the setting up of the Truth and Reconciliation Commission in South Africa under the chairmanship of Bishop Desmond Tutu. In the Haddon-Cave report it is pointed out the part that a *just culture* plays in promoting safety "where it is clear to everyone what is acceptable"[31] and what is not. (Reason differentiates a *just culture* from a "no-blame" culture as he sees the latter as being "neither feasible nor desirable (because) a small proportion of human unsafe acts are egregious ... and warrant sanctions".[32]) The benefits to the learning process of openness have been discussed earlier. As in all cases of motivation there are two approaches, the stick (such as the jeopardy associated with taking an oath) and the carrot. In order to motivate people to be open and not to "cover-up", those conducting inquiries need to consider whether it was clear to everyone what was or was not acceptable and, when selecting the style of the inquiry, that only a small proportion of acts are egregious. Once again we must question whether the adversarial approach promotes positive learning. The fact that the police tried to cover-up what happened seems not to be in doubt. However what is not clear is why the police felt it necessary to conduct a cover-up and what this tells us about our ability to prevent unwanted occurrences in the future and our ability to learn from them.

In the case of the Hillsborough tragedy, we can see inquiries into inquiries which, in the end, still do not promote the learning desired. We can see that, as in all facets of human activity, judicial inquiries have their limitations and, when seen from a different perspective, might be judged to be (severely) flawed. In this section I have tried to offer a different perspective on some of the lessons that might have been taken away from this particular case. Again, I would like to emphasise that I am looking at these questions from the perspective of what can we learn from these events in order to prevent them happening again. The various Hillsborough inquiries have shown that, not only can judge-led inquiries fail to produce accurate findings but also some of the key lessons for preventing such occurrences in the future can be missed and this, in itself, is also a tragedy.

The Law and Risk

We have already seen in Chapter 2 where the interests of the judicial system and the interests of good risk management clash. I have also shown that others, such as Professor James Reason, have raised concerns over the judicial perspective on unwanted occurrences. We see that while academics now more often take a systems view, this perspective has yet to be adopted by the judicial system. This would appear to be a major mismatch in cross-understanding between those who strive to understand these phenomena and those who judge on behalf of society. In this penultimate section I will lay out other areas where there may be other serious differences which may lead to difficulties in learning from inquiries.

PROBLEM OR SOLUTION FOCUSED?

One approach to looking at the difference between the judicial and the learning perspectives comes from the world of coaching. Jackson and McKergow describe two ways of looking at issues that they call "problem focused" and "solution focused". The important differences[33] are listed in Table 6.2. Within the former we can recognise the judicial perspective and within the latter we can see the learning perspective. Experience from the coaching environment would suggest that having a problem focus adds another barrier to the successful implementation of solutions. In turn, this warns those conducting inquiries that they need to be aware of this potential barrier and to take positive steps to ensure that it does not have any adverse effect on the outcome they are trying to promote.

Table 6.2   Problem or Solution Focus

Problem Focus	Solution Focus
• What's wrong?	• What's wanted?
• What needs fixing?	• What's working?
• Blame	• Progress
• Control	• Influence
• Causes in the past	• Counters (blockers) in the past
• The expert knows best	• Collaboration
• Deficits and weaknesses	• Resources and strengths
• Complications	• Simplicity
• Definitions	• Actions

WHO BENEFITS, WHO PAYS?

Another set of barriers to learning might be scepticism over who benefits the most from the legal or quasi-legal procedures. One of the assertions I make in this book is that there is jeopardy associated with every benefit; when someone benefits, often someone else loses. Even when the benefit is social justice, other innocent parties may have to pay the price. For example take the case from October 2012 when female workers won the right to take their case for discrimination against Birmingham Council to the civil courts. This was depicted as a victory for female rights. But someone has to pay. The taxpayers of Birmingham will have to pay a sum estimated to be in excess of £757 million[34] for any future settlements. To pay for the settlements, the Council will have to take money from some other area of their funded services. The subsequence of any future settlements may be that female workers (as well as their male colleagues) may lose their jobs as services are cut. Female recipients (as well as male recipients) may lose, what are to them, vital services. We can see that justice can be a fickle friend.

Perrow sees marine law being for the benefit of maritime lawyers not for the benefit of those in peril on the seas. He says, "The marine courts exist to establish liability and settle material claims, not to investigate the cause of accidents and compensate seamen."[35] He also quotes the US National Transportation Saftey Board saying, "According to the court decisions, 99 per cent of all collisions are caused by failure to obey the rules of the road, and (yet) no one, not even an admiralty lawyer, fully understands the rules and their various legal interpretations".[36] This sentiment was endorsed by a senior practitioner interviewed as part of my own research (see Chapter 2). This may lead to another barrier to learning and that is suspicion amongst practitioners that any rules suggested are as much for the benefit of lawyers as they are there to assist practitioners avoid problems in the future.

The cost of inquiries may also alienate practitioners and society in general by perpetuating stereotypes of a rich elite benefiting from the misery of others. One has to question who benefits the most from inquiries ("follow the money") a point recognised by the PASC when they discussed how the legal costs might be reduced, such as "re-calculating legal costs and expenses in a way more appropriate to pay for guaranteed employment for several months or years, rather than at a daily rate".[37]

HUMILITY

The second of these is the need for humility. Barton and Sutcliffe talk of *situated humility*.[38] They see the need for humility because small fluctuations in events can have significant implications and when the events themselves are still unfolding, adjustments in approach are critical. It is precisely these situations in which pre-existing assumptions, planned actions and rationalisations are most dangerous if rigidly held. You can be confident in your skills but humble about the situation. Even the most experienced experts cannot know how a dynamic situation will unfold.

David Christenson (from the US Wildland Fire Lessons Learned Centre) wrote of how he and his organisation had learned from the work of Karl Weick and Kathleen Sutcliffe and recognised the need for *cultivated humility*:[39]

*Try to see the value of increasing organizational learning through a
healthy scepticism about your successes and a greater awareness of the
potential for failure. Success can breed overconfidence in the status quo
and makes people less tolerant of opposing viewpoints.*

The basic message is that we have to know our limitations and to keep an open
mind. Those in senior posts within the judiciary have the *problem of induction*
with which to contend. Every day they are faced with the fallibility of their fellow
humans. At the same time they are blessed with twenty-twenty hindsight; they
can see where the fault lies and know why they would not have made that error
because they can clearly see what should have happened. Over years of this
process they cannot help but start to feel smarter and superior to their fellow man
and their expectation of what is foreseeable is therefore likely to be constantly
adjusted upwards. While the judiciary may have a high opinion of their own
capabilities, this is not necessarily how they are perceived by others.

From the PASC report, we can see that judges consider themselves
equipped to undertake the task of inquiry. However, they do not seem so ready
to justify their judgement to those outside their own community; while the
judicial system seems to facilitate numerous reviews (appeals), in the case of
inquiries they seem to expect their recommendations to be accepted without
question. In this instance they can be perceived to lack humility; to accept that
they also may be fallible. For example, after a series of accusations of child
abuse, the adequacy of previous inquiries was questioned and the government
looked to appoint a "senior independent figure" to investigate whether "the
Waterhouse Inquiry was properly constituted and did its job".[40] From a
learning perspective this approach, known as *double-loop learning*, is a sensible
and necessary practice. Members of the House of Lords did not see it as such
and seemed to prejudge the case. Lord Lloyd of Berwick (a Lord of Appeal)
described the Waterhouse (a High Court judge) report as impeccable and
thorough. His comments were supported by a former member of the judiciary
who described Waterhouse "a very distinguished and conscientious judge".
The tone of these responses was that aspersions were being thrown at the judge
rather than accepting the possibility that a judge may not have got every aspect
of his work totally correct. To interpret even potential criticism of his work
as criticism of the man can be seen to be based on the construct that only bad
people do bad things.[a] For learning to take place all parties need to be prepared
to examine their own fallibility, to re-examine their own performance and to
look to learn from others.

---

a   See the work of James Reason and other who have addressed his issue.

CONSTRUCT OF NEGLIGENCE

One of the key differences between a learning and a judicial perspective is the construct of negligence. I have to be honest here that, despite numerous discussions, I do not understand this judicial construct. I have tried but it does not connect with my mental model of this subject. I have been advised that it is impossible to lay down rules which, if followed, would provide a clearly defendable position. This is due to the subjective nature of the *reasonable man* and *foreseeability* constructs which are at the heart of any judgement. I also see here a clear difference in my mental model about what might be *foreseeable* to a *reasonable man* from that used within the judicial process.

The more I learn about the human weaknesses that cause unwanted occurrences the less I consider it reasonable to expect others to comprehend (to see, appreciate and act appropriately) complex situations. This view seems to be distinctly at odds with the legal construct of negligence which seems to expect greater and greater competence from ordinary people; it seems to expect professionals to be perfect and ignores the issue of cognitive overload, slips and lapses which are an inevitable part of life.

Elsewhere[41] I have examined the issue of *failure of foresight* in more depth. Here I will reprise my argument. In 1961, Stanley Stark[42] set about describing the construct of "Executive Foresight" where he stated that, "Management has no choice but to anticipate the future" but "the ability to forecast is quite limited." He says, "planning is … the exercise of foresight" and "to see, in this context, means both to assess the future and make provision for it." But here is the problem; so many things can go wrong, for which do you make provision? Here we can refer back to Professor Reason's illustration of this point using of a bolt with eight nuts marked "A" to "H"[43] where he points out that while there is only one correct solution there are over 40,000 ways to assemble the combination in the wrong order. Stark concludes that, "Man tends to resemble the ostrich in that his preventive action is often more effective in quieting his fear than in removing him from danger." He describes the ability of foresight as:

> (1) the ability in any situation to think of a large number of consequences,
> (2) the ability to judge among consequences as to their probability,
> (3) the ability to judge among consequences as to their importance, and
> (4) the ability to decide the best course of action to pursue on consideration of all the consequences likely to follow.[44]

In Chapter 2 I have outlined some of the reasons why people might "fail to see". Within this idea of *foreseeability* is the inconceivable risk which is part of a family of risks that have been given a variety of labels. Taleb uses the term "Black Swans", to refer to these low-probability, high-impact events. Renn refers to these risks as a "sword of Damocles". Here the debate revolves around *foreseeability*, controllability, manageability and saliency of warnings. Current risk management processes, which look to balance probability of an event and its potential impact, lead to the exclusion of occurrences which are conceived as being very rare, even if their potential for damage or harm might be considered to be extreme. There is a school of thought (stereotyped as the "precautionary principle", but again this term has a wide range of meanings attributed to it), which advocates that these risks should just be avoided, some would say, at all costs. This approach, while being theoretically desirable, may be impractical as it may occur after the organisation considers the risk to have already been managed. Therefore, the focus of risk discourse should continually consider the implications of the potential to create harm and how organisations might try to justify their inactivity should the inconceivable manifest itself.

We can already see that foresight is not a simple task. Erik Hollnagel adds another layer of complexity to the problem. He regards accidents as being emergent. That is, that they cannot be predicted from the system's constituent parts; at this point Professor Reason admits to a failure of understanding.[45] When we consider the number of possible options, the possibilities of each option, and then have to consider all the possible consequences of each, it is now far easier to see why we tend to resort to "quieting our fear" rather than removing the dangers. When I read inquiry reports, while they may espouse otherwise, I see hindsight rather than foresight as being their key tool when reconstructing what happened and why. They are able to see all the available warning signs that were present and therefore how the tragedy should have been avoided. Few even try to recreate the white noise of data that faced those involved.

That is not to say that the judicial system just ignores such issues. If we use the case of the private prosecution, as reported by the HIP,[46] as an example of the logic employed we see the following:

> *1.256 The judge, Mr Justice Hooper, summarised the prosecution case for manslaughter as the failure by the officers to prevent a crush on the terraces and to divert fans from the tunnel. The risk of serious injury, therefore, had been foreseeable.*

1.264 At the conclusion of the evidence the judge identified four questions for the jury to consider. First, "Are you sure, that by having regard to all the circumstances, it was foreseeable by a reasonable match commander that allowing a large number of spectators to enter the stadium through exit Gate C without closing the tunnel would create an obvious and serious risk of death to the spectators in pens 3 and 4?" If "yes", they were to move to question 2; if "no", the verdicts should be "not guilty". Second, could a "reasonable match commander" have taken "effective steps ... to close off the tunnel" thus preventing the deaths? If "yes", they were to move to question 3; if "no", the verdicts should be "not guilty". Third, was the jury "sure that the failure to take such steps was neglect?" If "yes", it was on to question 4; if "no", the verdicts should be "not guilty". Fourth, was the "failure to take those steps ... so bad in all the circumstances as to amount to a very serious criminal offence?" If "yes", the verdicts should be "guilty"; if "no", they should be "not guilty".

In the end the issue of what is *foreseeable* for a *reasonable man* will come down to the subjective opinion of those judging the case. I would however question whether those given this task have the necessary *seat of understanding* to make those judgements or whether, like those they are judging, they are making of it the best they can while quieting their own fears of danger.

We can surmise the reasons for the increasing standard of reasonableness as each time an organisation accepts their "guilt" (often driven by the fact it would be a cheaper option than fighting the case) the expectation of what is reasonable increases. Therefore while a *reasonable man* and the *substitution test* are derived from the same desire, they are both seen as a test for fairness, there is a danger that what we are coming to expect from professionals or even other members of society is not even plausible. We may, in hindsight, be clear about what should have been done to ensure that a specific tragedy did not happen, but until we can devise failure proof ways of making them happen, many key inquiry recommendations will remain *fantasies*.

Within the construct of negligence and culpability is the consideration of the number of deaths that result from an act or omission. While this might be a significant issue from a social and political perspective (and therefore to judicial proceedings) it may be irrelevant to accident prevention. Given Perrow's *Union Carbide Factor*, we might see more important lessons being derived from near misses rather than those gained from major losses of life. However, if inquiries and related judicial proceedings focus more on events that lead to major losses of life, valuable lessons may be lost due to this prioritisation.

One of the key problems of the legal construct of negligence is that it is just one small step away from a major fallacy that seems to perpetuate within the judicial perspective. This is the fallacy that knowing, or having foresight of a problem is seen as being all that is required to prevent it.

COMPETENCIES

I do not question the competence of the people conducting these inquiries; I am however questioning whether they have the competencies necessary to fulfil the task as set. The core of my argument is the segregation of knowledge between the academic and the judicial worlds. When a phrase such as *failure of foresight* is used by those conducting an inquiry, we have to question whether they are using it because it is a catchy phrase or whether they are trying to communicate the meaning, subtlety and complexity that is argued within the academic literature. Do they appreciate what is really necessary to prevent such failures and the role that *failure of imagination* and the concept of *inconceivability* play? Do they understand how standard risk management practices contribute to forestalling or promoting *failures of foresight* or are their judgements only so clear because they had the benefit of hindsight?

The judicial system, due to its case by case nature, can only *muddle through*. The judicial perspective therefore has its own issues of *induction* and *normalisation of deviance* which might lead them to decisions that, to outsiders, seem to lack common-sense much in the same way as some decisions made by practitioners seem to lack common-sense to the judicial perspective. This is an issue of cross-understanding rather than competencies. The issue of competencies arises when judgements are made solely within the frame of reference of their previous experience without any attempt to examine the body of knowledge that exists on this subject, where you see the selective use of academic work to make a legal point while relying on the others involved to be equally uninformed so as to avoid challenge. This understanding of the issues may warrant the label used by Snook of being a "thin description".[47] This lack of competencies is then further overlooked due to the acclaim it might receive from other well-meaning but equally uninformed parties. In this context we see equal *failures of foresight* that lead to unintended consequences, which are rarely acknowledged. One *mea culpa* makes this point. The case is the report into junior doctor training which is seen by some to have had "a malign influence on medical training, and for putting patients at risk". In a letter to *The Times*, David Nunn wrote, "Who is to blame for the nonsense that is now surgical training? Who accepted the changes introduced by Calman? Who agreed … Who acquiesced to the farrago of modernising …? I am afraid it was me, and all my senior surgical colleagues." [48] If Calman and his medical colleagues can generate such unintended consequences how much more vulnerable are those who only have a passing acquaintance with a subject area and how are they then held accountable for their mistakes? Practitioners who are held accountable for their errors may be reluctant to learn from those who do not seem to understand and are not held accountable for their own errors and misjudgements.

CONTRADICTORY MESSAGES

The *muddling through* methodology used by judicial processes may have another damaging consequence. As we have seen earlier, the academic literature cites *amoral calculation* as a potential source of failure. However the courts send messages that morally questionable actions are not illegal and are therefore acceptable. Two examples of this can be seem in the McLaren, FI industrial espionage[49] and the way that banks fixed LIBOR rates. In the McLaren case a court decided to allow the fine imposed by the sport's governing body to be tax deductible[50] which, by implication means that it is acceptable behaviour. In the LIBOR case,[51] banks were fined but the regulator was powerless to take action against the individuals responsible; whether the banks could offset this fine becomes an interesting question. The point is that we see contradictory messages between what we learn from the academic literature and what we learn from the judicial system. This has implications for *risk assessment* and potential *failures of foresight*. Whereas these processes had a once simple test, "Are *amoral calculations* the basis of our decisions?" These examples add complexity in that they add the caveat "but it is fine if we get away with it". This must add potential hazard to the system from which only lawyers are likely to benefit!

Again, when judging the credibility of a recommendation, the credibility of the provider will be questioned either as an individual or as part of a generic group. In this context, the final outcomes of such cases do not matter. The perception of the judiciary being out of touch with reality has been set. The context within which people will view their judgements has been established. Where academics and practitioners see contradictory messages from an outsider group, such as an acceptance of *amoral calculation,* they will question the validity and relevance of any recommendations provided. It can be seen that foresight is difficult enough; such contradictory messages make these judgements even harder.

So, Why do we Fail to Learn?

So, why do we fail to learn from inquiries? As we have seen, there are a number of potentially significant barriers to society learning from inquiries. Here I will summarise what I see as being the main reasons that we fail to learn from inquiries. The first is the distorting nature of the need to allocate blame. The second is where knowing is falsely assumed to lead to the appropriate action. There third is the alienation of the potential audience by the approach taken by inquiries and finally deficiencies in the inquiries being part of an overall learning system.

THE NEED TO BLAME – FUNDAMENTAL ATTRIBUTION ERROR

According to Tim Gardner, the instinct to blame and punish is a critical component in our reactions to risks.[52] As a psychologist, James Reason tries to explain this.[53] Reason sees part of the problem as the *illusion of free will* where people believe that they "are free agents, the captain of their own fate". In this belief they see that others are also free agents "able to choose between right and wrong, between correct and error-prone paths of action" and therefore "their errors are seen as being, at least in part, voluntary actions". He explains that if warnings have been offered and yet errors still occur, the psychological need to blame and punish is multiplied. Reason then spends the rest of his book explaining why slips, lapses and some other errors are, in fact, involuntary but how the shattering of the *illusion of free will* may have some very real harmful side effects.

Tied into the need to blame is the need to find someone else to find at fault, a scapegoat. In finding a scapegoat, suffering and others' feelings of guilt, aggression, blame can be transferred from a person or group to another person or group in order to reduce the distress on the first group; this seems to help them find "closure". Psychologists consider that this process is often an unconscious one which is more likely to be denied by the perpetrator but it does enable the "self-righteous discharge of aggression" and tends to have extra-punitive characteristics. In summary, because of our own mental make-up we need to transfer unsettling emotions to others in order to assuage our own pain. The problem is that this might hinder rather than help us learn from these experiences.

As we see from our earlier examination of the purpose of inquiries, in general they seek to learn in order to prevent, rather than to blame. However, the Rt. Hon Lady Justice Hallett still feels that she has to remind her readers that:

> *It is not generally a proper function of an inquest to attribute blame or apportion guilt to individuals, nor is it a proper function of a Coroner to express opinions in the verdicts returned.*[54]

The separation of finding fault and blaming is a very fine line and may come down to an issue of writing style. I can illustrate this point by contrasting the book by Scott Snook[55] on the loss by friendly fire of two US helicopters and the report by Charles Haddon-Cave[56] on the loss of a Royal Air Force Nimrod aircraft. To be fair to both authors, the book by Snook was based on his doctoral thesis and the terms of reference for Haddon-Cave required him "to assess where responsibility lies" but even having said this I feel my main point still stands. The way Snook narrates the story exposes the uncertainty, the ambiguity and his own reflections and learning. He admits to wanting to allocate blame and his visceral feeling on this subject due to his own experience, all of which enables you to see how he evaluates the complexity of the situation presented to those involved. At the end of the book I feel that I understood not only what the author was saying, but what each of the participants had been thinking at the time. In turn this enabled me to translate the lessons learnt that day to my own experience and working life.

The Snook book provides a sharp contrast to the Haddon-Cave report. To give the report its due, it provides a superb investigation and analysis of the technical aspects of the accident which left me in no doubt that he had exposed the mechanical issues that lay behind the tragedy. However, when he came to the systems and organisational causes, I found his arguments less convincing. It is not to say that I doubted any of the issues of fact; what I had difficulty with was his interpretation of those facts. I have to admit that doubt started to creep into my mind in his use of the work by Professor Reason. It was not in the elements he selected but in the elements he left out; his use of Reason's work did not resonate with my reading of the nuances found within his overall body of literature. I have to accept the possibility that I have misunderstood what Reason was trying to say, however, if that is the case, that debate is for another day. My point is the language used by Haddon-Cave, the certainty that he projected and the confidence with which he allocated blame, made me doubt whether he truly understood the subtleties and complexities of the situation that faced the organisation. The clarity and confidence suggested to me a rather simplistic mental model which, in turn, made me question whether I would have enough confidence in his recommendations to take the time to even try to transfer them into my working life. Gerd Gigerenzer advises that, "In an uncertain world, certainty can be a dangerous ideal";[57] I am conscious of this warning. By the end of the report I still had no idea of the dilemmas and pressures faced by the people he criticised. I knew only what they had missed. I felt no better informed about how this situation might be avoided in the future as I had only the minimal reference points against which I could evaluate his recommendations. From a judicial perspective, Haddon-Cave may have found the appropriate answers, however from the perspective of learning practical lessons, any valuable lessons that he had to offer may have been lost by the way he delivered his message.

In my desire to learn, I need to reflect on whether we are starting to lose the necessary focus on causes and whether blame has a useful function in militating against the causes. In 2008 James Reason asked, "Has the pendulum swung too far?"[58] whether "the process (has) gone too far towards collective responsibility and away from individual responsibility?" He sees the argument in terms of *universals*, *conditions* and *causes* and which might be addressed in order to be most effective in the prevention of future unwanted occurrences. Should we understand more and condemn less or do we need to understand less and condemn more? Is it even possible to establish facts without allocating blame? Phil Scraton, a professor of criminology, does not think so.[59] As part of this debate I would suggest we need to consider two factors. The first is, when judging, do we fall prey to social and media pressure, do we fall prey to what seems like the inevitable flow in the judicial system to equate errors without intent (as in *mens rea*) to a criminal act and whether it is valid to take hindsight as an appropriate reference point (those allocating blame need to take scrupulous care to ensure that the judgements being criticised are not being evaluated based on hindsight; this test is often espoused but failed in practice)?

While blame has a useful social purpose, how can we be sure we are using it for the greater good? In this section I have only made a brief excursion into a very complex subject and it is probably more suited to psychologists,[60] social ethicists and lawyers to explore the social function of blame when a death is caused. From the perspective of learning from these tragic events my concern is that the judicial actions seem increasingly to be at odds with what we know about such events from an academic and practical perspective. My concern is that the actions taken within a judicial context may have the unintended consequences which are counter to their intent and that recommendations created within a judicial perspective may have some fundamental flaws.

KNOWING IS NOT ENOUGH

The question now becomes whether knowing that something might possibly happen is enough to ensure it will not happen? I discuss this at greater length elsewhere,[61] suffice to say here that it is not. If we take an extreme example, we all know that we are going to die at some time in the future but, so far, we have not found a way of preventing this from happening. This issue should not be seen as only a difference of perspectives between the judicial and the practitioner. This difference can also be seen with two different academic fields as well. I divided risk management literature into three paradigms which I called *line, circle* and *dot* that provide metaphors roughly equated to project risk management, process risk management and accident (scenario) risk management. Here we see those who employ the *dot* perspective have a different attitude to those who employ the *line* perspective. This issue comes down to having differing perspectives as to the gap between understanding and resolution. In a discussion about *organisational learning*, one set of scholars sees that, "As an outcome, learning represents the acquisition of new repertoires, representing a change in a group's potential behaviors."[62] However, in the same volume other scholars warn that, "The gap between analysis and implementation is considerable and poorly understood."[63] We can see this manifesting itself within the difference between the *line* and *dot* perspectives.

The impression given by many *dot*-based writers is that, in Pareto's construct, finding the cause of an accident, for example, means that an organisation is 80 per cent of the way towards preventing the next one (writers often express the sentiment that if an organisation had understood the cause and potential for an accident, why did they not prevent it?) Hopkins for example says, "NASA had already been told very clearly in the Stephenson report that it was dangerously close to the boundary. In my view the problem was that NASA's organisational structure prevented it from acting on this knowledge."[64] His assumption is that as they knew they were "close to the boundary", they knew where they needed to draw back and how to go about it; this assumption should be questioned. *Line*-based writers appear to be at the opposite end of the spectrum. In their writings they see that understanding an issue is barely a start (20 per cent) in trying to resolve it and hence the emphasis placed on project risk management.

Learning as an organisation, like *high reliability*, is no easy task. The complexity of this issue can be seen in that it has spawned an entirely separate area of academic study. There are many relevant lessons available to those conducting inquiries from this body of academic literature. However, I have neither the space in this book nor the expertise to do the subject justice. Suffice to say that the first step in this process is for future report authors to develop a clear idea in their own minds of the links within and between the 26 building blocks that they already use (as indicated in Chapter 4). The question therefore becomes one of whether those making the recommendations have a clear picture of how they see recommendations moving from the page to being an effective end result, whether they can envisage the steps required, whether they envisage that they have any responsibility, whether they see it all being delegated to someone else, or whether they are just hope for a miracle? (See Figure 6.1.)

Lord Puttnam, in a lecture on pre-legislative scrutiny, points to an important issue. He explains that the problem is that, "How a bill is to be implemented is often not defined, and the key challenges are sometimes not

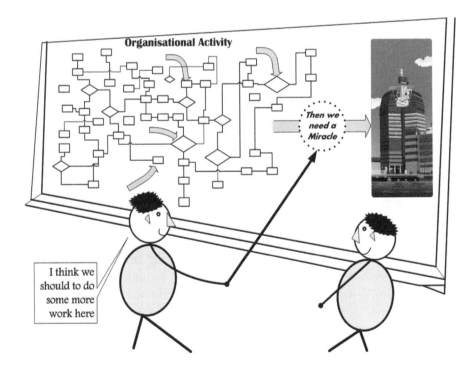

Figure 6.1   Miracle Cartoon

described (and) there is no objective test against which to judge the efficacy of an Act following implementation." The same criticism might be made of inquiry recommendations. Lord Puttnam also points to the tendency to challenge strategy when something does not work (goes wrong) rather than appreciating the importance of effective implementation in preventing *the unwanted*.[65] Without a clear idea by those making the recommendations of how they see the effect being enacted, the report might fall prey to the accusation that they are just *fantasy documents*. Without such clarity the authors may harm their own credibility when they admonish another organisation for having not learned, for example, by saying that poor leadership or poor communication might cause problems. In the case of poor leadership, when those at the top of the organisation (the leadership) are inadequate, the report needs to be clear about where the impetus for change should have come for it could not have come from the poor leaders themselves.

ALIENATING THEIR AUDIENCE

We have already discussed how humans tend to dissociate themselves and their circumstances from previous calamitous events. This is done to provide themselves with a shield of protection against the dangers and uncertainty of everyday life. This tendency to dissociate may be magnified by some of the language used within inquiry reports. Those who have had the advantage of hindsight label those not as fortunate as "sloppy",[66] as "banal examples of organisational elites not trying very hard"[67] or highlight "complacency".[68] The Taylor report on the Hillsborough Disaster asserts the "failure to give that order was a blunder of the first magnitude".[69] While those inquiring may feel justified in making such comments, they need to be aware of the subsequence of doing so. While these terms may be carefully defined in the various chapters, the impression created is one where the responsible manager is seen to be inadequate and, if they had just applied themselves a bit more, the problem would have been identified and the accident/disaster prevented. While this may be unfair to those involved, there is also a more important issue.

Cook and Woods[70] talk of *distancing through differencing*. Here people distance (disassociate) themselves from the situation by noticing the differences rather than similarities. If managers involved in accidents or other crises are labelled "sloppy" and so on, those who have yet to be involved will distance themselves from such events because they do not see themselves in that way. If foresight is to be available to them, they have to be open to the possibility that the worst might happen to them and their organisation. Therefore, the premise underlying this book is why might, clever, dynamic and capable people be induced to miss relevant clues or make a flawed decision necessary to produce a significant *failure of foresight*? Why do they fail to see that such failure could happen to them and how might barriers to learning, such as language affect this process? For, should the recommendations be read by others than those directly affected, the likely result of such statements is that the reader will distance themselves from the events because they do not see themselves as being either sloppy or complacent. This mechanism allows the person to think "well, this does not apply to me because…" The people using such words have erected the first barrier to any lessons being learnt. Therefore, an important step within this process is for those suggesting the lessons to be learnt to take care when making their recommendations to avoid alienating their potential audience.

Some of the language used within reports also undermines the writer's credibility. For example, the Bichard report stated, "The inquiry did find errors, omissions, failures and shortcomings which are deeply shocking."[71] For any student of organisational failure, the errors, omissions, failures and shortcomings reported are not shocking; quite the contrary, they are depressingly familiar. Statements such as these can only lead to questions as to the naivety or pomposity of those writing the reports or whether the wording was chosen more to dramatise the subject matter.

The Hillsborough Independent Panel[72] provides another example. It states that these reports "illustrate how different interpretations of events emerge from similarly experienced 'experts' evaluating the same evidence but from different perspectives and contrasting interests". It is not clear at whom this statement is aimed. While it is an important realisation that has implications for the interpretation of data and what is learnt from any series of events, as written it comes across as a naïve realisation that does harm to the credibility of the panel.

If recommendations are to be adopted by people other than those directed to do so, those making the recommendations must have credibility. This credibility can easily be lost either by giving the potential recipients enough differentiation so they are able to distance themselves from the events or by those making the recommendations seeming to be outside of their own area of expertise.

THE PROCESS OF LEARNING

We can see from those who write about *organisational learning* that learning is most effective when all the necessary components form a coherent system. From our examination of the top-level inquiry process we see little evidence of it being viewed as a coherent system. Here I examine three aspects. The first is the Parliamentary governance process, the second is the construction of the lessons learnt and the final is one of collating lessons learnt.

If we take as our focus the 2005 Inquiries Act,[73] we see that it was preceded by a Select Committee report[74] to which the Government responded[75] and then the production of statutory instructions and standards notes. While this may be a conventional process for government, it is not an obvious way of promoting learning. It should be noted that the Select Committee has not conducted any review of how their report was implemented or whether the results desired were achieved. This issue is also raised by a submission to the Justice Select Committee in October 2010. The submission confirmed that the aim of the Inquiries Act (2005) "was to ensure that inquiries were conducted efficiently within a reasonable timeframe and at a reasonable cost and that they were effective at making findings of fact and delivering valuable and practicable recommendations";[76] that, "the aim of an inquiry is rather to help restore public confidence in systems or services by investigating the facts and making recommendations to prevent recurrence."[77] The report stated that they "believe that overall the Act has been successful in meeting its objectives of enabling inquiries to conduct thorough and wide ranging investigations, as well as making satisfactory recommendations."[78] In light of what we now know from the previous chapter we have to question the basis on which "reasonable cost", "thorough" and "satisfactory recommendations" were judged.

In its response to the original Public Administration Select Committee report in 2005, the Government specifically excluded two important considerations in the context of learning. Where the report recommended that the "Government should consider whether research should be undertaken by an appropriate body, such as the National Audit Office, into the value for money which inquiries represent", the response, while emphasising the importance of encouraging good budgeting, rejected the recommendation for research;[79] one therefore has to question the basis on which the "reasonable cost" judgement is made. The report also recognised that "recommendations need to be workable in practice". In its response the Government left this issue to the panel; its concern was with practical difficulties in testing any recommendations and how any consultation might be seen to undermine the independence of the inquiry panel.[80] It is noted that no concern is expressed over potential unintended consequences generated by poor recommendations. Again one has to question the basis on which the recommendations are assessed as being satisfactory. Finally, it is noted that the issue of thoroughness is not addressed. From an academic perspective we are reminded that quantity (for some of these reports are very long) does not necessarily equate to thoroughness. If inquiry reports are now re-examined using the questions set out in Chapter 2, it can soon be established that the reports still leave many questions unanswered. It is clear from the Government paper on this subject that their focus is on the function of the act; this focus is understandable when it is seen to be driven by their quasi-judicial perspective and their *localised rationality*. This focus does mean that they fail to examine the wider questions about whether this process (system) is achieving the results required of it, whether this is to prevent future tragedies or "restore public confidence in systems or services". This leaves us with a question as to whether the parliamentary governance process fits the criteria for it being an effective part of a learning system.

The second issue is whether those who construct the lessons to be learnt see themselves as part of an overall learning process or as being independent of the learning process. We have seen how the Government has passed the responsibility for making any recommendations workable to the inquiry panel but the panels do not have any responsibility placed upon them to ensure that their recommendations are workable. In their turn, inquiry panels often can be seen to produce quite abstract recommendations and pass the responsibility for implementing them back to the practitioners with apparently little consideration for what might be involved or whether they are workable. We can see that they do not see themselves as part of the overall process that examines or ensures that recommendations are workable before they are proposed or accepted (remembering, as discussed previously, that it may be easier to accept rather than question recommendations offered). From a learning perspective I see each part of the process as being part of the overall systems that will affect whether any proposed *organisational learning* is successful or not. Within the inquiry process I see a number of components that do not see themselves as being part of an overall system and therefore see how even something that they do in good faith may have unintended consequences and so adversely affect future learning.

The third issue is another issue of complexity. In this context the complexity arises from the number of issues highlighted by inquiries and other investigative processes. We see in Chapter 4 over 1,100 recommendations from only 20 inquiries. Even when we group these recommendations we have 24 major categories (I exclude the last two: comments and admonish) to monitor and address. Where organisations try to track the action taken to implement the recommendations of even their internal inquiries, the matrix required becomes very difficult to manage let alone overcome each and every organisational weakness. This complexity multiplies when they try to learn from external experience and this complexity becomes a further barrier to learning. There appears to be little effort to try to collate and learn holistically from these events. Therefore, again, when an individual is condemned for an apparent *failure of foresight*, those providing the condemnation need to be able to show how they would have benefited from some previous misfortune.

In these three aspects of the overall learning system we can see some of the potential barriers to learning that might pervade the system. Without appreciating and then acting to remove these barriers we, as a society, can only expect further failures of our systems and processes in the future.

FUTURE RESEARCH

In this analysis we can see a number of gaps in the current system that is meant to help us learn from unwanted occurrences. We may therefore be advised to try to close these gaps if we are to have hope that the system might achieve its aim of promoting societal learning. If we do not close these gaps we cannot be surprise that others "fail to learn the lessons from the past". I see four important gaps in our understanding of this subject. The first is our level of understanding of inquiry practices as seen from a learning perspective. The second is the ability (or more accurately the inability) of those who seek to understand organisational failure to communicate their understanding to both practitioners and the judiciary. The third area of work are the practices required to produce workable and effective recommendations and finally, as it has implications for consideration of what is reasonable and practicable, is the requirement to analyse improved criteria for deciding the cost effectiveness of any recommendations.

In this book I have provided an initial examination of the inquiry process from a learning perspective. While I see my analysis as being appropriate to the purpose of this book, I do accept that it is far from definitive. It would be interesting to see whether a larger sample changed the proportion attributed to each type of recommendation or whether an analysis of the secondary purpose of each recommendation would change our understanding in any way. I see a richer understanding might also be obtained by analysing the processes by type and by whether the chair was a member of the judiciary or not, male or female or by nationality. As a result of my analysis I see us being only at the start of the understanding of how inquiry practices affect subsequent learning.

What is also clear from my research is that there is a considerable body of relevant knowledge that does not reach those who need to know it. In classic communication theory it is the responsibility of those with the message (the new knowledge) to communicate it to others. However in the context of inquiries, it may be fully justifiable to reverse this proposition. We know that ignorance of the law is no defence. We see this stance taken by those who conduct inquiries in their criticism of any parties to their inquiry who did not know or failed to ask about a particular issue that in hindsight turned out to be critical; sometimes this behaviour is deemed to be reckless. The question that this raises is whether this same standard might be applied to inquiry panel members where their recommendations can be shown to have had unintended consequences? In order to be deemed competent to conduct an inquiry should the panel have a basic or extensive understanding of the subject on which they are passing judgement? In particular, panels need to display a fuller understanding of issues such as what is possible and not possible with foresight rather than hindsight.

The premise of inquiries is that we should learn from the misfortune of others to ensure that "it never happens again". However, as we have seen, the link between the two can be somewhat tenuous. There is surprisingly little emphasis on recommendations being workable and effective. This is taken as a given rather than testing this assumption for its validity. Despite recommendations being ubiquitous, there has been very little research conducted into the production of recommendations either in a practical or an academic context.

In a world where there are not infinite resources, cost is and must always be a consideration. A previous mentor often reminded me that "aspirations without resources are simply fantasies". Therefore, those involved in inquiries need to consider cost from two angles. The first is the cost effectiveness of the process that produces the recommendations; after the Saville Inquiry into Bloody Sunday[81] it is clear that Parliament and Government are trying to address this issue. This inquiry took 12 years and cost £192 million[82] compared to the average cost of all the other inquiries which is £7 million.[83] The second issue is the cost effectiveness of implementing inquiry recommendations. This is a complex issue as it needs to consider not only the direct costs of implementation but also the cost of implementing recommendations that fail to deliver the intended results and the costs created by any unintended consequences. If inquiry recommendations are to be considered as a serious attempt to learn, rather than being seen as just politically expedient, serious consideration needs to be given to the costs necessary to learn from them.

Conclusions

And so, what conclusions can we draw? We have seen that in the prelude to many inquiries you will often hear demands for them to be held to ensure that "this will never happen again" but we have to question whether this goal is achievable. There can be no doubt that inquiries serve an important social purpose. These include discovery, catharsis, accountability and learning. A further complicating factor however is that inquiries are driven by three quite different social imperatives: the political, the judicial and the desire to learn. While I have concentrated on high-level inquiries, many of the lessons identified here may be equally applicable to inquiries conducted at every level of an organisation. These purposes and imperatives create different perspectives and starting points from which to construct a picture of what happened, why it happened, what lessons might be learnt and what might be done to prevent a reoccurrence. The results and recommendations from these inquiries do affect society and the factors that shape it both for the good and, unfortunately, to its detriment. We want to be safe while we go about our everyday business, but do we want to stop extraordinary people doing very brave things?

Pidgeon and O'Leary warns us that, "It may be impossible to insulate an otherwise well run and negotiated intra-organization learning system from the powerful and symbolic external legal and social blaming processes which inevitably follow any disaster."[84] Therefore, we need to make significant efforts to align the two.

ACCIDENTS WILL HAPPEN

There is a very long journey between understanding the causes of unwanted events and ensuring that they never happen again. As Peter Madsen remarks in concluding his paper on learning from Disaster in the US Coal Mining industry, "It may be unrealistic to hope that accidents similar to the Sago Mine disaster will 'never happen again'. I would go one step further to suggest that it may be totally unrealistic and even dangerous to expect that any such disasters 'will never happen again'."

No matter how we all may wish it was different, accidents will happen (whatever we may call them). One of the key differences between judicial and academic thinking is whether we can avoid them. I find it ironic that, within reports that admonish individuals for errors, lapses and mistakes you will often find errors, lapses and mistakes (see Table 6.3). To me this only goes to reinforce the fact that, no matter how good an individual's credentials or intentions are, such slips are too easy to make and so mistakes will happen. (Any lack of such errors in this book I must put down to my editors rather than my own efforts!) This attitude is supported by both Charles Perrow's idea of *normal accidents* and writers on *high reliability organisations*.

Table 6.3   Examples of Errors in Reports

Haddon-Cave (2009) page 260 para 10 states:

"The general standard of BAE Systems' work on the Nimrod Safety Case was lamentable. It was riddled with errors and of generally poor quality throughout."

However typographical errors can be found within his report at: page 290, para. 11.120 sub-para. are numbered 11.118: page 293: para. 11.128: sub-para. are numbered 11.126: error repeated in para. 11.129, 11.130, 11.131, 11.184; page 373, para. 13.72 "into to"; page 14 note 16 says the Gray report was published on 16 Oct 09, notes on pages 402, 408 and 568 say that the Gray report was published on 15 Oct 09; page 454: note 38 is missing: page 454: uses spelling of "Zebrugge" and "Zeebrugge" in the same paragraph; p.459; references are in wrong order.

Scraton (1999), loc 626 comment how the police reissued the operational order "complete with uncorrected spelling mistakes" yet his own book contained:

Fan spelt "fen" on three occasions (loc 383, 635, 991); beating spelt "bearing" (loc 591), ticketless spelt "ricketless" (loc 4648), unforeseeable spelt "unforesceable" (loc 4749) and there was a missing full-stop (loc 2415).

Charles Perrow expounds the idea of *normal accidents*; others have labelled it *normal accident theory* or NAT. Perrow does not see his work as a theory but a warning.[85] He warns that if systems are complex and closely coupled, accidents will happen. Therefore, he warns that if the system has a potential of a disastrous failure, you should think twice about creating it. In Chapter 2, under the heading "Failure to See", we see how even writers who espouse the concept of *high reliability* understand that accidents will happen, that safety and reliability are both fragile constructs.

Marc Gerstein says, "The challenge of eliminating accidents is formidable, and perhaps impossible."[86] He goes on to describe the work of Per Bak on complex systems and the accidents to which they are prone and here he provides another warning. He says that, "True complexity ... arises over an extended period through the complex interplay of driving and restraining forces" (I described a number of these forces in Chapter 2) and how they evolve towards a "critical point". At the critical point the power law is evoked. This means that the longer the crisis is delayed, the larger the crisis is that ensues and, as the time extends, the size of the crisis increases on a logarithmic scale. This point is also explored by Peter Ormerod (an economist) in his book *Why Most Things Fail*.[87] The issue this raised for inquiries is that by discouraging small failures we are just storing up trouble for the future so that when the tragedy happens the consequences of this are more pronounced. This raises difficult issues for society and leads to questions about where the balance should lie between what is good for the individual, what is good for society as a whole and the damage caused to the many by focusing on what might benefit a single individual. These complex issues have implications for every recommendation that an inquiry makes. However they are difficult to discuss as they might be seen as bordering on the *taboo* as can be seen in the reaction of one reviewer to Taleb's book *Antifragile*.[88] This makes it very difficult to "learning the right lessons" as there will always be questions about what actually is the right answer.

I consider that aspiring to be a *high reliability organisation* is an admirable objective yet it is an uncommon state for organisations to achieve. As a result of my work in this area, my mental model might be characterised by what Snook refers to as *practical sailing. Practical sailing* is the "continuous intelligent adjustments and adaptations to changing conditions and goals".[89] I see the mechanisms that create *practical sailing* as being that people and organisations normally *muddle through*, having to adapt to changing situations through *mutual adjustment*, learning by *trial and error*, using rules of thumb (*heuristics*), *compound abstraction, local rationality* and managing to avoid disaster by dint of the *Union Carbide Factor* (good fortune); this might be seen as a normal state of chaos *(normal chaos)*. What in hindsight is seen as drift looks, at the time, like sensible adaptation. This expectation sets the basis for my mental model of how organisations learn. I see my model as being at odds with the judicial model and therefore I do not immediately trust their recommendations (here I am referring to the "trust" required to accept virtual data as in the unsubstantiated advice of others). Critical to this process are our expectations.

FAILURE OF EXPECTATIONS

One final reason for our failure to learn may derive from a failure of expectations; in this case, expecting too much. We fail to recognise that what we see as chaos is a more natural state than is order and that entropy eventually overwhelms all systems. To create order takes a great deal of energy and an equal amount of good fortune however we still express surprise when chaos manifests itself. We are able to trace the development of these expectations through our daily life and our court processes. When we conflate findings of negligence in law against what is practically possible, we see that the legal test seems to be moving further and further away from what we are actually able to achieve as understood through both academic study and practical experience. This expectation of an error-free world is further reinforced by the media. General reporting of these events, for understandable reasons of rating and sales, tend to focus on the sensational and dramatic. They frequently also includes the question "who is to blame" as if this is the most important aspect. While the allocation of responsibility is important, this focus on "others" can bring with it unintended consequences. By creating a societal expectation that someone else is responsible, the individual may overlook their own responsibility for having good judgement and thereby unwittingly putting themselves at unnecessary jeopardy. For example, when being part of a crowd each individual needs to remain aware that their behaviour may have consequences for other people within that group. At the heart of this issue is the social role of the police. Scraton raises this issue when he talks of the police at Hillsborough being "committed to regulation and enforcement rather than safety and management; the police as a *force* rather than a *service*".[90] This was a debate that I was introduced to in Northern Ireland in the 1970s where the Constabulary saw that they "policed with the consent of their community". While the wording may be seen as semantic, the underlying issue is fundamental. Society must decide the basis on which they are policed, by a force or a service; this will have a fundamental effect on the way they do their work, the mindset with which they approach their work. Where inquiries report a flip between these two paradigms, they need to be aware of these inconsistencies and the effect this will have on any lessons that emerge.

We also expect people to work in ways that are alien to normal human behaviour (we are neither rational nor driven by rules-based logic). By labelling someone as professional we have come to expect them suddenly to be able to avoid the slips, lapses and errors that make us human. We give people multiple roles, many of which are very complex, and then expect people to switch between roles without having an appropriate period of adjustment and yet we still expect them to operate error-free. What is the alternative to giving people multiple roles? The answer is that everyone should specialise in a single role; however, who decides how complex a single role can be? How quickly would society grind to a halt awaiting the arrival of the appropriate specialist? Can we afford to specialise? Can we afford not to specialise? I do see a simple test that might help us to calibrate our expectations. When you see an error and are tempted to allocate blame to an individual, consider then list everything that they would have needed to know and everything that would need to have been done correctly, allocate each of them a 99 per cent probability of a positive outcome and you will see how failure becomes a strong possibility. With ten independent interrelating phenomena there is about 1 per cent probability of failure, at 20 it is nearly 20 per cent, at 50 it is nearly 40 per cent and at 70 there is a better than evens chance of something going wrong. (If these "independent interrelating phenomena" are people, the size of the problem becomes immediately apparent!) Yet we expect perfection in others or we call it negligence. We need to consider the unintended consequence for our society of having such false expectations.

In such circumstances it is also easy to underestimate how many thoughts, interpretations and actions need to be combined to ensure a positive outcome. For example Professor Scraton states, "The prosecution maintained that Duckenfield and Murray had enough time to respond to the simple questions regarding the consequences of opening exit gates: where people would go, what would happen on the terrace and who would organise the crowd in such an unusual situation."[91] Here we see three questions constructed and refined with the benefit of hindsight. However without this advantage, other questions, such as those in Table 6.4, might also come to mind.

As we have discussed earlier, the *recovery window* for such events (the time when the normal becomes abnormal and before it is too late to avoid *the unwanted* occurrence) can be short. In the case of Hillsborough, depending on your viewpoint, it was between ten and 30 minutes. As this list of questions demonstrates, it is easy to see that this time can be quickly consumed by the formulation and analysis of questions such as these. Within the *recovery window* those involved not only need to act appropriately but they needed to see and appreciate the requirement to formulate a well-considered plan in order to act appropriately. How this is done is a matter of training, experience and *anticipation* (that is how you might expect people to act or react). However, we need also to be aware that people might not react in the way we might expect.

Table 6.4   Hillsborough Questions

- How did this build up occur?
- What else is going on in the stadium and therefore where do I need to focus my energy?
- What are the options open to me to address the build up?
- What are the advantages and disadvantages of each option?
- From where do I collect the data necessary to make the decision?
- For what are my people programmed (trained and prepared) to do?
- What do I need to do to make each option happen?
- What might be the unintended consequences of each option?
- Which parts of the terrace do I need to be concerned with?
- What is their current state?
- What is the flow pattern to each?
- How might people react if we try to close the tunnel?
- Are the people in place to take the necessary action?
- To whom do I need to communicate?
- What do I need to tell them?
- How do I communicate with them?
- How long will it take to communicate and for them to react?

Expectations can mislead whether these expectations are held by society in general, whether they are about what we expect an individual to do successfully or the complexity of the issues that we face. Such false expectations are likely to create significant vulnerabilities within any system.

FAILURE OF THE INQUIRY PROCESS

We can see that the inquiry process does serve a useful purpose but that it does have distinct weaknesses. They are adept at preventing the last crisis and affecting the discipline into which they inquire, they have, with some notable exceptions, a very limited effect on future accidents. In many cases their findings could have been foreseen by the reading of a crisis management textbook. With the exception of the specifics of the case, they provide little that is new and what is new is often hidden within the mass of data presented. This might suggest that they do not really understand what is required to fulfil their remit to provide lessons to prevent the situation reoccurring.

So, to use their own language, who is to blame? Is it the academics for failing to communicate their ideas to a wider audience, is it the politicians for failing to provide the appreciate framework or is it those conducting inquiries for failing to avail themselves of the knowledge that exists? Should such a failure lead to a recommendation that unintentionally becomes a latent cause contributing to some future mishap, should the panel be held liable for this consequence, especially if they insisted that their recommendations are enacted? If yes, by what standard should this omission to avail themselves of the necessary knowledge be judged, especially if the result was a death? If judged by the standards that they judge others, is their omission grossly negligent and therefore bordering on the criminal? If not, why not? From a learning perspective, if those making the recommendations are not held to the same standard as those they judge, why should we take their advice as being valid?

KEY LESSONS FOR INQUIRIES

Even if we did teach this subject, I am not sure, amongst everything that we know, what we should teach, how and to whom. This requires a more systematic approach. I will use as my example to illustrate this point the Haddon-Cave report, which recommended that the MOD teach the appropriate lessons learnt to their senior staff. Using a Freedom of Information request, I asked the MOD about the specifics of what was taught. Having told them why I was asking the question, I received the reply detailed in Table 6.4. In this reply you will be see the same bureaucratic summation as we see in the lessons learnt for the Anderson Inquiry (see Table 6.1). In defence of the MOD, it might be said that this reply only provided a top-level overview of the lessons learnt. However, I am also aware of what lies beneath this layer as my doctoral study was sponsored by the relevant part of the Defence Academy and so I am aware of the practical difficulties they faced in distilling and disseminating these lessons, let alone ensuring that they are effectively implemented. You might now compare these lessons to the multitude of other issues addressed within this book. I do not consider the MOD any worse than other large organisations which have to struggle with these issues. We have to ask whether what is being asked of them is even possible.

While acknowledging this caveat, should we at least try to learn? The answer must be "yes". And so, why do we fail to learn from inquiries? The answer has to start with how we as humans tackle our day-to-day tasks. How we employ the approach of *muddling through*, and developing our understanding of the world around us based on *trial and error learning* and employing *compound abstraction* in our thinking. This can be seen to be the only option realistically open to us as we have not yet developed a systematic approach to conducting and learning from life let alone inquiries. That having been said, we can see that there are areas of inquiry practice that are open to improvement.

Table 6.5   Ministry of Defence Lessons Learnt

In general terms, the lessons that MOD have taken from the disasters you mention, plus others we have looked at such as Texas City, can be assigned to five areas:

1. Leadership and commitment, including developing a strong safety culture, a questioning attitude and removing organisational pressures which could lead to attempts to save time and money.
2. Thorough reporting, recording, investigation and learning from accidents and incidents.
3. Developing and maintaining the required levels of competence.
4. Comprehensive risk management processes.
5. Effective supervision and scrutiny of both people and processes.

The MOD's Safety Targets, which are aimed at MOD's Top Level Budget Holders (that is, our senior managers), explicitly address the first four areas detailed above, as well as other areas. As such we have a link from the lessons learnt from major disasters to the responsibility of our senior leaders for delivering improvements.

In this book I have examined the subject of inquiries from the perspective of potential learning in order to discover why we seem to fail to learn from this hard-won experience. I have focused on factors within the inquiry itself which might militate against such learning. I have identified a number of issues that might be addressed if we, as a society, are to gain maximum benefit from these pieces of work. My main points are:

- We need to recognise that the imperatives that drive inquiries conflict. What is necessary for justice often conflicts with what is necessary to learn. Therefore, those who vigorously advocate one end need to be aware of the barriers that their approach might create for others.

- We need to accept that politics are unavoidable within any inquiry process. If we are to learn, this issue needs to be tackled directly each time. Reports need to identify and address the interests of all concerned parties pragmatically and recognise how their views might wish to shape the findings and recommendations.

- We need to stop merely relearning what we already know. While inquiries are required to explain why the events occurred, they also need to be able to differentiate between the commonplace and the extraordinary. They need to be able to move the focus of learning away from the direct causes to understanding more about the indirect causes; what causes the causes. More particularly, they should look to explain why intelligent hardworking individuals thought, at the time, that the course of action taken was appropriate. Simply identifying mistakes and errors and labelling them as incompetent or complacent is in itself, and to use their own words, banal.

- If society is to learn from the experience of others then those conducting inquiries also need to learn from and about what has gone before. Those commissioning and conducting inquiries need not only to learn lessons about conducting inquiries but also look into lessons we have learnt about what causes these occurrences. Those who judge need to have the training and experience in order to start their task with the appropriate *seat of understanding*.

- As part of any inquiry, we need to differentiate between two distinct gaps in knowledge. The first is what those involved did not know which was already known elsewhere (and understanding why these lessons had not percolated down to that point at that time). The second is what was not known as identified by the inquiry as the need for further review. Confusing these two gaps may not only lead to unfair findings but may also precipitate poor recommendations.

- Any inquiries can only present a partial view of the events that occurred and why they occurred. We need to recognise that the form of the inquiries and the structure of the inquiry team will shape the report they produce.

- Those conducting inquiries should expect to have to justify their analysis and judgement as they are not all knowing and neither are they infallible. They will suffer, like everyone else, from local rationalisation and will privilege certain aspects of the debate. They need to be prepared to justify these opinions if they expect society to heed their warning and resource the changes they recommend and such scrutiny mechanisms need to be put in place.

- Those making the findings need to communicate their findings and recommendations clearly to the various different audiences involved. If society as a whole is to learn, those offering the new learning need to be conscious of how they are presenting their work.

They need to understand such phenomena as cross-understanding and develop methods to overcome these blockages. Without an appropriate effort in this area, learning will be lost and similar mishaps will happen again.

- We, as a society, need to be more realistic about what can be expected. Even within perfect systems, if there could ever be such a thing, components will fail, and people will make slips and have lapses; accidents will happen.

- Report authors need to be more realistic about how change will be achieved and in what timeframe. In framing recommendations they need to consider soliciting the support from experts in *organisational learning* and change as well as from those wishing to make the changes.

- Report authors should consider differentiating Macro, Mezzo and Micro recommendations as well as between specific technical changes and specifying the changes in outcome required.

- After a crisis, criticism of those involved is too easy; true understanding and constructive criticism are much harder and more difficult to achieve. Whenever authors are tempted to say things like "they failed to learn from the past" inquiry members should be prepared to explain how they envisage that piece of knowledge could or should have been known to those involved.

- The action or inaction being criticised needs to be viewed in the context of the time. If we are to learn for the future we should resist seeing the world as we would like to see it. We need see the world as it is and as it is likely to be seen by the next person who is placed in such an invidious position.

- One of the more difficult issues facing inquiries is the separation of liability from understanding. We see very different attitudes to this issue even amongst academics. As we have seen, Professor Scraton (a criminologist) thinks this to be nearly impossible. On the other hand Professor Snook (a social scientist) found it nearly impossible to allocate blame and liability once he really understood the circumstances around his case study. From my point of view,

I have no interest in allocating blame as my interest is why good people are led to think an action may be appropriate where at another time or in another space they might think it inappropriate. For this reason inquiries should be kept separate from criminal investigation unless it is specifically set up to determine liability and blame. It may even be appropriate to screen panel members for their propensity to correlate inquiry with liability. Where an inquiry is set up to allocate responsibility, there needs to be recognition that the learning value of such procedures will be greatly, if not totally diminished.

- Finally, the structure of the report will have an effect on the message communicated. There are basically two choices. The first is a narrative structure that leads to the findings and recommendations. The second structure starts with the recommendations and then uses the evidence to justify the recommendations. (It should be noted that this is different from just placing the recommendations that follow a narrative report at the beginning of the report document!) The first has the advantages of being seen to set out the whole story in a logical manner; this is recognised within the judicial system, for "in court, it appears that the best story ... wins the case".[92] However, a disadvantage of this approach is that the recommendations can appear to be an exhausted "add-on". The latter approach has the advantage of placing the transfer of learning at the heart of the inquiry's purpose where the recommendations become the central focus of the work. A disadvantage of this approach however may be that the narrative is obscured. The report authors need to justify their approach. This needs to be based on the purpose of the inquiry (explain or prevent) and the audience being addressed rather than on the background of those conducting the inquiry.

So why do we fail to learn, why do we suffer the same crises time and again? In summary:

- There are basic issues of leadership and communications as there are in all circumstances of failures.

- Blame and politics both internal and external to any organisation are rife.

- We do not trust the intent of those making the recommendations; they are often seen just as more rules to catch us out in the future.

- We do not trust the expertise of those making the recommendations: they may be expert in their own field but they do not seem to understand how systems and people actually work.

- We do not see the world in the same way as those producing the recommendations and so we fail to generate the necessary cross-understanding.

- Recommendations are too context specific: they probably would have stopped the specific case in question, they may stop such an event happening to the same group, they might stop such an event within the same industry but are unlikely to have much effect outside of the industry even if the lessons are applicable to them.

- There is also the question of follow-through; this covers all the issues ranging from:
  - how recommendations are evaluated, selected and resources allocated for their adoption;
  - how we allocate responsibility for implementation;
  - how we allocate responsibility for governance.

- There are questions about how we learn lessons in a wider societal context:
  - across academic disciplines;
  - from the way we run inquiries and the way we make recommendations.

- These lessons are not taught as part of basic organisational or business studies. We therefore need to consider:
  - whether we are asking the wrong questions and whether we are dealing with the world as it is or the world as we would like it to be;
  - how we might collate and disseminate these lessons through government sponsored documentation and codes of practice;
  - how we conduct basic training for those who judge these issues;
  - how managers and others are trained in risk management (as distinct from health and safety issues) from the most basic level up to that required for effective *risk governance*.

One final point, I do not see this book as being definitive, but rather as being at the opposite end of this scale. I do not see its success as being the universal adoption of the ideas that I set out here. In the spirit of examination and review, what I would now like to see is a vigorous debate of these issues which may lead to more effective management of inquiries in the future. I hope to see the inclusion of the other disciplines necessary to understand this complex area more fully and I would like to see the issue of learning taking equal prominence alongside discovery, catharsis and accountability in our quest to stop unwanted occurrences from ever happening again. However we always have to remember that, and here I quote the psychologist Marc Gerstein, "Reality is often capriciously nonlinear."[93]

Endnotes

1   Smith (2005), Report 3, Recommendation 2.
2   PASC HC51-I (2005), page 41.
3   Grayson and Exter (2012).
4   http://www.mod.uk/NR/rdonlyres/B53F6F66-AD2C-40B6-A460-456C96ECCC8D/0/service_
        inquiry_flooding_hms_endurance.pdf, accessed 5 October 2012, pages 19 and 20.
5   Ibid, page 28.
6   Senge et al. (1990).
7   PASC HC51-I (2005), page 8, para.7.
8   Taylor (Interim in 1989; final 1990).
9   Stuart-Smith (1998).
10   HIP, page 54, para.1.232.
11   See page 178 of the HIP report.
12   See page 178 of the HIP report.
13   Taylor (1989), page 11, para.64.
14   HIP, page 356, para.2.12.123.
15   HIP, page 57, para.1.266.
16   Edmondson et al. in Starbuck and Farjoun (2005), pages 220–243.
17   HIP, page 94, para.2.2.60.
18   HIP, page 169, para.2.5.78.
19   HIP, page 139, para.2.4.72.
20   Roger's Commission (2011), page 122.
21   Bea (2012), page 17.
22   Scraton (1999), e-book loc 707.
23   HIP, page 8, para.13 and 100.
24   HIP, page 36, para.1.67.
25   Scraton (1999), e-book loc 273.
26   HIP, page 100.
27   Scraton (1999), ebook loc 4698.
28   HIP, page 42, para.1.125.
29   HIP, page 110, para.2.3.50.
30   HIP, page 37, para.1.76.
31   Haddon-Cave (2009), page 569.
32   Reason (1997), page 195.
33   Jackson and McKergow (2006), page 3.

34   http://www.bbc.co.uk/news/uk-england-birmingham-20294633, accessed 13 November 2012.
35   Perrow (1999), page 173.
36   Perrow (1999), page 191.
37   PASC HC51-I (2005), page 18, para.38.
38   Barton and Sutcliffe (2010), pages 73 and 75.
39   Christenson (2007).
40   http://www.publications.parliament.uk/pa/ld201213/ldhansrd/text/121114-0001.htm#12111438000734, accessed 15 November 2011.
41   Lauder (2011), pages 98 to 107.
42   Stark (1961).
43   Reason (1997), page 93.
44   Stark (1961), page 35.
45   Reason (1997), page 94.
46   HIP, pages 56–57.
47   Snook (2000), page 22.
48   Goddard and Eccles (2012), page 147.
49   http://news.bbc.co.uk/1/hi/business/7220063.stm, accessed 26 November 2012.
50   http://www.taxation.co.uk/taxation/Articles/2012/11/07/49471/spygate-scandal, accessed 26 November 2012.
51   http://www.telegraph.co.uk/finance/libor-scandal/9573119/Libor-reforms-Bankers-must-pay-the-price-with-jail-for-fixing-interest-rates-says-FSAs-Martin-Wheatley.html, accessed 26 November 2012.
52   Gardner (2008), page 81.
53   Reason (1997), page 127.
54   Coroner's Inquest into the London Bombings of 7 July 2005, para.8, accessed 17 October 2012.
55   Snook (2000).
56   Haddon-Cave (2009).
57   Gigerenzer (2003), page 90.
58   Reason (2008), page 136.
59   Scraton (1999), e-book loc 2497.
60   For example Professor Reason raised this issue in 1997, see pages 206–210.
61   Lauder (2011), Chapter 3.
62   Ramanujam and Goodman (2011), page 85.
63   Carroll and Fahlbruch (2011), page 3.
64   Hopkins (2009), page 510. Also see Toft and Reynolds (2005) for other examples.
65   http://www.parliament.uk/get-involved/outreach-and-training/resources-for-universities/open-lectures/the-role-and-importance-of-pre-legislative-scrutiny-in-parliamentary-life/, accessed 10 Jan 2013.
66   Turner (1994).
67   Perrow (1994), page 218.
68   Hopkins (2001), page 70.
69   Taylor (1989), page 40.
70   Cook and Woods (2006).
71   Bichard (2004), page 1, para.6.
72   HIP (2012), page 204, para.2.6.176.
73   http://www.legislation.gov.uk/ukpga/2005/12/pdfs/ukpga_20050012_en.pdf, accessed 3 December 2012.
74   PASC HC51-I (2005).
75   http://www.archive2.official-documents.co.uk/document/cm64/6481/6481.pdf, accessed 3 December 2012.
76   MoJ Cm 7943 (2010), page 3, para.2.
77   MoJ Cm 7943 (2010), page 5, para.14.
78   MoJ Cm 7943 (2010), page 18, para.70.

79   Cm 6481 (2005), page 17, para.10.
80   Cm 6481 (2005), page 19, para.13.
81   http://webarchive.nationalarchives.gov.uk/20101103103930/http://report.bloody-sunday-inquiry.org. accessed 12 December 12.
82   MoJ, Cm7943, page 3, para.4.
83   PASC, HC51-I (2005), page 45, para.125.
84   Pidgeon and O'Leary (2000), page 27.
85   Private email of 1 November 2010, Professor Perrow confirmed that this reading correctly represented his views.
86   Gerstein (2008), pages 112 and 113.
87   Ormerod (2005), page 165–187.
88   Taleb (2012).
89   Snook (2000), page 228.
90   Scraton (1999), e-book loc 5100.
91   Scraton (1999), e-book loc 4702–4704.
92   Gerstein (2008), page 27.
93   Gerstein (2008), page 237.

Annex:
Recommendations Per Report

This annex shows the result of the analysis which provides the basis for Chapter 3. In this annex I reproduce the table that lists the number of each type of recommendation (see Table 3.2 for types of recommendations) made for each inquiry (see Table 3.1 for a list of the inquiries analysed). As the original table was too large for the format of this book I have separated it out over the next four pages. The original table was, in effect, quartered as follows.

Tables 1 and 2 are the recommendations per report.
Tables 3 and 4 shows the percentage of recommendations per report.

It should be noted that the totals at the right hand side and at the bottom of each page are the totals for the total sample, not the totals for the page.

Annex: Recommendations per Report – 1

Inquiry	Governance	Purpose	Planning				Political			Capability			TOTAL
			[1]	[2]	[3]	[4]	[1]	[2]	[3]	[1]	[2]	[3]	
US – Roger's Com (1989) – Challenger			2	3	1		1				1	2	28
UK – Taylor(1989&90) – Hillsborough			1	2	1	2		1	5		2	30	124
UK – Donaldson (2000) – NHS										1	1	2	10
UK – Cullen Inquiry (2001) – Part 1+2	1		4	1	12	1	1	1	1	1	7	13	162
US – Pres Com (2002) – 9/11 attack				2		1	3	1	1			7	41
US – Columbia (2003)				3			1				1	11	29
UK – Laming (2004) - Climbie			2		2		2				5	5	108
UK – Smith (2005) – Shipman 3		3			4	1			3		6	2	48
UK – Smith (2005) – Shipman 4					1				1			4	33
UK – Smith (2005) – Shipman 5		1	1		4	2		13	9		5	7	109
US – Baker(2007) – Texas City										1	1	3	10
UK – Wolfe (2008) – Bae			4		4						2	1	27
UK – Haddon-Cave (2009)	1			2	2		9	3	1	4	7	5	90
UK – Walker (2009) – Banking	5						2				1	1	39
UK – Donaghy (2009) – Construction							2		2			4	28
Aus – Borthwick (2010) – Montara			1	4	2		1	3	4	1	3	1	105
US – President Com (2011) – BP			1	2	4		3		4		1	5	29
UK – FSA (2011) – RBS			2		3	2	1		1		2	4	37
Fr – Bea (2012) – AF447					1		4		3		1	2	41
Norway – 22 July Commission (2012)			1	5	1				5	1	2	5	32
	7	4	19	24	42	9	30	23	40	9	48	114	1,130

Annex: Recommendations per Report – 2

Inquiry	Performance Management [1]	[2]	[3]	Bureaucracy [1]	[2]	[3]	[4]	Standards [1]	[2]	Technical [1]	[2]	Comment	Further Review	Admonish	TOTAL
US – Roger's Com (1989) – Challenger	1	2		5	1	1		2			4		3		28
UK – Taylor(1989 and 1990) – Hillsborough		7		7	5	5		3		18	7	3	14	10	124
UK – Donaldson (2000) – NHS		4											2		10
UK – Cullen Inquiry (2001) – Part 1+2	2	3		30	21	2	1	13		3	3	9	36	1	162
US – Pres Com (2002) – 9/11 attack	3			3	6			1		2		2	1	4	41
US – Columbia (2003)		1	1	3		1	1				5				29
UK – Laming (2004) – Climbie	9	22	3	7	4			2	1	29	1		9	5	108
UK – Smith(2005) – Shipman3	1			4	7	2		1		9		2		2	48
UK – Smith(2005) – Shipman4	1				2			7		10	4		3		33
UK – Smith(2005) – Shipman5	1	3	2	6	7	5		2		30		1	10		109
US – Baker(2007) – Texas City	1	3			1				1						10
UK – Wolfe (2008) – Bae	2	2		2	4			5							27
UK – Haddon-Cave (2009)	1		1	24	14	2	6	1	1	1			6		90
UK – Walker (2009) – Banking	5	3	3	7	8			1		3					39
UK – Donaghy (2009) – Construction				2	2			2					9	5	28
Aus – Borthwick (2010) – Montara		2	3	8	6		1	9		36	3	5	10	2	105
US – President Com (2011) – BP					1			2		3	1		1	1	29
UK – FSA (2011) – RBS	12	2			1								7		37
Fr – Bea (2012) – AF447	2	4		1	1			5	2	1	3		15		41
Norway – 22 July Commission (2012)		1		2	2								1	2	32
	41	59	13	111	93	18	9	56	4	145	31	22	127	32	1130

Annex: Percentage of Recommendations per Report – 3

Inquiry	Governance	Purpose	Planning				Political			Capability			TOTAL
			[1]	[2]	[3]	[4]	[1]	[2]	[3]	[1]	[2]	[3]	
US – Roger's Com (1989) – Challenger	0.0	0.0	7.1	10.7	3.6	0.0	3.6	0.0	0.0	0.0	3.6	7.1	100.00
UK - Taylor(1989 and 1990) – Hillsborough	0.0	0.0	0.8	1.6	0.8	1.6	0.0	0.8	4.0	0.0	1.6	24.2	100.00
UK – Donaldson (2000) – NHS	0.0	0.0	0.0	0.0	0.0	0.0	0.0	0.0	0.0	10.0	10.0	20.0	100.00
UK – Cullen Inquiry (2001) – Part 1+2	0.6	0.0	0.0	0.6	7.4	0.6	0.6	0.0	0.6	0.6	4.3	8.0	100.00
US – Pres Com (2002) – 9/11 attack	0.0	0.0	9.8	4.9	0.0	2.4	7.3	2.4	2.4	0.0	0.0	17.1	100.00
US – Columbia (2003)	0.0	0.0	0.0	10.3	0.0	0.0	3.4	3.4	0.0	0.0	3.4	37.9	100.00
UK – Laming (2004) – Climbie	0.0	0.0	1.9	0.0	1.9	0.0	1.9	0.0	0.0	0.0	4.6	4.6	100.00
UK – Smith(2005) – Shipman3	0.0	6.3	0.0	0.0	8.3	2.1	0.0	2.1	6.3	0.0	12.5	4.2	100.00
UK – Smith(2005) – Shipman4	0.0	0.0	0.0	0.0	3.0	0.0	0.0	0.0	3.0	0.0	0.0	12.1	100.00
UK – Smith(2005) – Shipman5	0.0	0.9	0.9	0.0	3.7	1.8	0.0	0.0	8.3	0.0	4.6	6.4	100.00
US – Baker(2007) – Texas City	0.0	0.0	0.0	0.0	0.0	0.0	0.0	0.0	0.0	10.0	10.0	30.0	100.00
UK – Wolfe (2008) – Bae	0.0	0.0	14.8	0.0	14.8	0.0	0.0	0.0	0.0	0.0	7.4	3.7	100.00
UK – Haddon-Cave (2009)	1.1	0.0	0.0	2.2	2.2	0.0	10.0	3.3	1.1	4.4	7.8	5.6	100.00
UK – Walker (2009) – Banking	12.8	0.0	0.0	0.0	0.0	0.0	5.1	0.0	0.0	0.0	2.6	2.6	100.00
UK – Donaghy (2009) – Construction	0.0	0.0	0.0	0.0	0.0	0.0	7.1	0.0	7.1	0.0	0.0	14.3	100.00
Aus – Borthwick (2010) – Montara	0.0	0.0	1.0	3.8	1.9	0.0	1.0	2.9	3.8	1.0	2.9	1.0	100.00
US – President Com (2011) – BP	0.0	0.0	3.4	6.9	13.8	0.0	10.3	0.0	13.8	0.0	3.4	17.2	100.00
UK – FSA (2011) – RBS	0.0	0.0	5.4	0.0	8.1	5.4	2.7	0.0	2.7	0.0	5.4	10.8	100.00
Fr – Bea (2012) – AF447	0.0	0.0	0.0	0.0	2.4	0.0	0.0	0.0	7.3	0.0	2.4	4.9	100.00
Norway – 22 July Commission (2012)	0.0	0.0	3.1	15.6	3.1	0.0	12.5	0.0	15.6	3.1	6.3	15.6	100.00
percentage of total	**0.62**	**0.35**	**1.68**	**2.12**	**3.72**	**0.80**	**2.65**	**2.04**	**3.54**	**0.80**	**4.25**	**10.09**	**100.00**
percentage of percent	0.73	0.36	2.41	2.84	3.75	0.70	3.28	1.34	3.81	1.46	4.64	12.37	100.00

Annex: Percentage of Recommendations per Report – 4

Inquiry	Performance Management [1]	[2]	[3]	Bureaucracy [1]	[2]	[3]	[4]	Standards [1]	[2]	Technical [1]	[2]	Comment	Further Review	Admonish	TOTAL
US – Roger's Com (1989) – Challenger	0.0	7.1	0.0	17.9	3.6	3.6	0.0	7.1	0.0	0.0	14.3	0.0	10.7	0.0	100.00
UK – Taylor(1989 and 1990) – Hillsborough	0.8	5.6	0.0	5.6	4.0	4.0	0.0	2.4	0.0	14.5	5.6	2.4	11.3	8.1	100.00
UK – Donaldson (2000) – NHS	0.0	40.0	0.0	0.0	0.0	0.0	0.0	0.0	0.0	0.0	0.0	0.0	20.0	0.0	100.00
UK – Cullen Inquiry (2001) – Part 1+2	1.2	1.9	0.0	18.5	13.0	1.2	0.6	8.0	0.0	1.9	1.9	5.6	22.2	0.6	100.00
US – Pres Com (2002) – 9/11 attack	7.3	0.0	0.0	7.3	14.6	0.0	0.0	2.4	0.0	4.9	0.0	4.9	2.4	9.8	100.00
US – Columbia (2003)	0.0	3.4	3.4	10.3	0.0	3.4	3.4	0.0	0.0	0.0	17.2	0.0	0.0	0.0	100.00
UK – Laming (2004) – Climbie	8.3	20.4	2.8	6.5	3.7	0.0	0.0	1.9	0.9	26.9	0.9	0.0	8.3	4.6	100.00
UK – Smith(2005) – Shipman3	2.1	0.0	0.0	8.3	14.6	4.2	0.0	2.1	0.0	18.8	0.0	4.2	0.0	4.2	100.00
UK – Smith(2005) – Shipman4	3.0	0.0	0.0	0.0	6.1	0.0	0.0	21.2	0.0	30.3	12.1	0.0	9.1	0.0	100.00
UK – Smith(2005) – Shipman5	0.9	2.8	1.8	5.5	6.4	4.6	0.0	1.8	0.0	27.5	0.0	0.9	9.2	0.0	100.00
US – Baker(2007) – Texas City	10.0	30.0	0.0	0.0	10.0	0.0	0.0	0.0	0.0	0.0	0.0	0.0	0.0	0.0	100.00
UK – Wolfe (2008) – Bae	7.4	7.4	0.0	7.4	14.8	0.0	0.0	18.5	3.7	0.0	0.0	0.0	0.0	0.0	100.00
UK – Haddon-Cave (2009)	1.1	0.0	1.1	26.7	15.6	2.2	6.7	1.1	0.0	1.1	0.0	0.0	6.7	0.0	100.00
UK – Walker (2009) – Banking	12.8	7.7	7.7	17.9	20.5	0.0	0.0	2.6	0.0	7.7	0.0	0.0	0.0	0.0	100.00
UK – Donaghy (2009) – Construction	0.0	0.0	0.0	7.1	7.1	0.0	0.0	7.1	0.0	0.0	0.0	0.0	32.1	17.9	100.00
Aus – Borthwick (2010) – Montara	0.0	1.9	2.9	7.6	5.7	0.0	1.0	8.6	0.0	34.3	2.9	4.8	9.5	1.9	100.00
US – President Com (2011) – BP	0.0	0.0	0.0	0.0	3.4	0.0	0.0	6.9	0.0	10.3	3.4	0.0	3.4	3.4	100.00
UK – FSA (2011) – RBS	32.4	5.4	0.0	0.0	2.7	0.0	0.0	0.0	0.0	0.0	0.0	0.0	18.9	0.0	100.00
Fr – Bea (2012) – AF447	4.9	9.8	0.0	2.4	2.4	0.0	0.0	12.2	4.9	2.4	7.3	0.0	36.6	0.0	100.00
Norway – 22 July Commission (2012)	0.0	3.1	0.0	6.3	6.3	0.0	0.0	0.0	0.0	0.0	0.0	0.0	3.1	6.3	100.00
percentage of total	3.63	5.22	1.15	9.82	8.23	1.59	0.80	4.96	0.35	12.83	2.74	1.95	11.24	2.83	100.00
percentage of percent	4.62	7.33	0.99	7.77	7.73	1.16	0.58	5.20	0.48	9.03	3.28	1.13	10.18	2.83	100.00

References

Adams, J. (2007), "Risk Management: It's Not Rocket Science … It's Much More Complicated", *Risk Management*, Vol.54, No.5, pp.36–40.

AJP-01(D). (2010), *Allied Joint Doctrine*, NATO, Brussels.

Anderson, I. (2002), *Foot and Mouth Disease 2001: Lessons to be Learned Inquiry Report*, The Stationary Office, London.

Ashby, W.R. (1956), *An Introduction to Cybernetics*, Chapman and Hall, London.

Baker, J. (2007), *The Report of the BP US Refineries,* Independent Safety Review Panel.

Baldridge, D.C., Floyd, S. and Markóczy, L. (2004), "Are Managers from Mars and Academicians from Venus? Toward an Understanding of the Relationship between Academic Quality and Practical Relevance", *Strategic Management Journal*, Vol.25, No.11, pp.1063–1074.

Barber, R. (2008), An investigation of the role of internally generated risks in complex projects. Unpublished PhD thesis, University of NSW, Australia.

Barton, M.A. and Sutcliffe, K.M. (2010), "Learning When to Stop Momentum", *Sloan Management Review*, Vol.51, No.3, pp.68–76.

Behn, R.D. (2003), "Why Measure Performance? Different Purposes Require Different Measures", *Public Administration Review*, Vol.63, No.5, pp.586–606.

Bichard, M. (2004), *The Bichard Inquiry HC653,* Stationary Office, London Report.

Blockey, D. (1998), "Managing Proneness to Failure", *Journal of Contingencies and Crisis Management*, Vol.6, No.2, pp.76–79.

Boin, A. and Schulman, P. (2008), "Assessing NASA's Safety Culture: The Limits and Possibilities of High-Reliability Theory", *Public Administration Review*, Vol.68, No.6, pp.1050–1062.

Borthwick, D. (2010), *Montara Commission of Inquiry*, Commonwealth Copyright Administration, Barton.

Bourne, M. and Bourne, P. (2011), *Handbook of Corporate Performance Management*, Wiley, Chichester.

Bourrier, M. (2005), "An Interview with Karlene Roberts", *European Management Journal*, Vol.23, No.1, pp.93–97.

Boyer, E.L. (1990), *Scholarship Reconsidered: Priorities of the Professoriate*, Carnegie Foundation for the Advancement of Teaching, Menlo Park, CA.

BS31100:2008 *Risk Management. Code of Practice*, British Standards Institute, London.

Bureau d'Enquêtes et d'Analyses (2012), *On the Accident on 1st June 2009 to the Airbus A330-203 Registered F-GZCP Operated by Air France, Flight AF 447 Rio de Janeiro – Paris, Final Report*, Ministere de L'Ecologie, du Developpement durable, des Transport et du Logement, Paris.

Calandro, J. Jr. and Lane, S. (2006), "An Introduction to the Enterprise Risk Scorecard", *Measuring Business Excellence*, Vol.10, No.3, pp.31–40.

Campbell, C.P. (1998), "Training Course/Program Evaluation: Principles and Practice", *European Journal of Training and Development*, Vol.22. No.8, pp.323–344.

Carroll, J.S. and Fahlbruch, B. (2011), "The Gift of Failure: New Approaches to Analyzing and Learning from Events and Near-misses. Honoring the Contributions of Bernhard Wilpert", *Safety Science*, Vol.49, No.1, pp.1–4.

Choo, C.W. (2008), "Organizational Disasters: Why They Happen and How They May be Prevented", *Management Decision*, Vol.46, No.1, pp.32–45.

Christenson, D. (2007), *Build a Healthy Safety Culture Using Organizational Learning and High Reliability Organizing*, Wildfire, Sevilla, Spain.

Clarke, L. and Perrow, C. (1996), "Prosaic Organizational Failure", *American Behavioral Scientist*, Vol.39, No.8, pp.1040–1056.

Cm 6481 (2005), *Government Response to the Public Administration Select Committee's First Report Of The 2004–5 Session: "Government By Inquiry"*, HMSO, London.

Coleman, T.S. (2011), *A Practical Guide to Risk Management*, CFA Institute, Charlotteville.

Colligan, M.J. and Murphy, L.R. (1979), "Mass Psychogenic Illness in Organizations: An Overview," *Journal of Occupational Psychology*, Vol.52, No.2, pp.77–90.

Columbia Accident Investigation Board (2003), *Columbia Accident Investigation Board Report*, Washington, DC (also see http://caib.nasa.gov/, accessed 1 April 2012).

Cook, R.I. and Woods, D.D. (2006), "Distancing through differencing: an obstacle to organisational learning following accidents", in Hollnagel, E., Woods, D. and Leveson, N. (Eds), *Resilience Engineering: Concepts and Precepts*, Ashgate, Aldershot, pp.329–338.

Corley, K.G. and Gioia, D.A. (2011), "Building Theory about Theory Building: What Constitutes a Theoretical Contribution?", *Academy of Management Review*, Vol.36, No.1, pp.12–32.

Cox, S., Jones, B. and Collinson, D. (2006), "Trust Relations in High-Reliability Organisations", *Risk Analysis*, Vol.26, No.5, pp.1123–1138.

Cullen, P.C. (2001a), *The Ladbroke Grove Rail Inquiry Part 1 Report*, HSC, London.

Cullen, P.C. (2001b), *The Ladbroke Grove Rail Inquiry Part 2 Report*, HSC, London.

Dallas, M. (2006), *Value and Risk Management: A Guide to Best Practice*, Blackwell, Oxford.

Dechy, N., Dien, Y., Funnemark, E., Roed-Larsen, S., Stoop, J., Valvisto, T. and Arellano, A.l.V. on behalf of ESReDA's Accident Investigation Working Group (2012), Results and lessons learned from the ESReDA's Accident Investigation Working Group, Introducing article to "Safety Science" special issue on "Industrial Events Investigation" *Safety Science*, Vol.50, p.1387.

Dekker, S. (2011), *Drift into Failure*, Ashgate, Farnham.

Dien, Y., Dechy, N. and Guillaume, E. (2012), "Accident Investigation: From Searching Direct Causes to Finding In-depth Causes – Problem of Analysis or/and of Analyst?", *Safety Science*, Vol.50, pp.1398–1407.

Donaghy. R. (2009), *One Death is Too Many, Inquiry into the Underlying Causes of Construction Fatal Accidents*, Stationary Office, London.

Donaldson, L. (2000), *An Organisation with a Memory, Report of an Expert Group on Learning from Adverse Events in the NHS*, Stationary Office, London.

Dunbar, R. and Garud, R. (2005), "Data Indeterminacy: one NASA, two modes" in Starbuck, W.H. and Farjoun, M. (Eds), *Organization at the Limit*, Blackwell, Oxford, pp.202–219.

Easterby-Smith, M., Thorp, R. and Jackson, P.R. (2008), *Management Research*, Sage, London.

Editor's Comments (2011), "The Challenges of Building Theory by Combining Lenses", *Academy of Management Review*, Vol.36, No.1, pp.6–11.

Elliot, D. (2006), "Crisis management in practice", in Smith, D. and Elliot, D. (Eds) *Crisis Management: Systems and Structure for Prevention and Recovery*, Routledge, Abingdon, pp.393–412.

Elliott, D., Smith, D. and McGuinness, M. (2000), "Exploring the Failure to Learn: Crises and the Barriers to Learning", *Review of Business*, Vol.21, Iss.3/4, pp.17–24.

Enzer, S. (1980), "Energy Policy: Failure of Foresight", *Los Angeles Business and Economics*, Vol.5, No.1, pp.12–17.

ESReDA Working Group on Accident Investigation (2009), *Guidelines for Safety Investigations of Accidents*, European Safety Reliability and Data Association, Oslo.

Farjoun, M. (2005), "Organizational learning and action in the midst of safety drift" in Starbuck, W.H. and Farjoun, M. (Eds), *Organization at the Limit*, Blackwell, Oxford, 60–80.

Farjoun, M. (2010), "Beyond Dualism: Stability and Change as a Duality", *Academy of Management Review*, Vol.35, No.2, pp.202–225.

Feigenson, N. and Park, J. (2006), "Emotions and Attributions of Legal Responsibility and Blame: A Research Review", *Law and Human Behaviour*, Vol.30, No.2, pp.143–161.

Financial Reporting Council (2010), *The Failure of the Royal Bank of Scotland*, Financial Reporting Council, London.

Financial Reporting Council (2010), *The UK Corporate Governance Code*, Financial Reporting Council, London.

Fischhoff, B., Lichtenstein, S., Slovic, P., Derby, S.L. and Keeney, R.L. (1981), *Acceptable Risk*, University Press, Cambridge.

Flavell-While, C. (2009), "Laying down the law", *TCE*, Dec-Jan, pp.24–25.

Francis, R. (2013), *Report of the Mid Staffordshire NHS Foundation Trust Public Inquiry,* The Stationary Office, London.

Gardener, D. (2008), *Risk, The Science and Politics of Fear*, Virgin Books, London.

Gauthereau, V. and Hollnagel, E. (2005), "Planning, Control, and Adaptation: A Case Study", *European Management Journal*, Vol.23, No.1, pp.118–131.

Gerstein, M. (2008), *Flirting with Disaster: Why Accidents are Rarely Accidental*, Union Square, London.

Ghaffarzadegan, N. (2008), "How a System Backfires: Dynamics of Redundancy Problems in Security", *Risk Analysis,* Vol.28, No.6, pp.1669–1687.

Gigerenzer, G. (2003), *Reckoning with Risk: Learning to Live with Uncertainty*, Penguin, London.

Gjorv, A.B. (2012), *Rapport fra 22. Juli-kommisjonen*, see: http://22julikommisjonen. no/en, accessed 15 August 2012.

Goddard J. and Eccles T. (2012), *Uncommon Sense, Common Nonsense*, Profile Books, London.

Grayson, D. and Exter, N. (2012), *Cranfield on Corporate Sustainability*, Greenleaf, Sheffield.

Grint, K. (2010), "Wicked Problems and Clumsy Solutions: the Role of Leadership", *The New Public Leadership Challenge* (2010) Ch11: pp.169–186.

Haddon-Cave, C. (2009), *The Nimrod Review*, The Stationery Office, London.

Hallett, The Rt. Hon Lady Justice (2011), Coroner's Inquest into the London Bombings of 7 July 2005, para 8, see: 7julyinquests.independent.gov.uk/ docs/orders/rule43-report.pdf, accessed 17 October 2012.

Hancock, D. (2004), "Tame Problems and Wicked Messes: Choosing between Management and Leadership Solutions", *RMA Journal*, July-August, pp. 38–42.

Hancock, D. and Holt, R. (2003), *Tame, Messy and Wicked Problems in Risk Management*, Manchester Metropolitan University Business School, Manchester.

Hatry, H.P. (1999), *Performance Measurement: Getting Results*, Washington, DC, Urban Institute.

Heimann, C.F.L. (1997), *Acceptable Risks; Politics, Policy and Risky Technologies*, University of Michigan, USA.

Hillson, D. (Ed.) (2007), *The Risk Management Universe: A Guided Tour*, 2nd edn, BSI Business Information, London.

Hirschhorn, L. (1993), "Hierarchy versus Bureaucracy: the case of a nuclear reactor" in Roberts, K.H. (Ed.), *New Challenges to Understanding Organization*, Macmillan, New York, pp.137–149.

HM Treasury (2004), *The Orange Book: Management of Risk – Principles and Concepts*, TSO, London.

Hollnagel, E. (1993), *Human Reliability Analysis, Context and Control*, Academic Press, London.

Hollnagel, E. (2009), *The ETTO Principle: Efficiency-Thoroughness Trade-off: Why Things That Go Right Sometimes Go Wrong*, Ashgate, Farnham.

Hollnagel, E. in Hollnagel, E., Woods, D.D. and Leveson, N. (Eds), *Resilience Engineering: Concepts and Precepts* (Symposium), 2004 October, Söderköping, Sweden, Ashgate, Aldershot, pp.9–17.

Hollnagel, E., Woods, D.D. and Leveson, N. (2006), *Resilience Engineering Concepts and Precepts*, Ashgate, Aldershot.

Hopkin, P. (2010), *Fundamentals of Risk Management*, Kogan, London.

Hopkins, A. (2001), "Was Three Mile Island a `Normal Accident'?", *Journal of Contingencies and Crisis Management*, Vol.9, No.2, pp.65–72.

Hopkins, A. (2008), *Failure to Learn: The BP Texas City Refinery Disaster*, CCH, Sydney, Australia.

Hopkins, A. (2009), "Reply to Comments", *Safety Science*, Vol.47, pp.508–510.

Horvath, M. (2001), "Who's to blame? An exploration of the role of blame perceptions as moderator of relationships between organizational perceptions and consequences", PhD thesis, Michigan State University.

House of Common Library (2011), *SN/PC/02599 – Investigatory Inquiries and the Inquiries Act 2005*, London.

House of Common Library (2012), *SN/PC/06410 – The Inquiries Act 2005*, London.

Hovden, J., Albrechtsen, E. and Herrera, I.A. (2010), "Is There a Need for New Theories, Models and Approaches to Occupational Accident Prevention?", *Safety Science*, No.48, pp. 950–956.

Hubbard, D.W. (2009), *The Failure of Risk Management: Why it's Broken and How to Fix It*, Wiley, Hoboken, NJ.

Huber, G.P. and Lewis, K. (2010), "Cross-Understanding: Implications for Group Cognition And Performance", *Academy of Management Review*, Vol.35, No.1, pp.6–26.

Huff, A.S. (2000), "Citigroup's John Reed and Stanford's James March on Management Research and Practice", *Academy of Management Executive*, Vol.14, No.1, pp.52–64.

Hutton (2004), *Report of the Inquiry into the Circumstances Surrounding the Death of Dr David Kelly C.M.G.*, The Stationary Office, London.

Irwin, R. (1977), Notes toward a model. In Exhibition Catalog for the Robert Irwin exhibition, Whitney Museum of American Art, April 16–May 29, 1977, pp. 23–31, Whitney Museum of American Art, New York.

Jackson, P.Z. and Mckergow, M. (2006), *The Solutions Focus: Making Coaching and Change SIMPLE*, Brealey, London.

Jaques, T. (2010), "Embedding Issue Management as a Strategic Element of Crisis Prevention", *Disaster Prevention and Management*, Vol.19, Iss.4, pp.469–482.

JSP832 (2008), *Guide To Service Inquiries*, MOD, London.

Kakabadse, A. (2010), Cranfield University School of Management, http://media.som.cranfield.ac.uk/vod/ki/topic/The%20Economic%20Downturn/0974/kakabadse5.mp4, accessed 24 November 2010.

Kaplan, R.S. and Norton, D.P. (2004), *Strategy Maps: Converting Intangible Assets into Tangible Outcomes*, HBS Press, Boston.

Kean, T.H. (2004), *The 9/11 Commission Report*, www.9-11commission.gov/report/911Report.pdf access 19 July 2012.

Kerfoot, K. (2003), "Attending to Weak Signals: The Leader's Challenge", *Nursing Economics*, Vol.21, No.6, pp.293–295.

Kieser, A. and Leiner, L. (2009), "Why the Rigour–Relevance Gap in Management Research Is Unbridgeable", *Journal of Management Studies*, Vol.46, No.3, pp.516–533.

Klien, G. (1998), *Sources of Power*, MIT Press, London.

Klien, G. (2009), *Streetlights and Shadows*, MIT Press, London.

Klein, G., Pliske, R., Crandall, B. and Woods, D. (2005). "Problem Detection", *Cognition, Technology and Work*, Vol.7, No.1, pp.14–28.

Klinke, A. and Renn, O. (2001), "Precautionary Principle and Discursive Strategies: Classifying and Managing Risks", *Journal of Risk Research,* Vol.4, No.2, pp.159–173.

Konrad, J. and Shroder, T. (2011), *Fire on the Horizon*, Harper, London.

Kutsch, E. and Hall, M. (2010), "Deliberate Ignorance in Project Risk Management", *International Journal of Project Management*, No.28, pp.245–255.

Lagadec, P. (1993), *Preventing Chaos in a Crisis*, McGraw-Hill, Maidenhead.

Laming, H. (2003), *The Victoria Climbié Inquiry*, HMSO, London.

Latané, B. and Darley, J.M. (1970), *The Unresponsive Bystander: Why Doesn't He Help?*, Appleton-Century Crofts, New York.

Latané, B. and Nidd, S. (1981), "Ten Years of Research on Group Size and Helping", *Psychological Bulletin*, Vol.89, No.2, pp.308–324.

Lauder, M.A. (1997), "The Viability of Multi-skilling", MDA Dissertation, School of Defence Management, Cranfield University.

Lauder, M.A. (2011), "Conceptualisation in preparation for risk discourse: a qualitative step towards risk governance", DBA Thesis, Cranfield University.

Law, S., Harper, C., Jones, N. and Marcus, R. (2003), *Research for Development*, Sage, London.

Le Porte, T. (1994), "A Strawman speaks up: Comments on The Limits of Safety", *Journal of Contingencies and Crisis Management*, Vol.2, No.4, pp.207–211.

Leveson, N., Dulac, N., Marais, K. and Carroll, J. (2009), "Moving beyond Normal Accidents and High Reliability Organizations: A Systems Approach to Safety in Complex Systems", *Organization Studies*, Vol.30, No2–3, pp.227–249.

Lovell, J. and Kluger, J. (1994), *Apollo 13*, Coronet, London.

Mack, A. and Rock, I. (1998), *Inattentional Blindness*, MIT Press, London.

Manning, P.K. (1999), "High Risk Narratives: Textual Adventures", *Qualitative Sociology*, Vol.22, No.4, pp.285–299.

Marais, K., Dulac, N. and Leveson, N. (2004), Beyond Normal Accidents and High Reliability Organizations: The Need for an Alternative Approach to Safety in Complex Systems, MIT. *ESD Symposium*, pp.1–16.

Marr, A. (2004), *My Trade: A Short History of British Journalism*, Macmillan, London.

Mckelvey, B. (2006), "Response: Van De Ven And Johnson's 'Engaged Scholarship': Nice Try, But…", *Academy of Management Review*, Vol.31, No.4, pp.822–829.

Merna, T. and Al-Thani, F.F. (2008), *Corporate Risk Management*, 2nd edn, Wiley, Chichester, England; Hoboken, NJ.

Micheli, P. (2013), "The Theory and Practice of Performance Measurement", *Management Accounting Research*, Vol.24, Iss 2.

Miller, G.A. (1956), "The Magical Number Seven, Plus or Minus Two: Some Limits on Our Capacity for Processing Information", *The Psychological Review*, Vol.63, Iss 2, pp.81–97.

Ministry of Justice (2010), *Post-Legislative Assessment of the Inquiries Act 2005*, Cm 7943, TSO, London.

Minns, S.E. (2010), "Strategic Change in Firms Following Private Equity Acquisition: An Ex Post Study of U.K. Technology, Industrial, and Communications Firms", *The Journal of Private Equity*, Vol.13, No.3, pp.22–31.

Mintzberg, H., Ahlstrand, B. and Lampel, J. (1998), *Strategy Safari*, Prentice Hall, London.

Mythen, G. (2004), *Ulrich Beck: A Critical Introduction to the Risk Society*, Pluto, London.

Mythen, G. (2006), *Beyond the Risk Society: Critical Reflections on Risk and Human Security*, Open University Press, Maidenhead.

Nadler, D.A. (2004), "Building Better Boards", *Havard Business Review*, Vol.82, No.5, pp.102–111.

National Commission on Terrorist Attacks Upon the United States (also known as the 9–11 Commission) see: http://9-11commission.gov/, accessed 6 September 2012.

National Commission on the BP Deepwater Horizon Oil Spill and Offshore Drilling, see: http://www.oilspillcommission.gov/, accessed 1 February 2012.

Nævestad, T.-O. (2008), "Safety Cultural Preconditions for Organizational Learning in High-Risk Organizations", *Journal of Contingencies and Crisis Management*, Vol.16, No.3, pp.154–163.

Nævestad, T.-O. (2009), "Mapping Research on Culture and Safety in High-Risk Organizations: Arguments for a Sociotechnical Understanding of Safety Culture", *Journal of Contingencies and Crisis Management*, Vol.17, No.2, pp.126–136.

Office of Government Commerce (2007), *Management of Risk: Guidance for Practitioners*, TSO, London.

Ormerod, P. (2005), *Why Most Things Fail*, Faber and Faber, London.

Panckhurst, G. (2012), *Royal Commission on the Pike River Coal Mine Tragedy*, Wellington New Zealand, Volume 1.

Peng, M.W. and Dess, G.G. (2010), "In the Spirit of Scholarship", *Academy of Management Learning and Education*, Vol.9, No.2, pp.282–298.

Perrow, C. (1994), "The Limits of Safety: The Enhancement of a Theory of Accidents", *Journal of Contingencies and Crisis Management*, Vol.2, No.4, pp.212–220.

Perrow, C. (1999), *Normal Accidents: Living with High-risk Technologies*, Princeton University Press, Princeton, NJ.

Perrow, C. (2007), *The Next Catastrophe*, Woodstock, Princeton, NJ.

Peters, T.J. and Waterman, R.H. (2004), *In Search of Excellence*, Profile Books, London.

Pidgeon, N. (1998), "Shaking the Kaleidoscope of Disasters Research – A Reply", *Journal of Contingencies and Crisis Management*, Vol.6, No.6, pp.97–101.

Pidgeon, N. and O'Leary, M. (2000), "Man-made Disasters: Why Technology and Organizations (Sometimes) Fail", *Safety Science*, Vol.34, pp.15–30.

Platts, K.W. (1993), "A Process Approach to Researching Manufacturing Strategy", *International Journal of Operations and Production Management*, Vol.13, No.8, pp.4–17.

Power, M. (2004), *The Risk Management of Everything; Rethinking the Politics of Uncertainty*, Demos, London.

Public Administration Select Committee (2005), *HC51-I, Government by Inquiry*, Stationary Office, London.

Public Administration Select Committee (2008), *HC473 Parliamentary Commissions of Inquiry*, TSO, London.

Qureshi, Z.H. (2007), "A Review of Accident Modelling Approaches for Complex Socio-Technical Systems", Defence and Systems Institute chapter appeared at the *12th Australian Workshop on Safety Related Programmable Systems (SCS'07)*, Cant. T. (Ed.) Adelaide. Conferences in Research and Practice in Information Technology, Vol.86.

Radell, W.W. (2006), "Storming and catastrophic system failure" in Smith, D. and Elliot, D. (Eds), *Crisis Management: Systems and Structure for Prevention and Recovery*, Routledge, Abingdon, pp.284–300.

Ramanujam, R. and Goodman, P.S. (2011), "The Challenge of Collective Learning from Event Analysis", *Safety Science*, Vol.49, No.1, pp.83–89.

Ramgopal, M. (2003), "Project Uncertainty Management", *Cost Engineering*, Vol.45, No.12, pp.21–24.

Rasmussen, J. (1997), "Risk Management in a Dynamic Society: A Modelling Problem", *Safety Science*, Vol.27, No.2/3, pp.183–213.

Reason, J. (1990), *Human Errors*, Cambridge University Press, Cambridge.

Reason, J. (1997), *Managing the Risks of Organizational Accident*, Ashgate, Aldershot.

Reason, J. (1998), "Achieving a Safe Culture: Theory and Practice", *Work and Stress*, Vol.12, No.3, pp.293–306.

Reason, J. (2008), *The Human Contribution, Unsafe Acts, Accidents and Heroic Recoveries*, Ashgate, Farnham.

Renn, O. (2008), *Risk Governance: Coping with Uncertainty in a Complex World*, Earthscan, London.

Rijpma, J.A. (1997), "Complexity, Tight-Coupling and Reliability: Connecting Normal Accidents Theory and High Reliability Theory", *Journal of Contingencies and Crisis Management*, Vol.5, No.1, pp.15–23.

Rizzi, J, (2010), "Risk Management; Techniques in search of a strategy", in Fraser, J. and Simkins, B.J., *Enterprise Risk Management*, Wiley, Hoboken, NJ, pp.303–320.

Roberts, K.H. (1990), "Some Characteristics of One Type of High Reliability Organization", *Organization Science*, Vol.1, No.2, pp.160–176.

Rochlin, G.I. (1991), "Iran Air Flight 655 and The USS Vincennes", in La Porte, T.R. (ed.), *Social Responses to Large Technical Systems*, Klinver, Netherlands, pp.99–125.

Roe, E. and Schulman, P.R. (2008), *High Reliability Management*, Stanford University Press, Stanford.

Roed-Larsen, S. and Stoop, J. (2012), "Modern Accident Investigation – Four Major Challenges", *Safety Science*, Vol.50, p.1395.

Roger Commissions (1986), Report of the Presidential Commission on the Space Shuttle Challenger Accident. See: http://history.nasa.gov/rogersrep/genindex.htm, accessed 5 September 2012.

Rumelhart, D.E. (1981), "Schemata: the building blocks of cognition" in Spiro, R., Bruce, B. and Brewer, W. (Eds), *Theoretical Issues in Reading Comprehension*, Lawrence Erlbaum Associates, Hilldale, NJ, pp.33–58.

Sagan, S.D. (1993), *The Limits of Safety*, PUP, Princeton, NJ.

Schobel, M. and Manzey, D. (2011), "Subjective Theories of Organizing and Learning from Events", *Safety Science*, Vol.49, No.2, pp.47–54.

Schulman, P.R. (1993), "The Negotiated Order of Organizational Reliability", *Administration and Society*, Vol.25, No.3, pp.353–372.

Scraton, P. (1999) [2009 e-book], *Hillsborough – The Truth*, Mainstream, Edinburgh: Random House, UK, Kindle Edition.

Senge, P. (2007), *The Fifth Discipline Fieldbook*, NB, London.

Shaw, J. (2005), "Managing All of Your Enterprise's Risks", *Risk Management*, Vol.52, No.9, pp.22–30.

Sheffi, Y. (2005), *The Resilient Enterprise: Overcoming Vulnerability for Competitive Advantage*, MIT Press, Cambridge, MA, London.

Slovic, P. (2000), *The Perception of Risk*, Earthscan, London.

Smart, C. and Vertinsky, I. (1977), "Design for Crisis Decision Units" reproduced in Smith, D. and Elliot, D. (2006), *Crisis Management: Systems and Structure for Prevention and Recovery*, Routledge, Abingdon, pp.321–342.

Smith, D. (2004), "For Whom the Bell Tolls: Imagining Accidents and the Development of Crisis Simulation in Organizations", *Simulation and Gaming*, Vol.35, No.3, pp.347–362.

Smith, D. and Elliot, D. (2006), *Crisis Management: Systems and Structure for Prevention and Recovery*, Routledge, Abingdon.

Smith, D. and Elliot, D. (2007), "Exploring the Barriers to Learning from Crisis: Organizational Learning and Crisis", *Management Learning*, Vol.38, No.5, pp.519–538.

Smith, E. (2012), *Luck*, Bloomsbury UK. Kindle Edition.

Smith, J. (2005), *The Shipman Inquiry* – Reports 1 to 6, HMSO, London.

Snook, S.A. (2000), *Friendly Fire: The Accidental Shootdown of US Black Hawks over Northern Iraq*, Princeton University Press, Princeton, NJ; Oxford.

Snook, S.A. and Connor, J.C. (2006), "The price of progress: structurally induced inaction" in Starbuck, W.H. and Farjoun, M. (Eds), *Organization at the Limit*, Blackwell, Oxford, pp.178–201.

Starbuck, W.H. and Farjoun, M. (2005), *Organization at the Limit*, Blackwell, Oxford.

Stark, S. (1961), "Executive Foresight: Definitions, Illustrations, Importance", *The Journal of Business*, Vol.34, No.1, pp.31–44.

Statutory Instrument (SI) (2006), *No.1838 The Inquiry Rules*, Stationary Office, London.

Stein, M. (2004), "The Critical Period of Disasters: Insights from Sense-making and Psychoanalytic Theory", *Human Relations*, Vol.57, No.10, pp.1243–1261.

Stockholm, G. (2011), "Insight from Hindsight: A Practitioner's Perspective on a Causal Approach to Performance Improvement", *Safety Science*, Vol.49, pp.39–46.

Sutcliffe, K.M. (2005), "Information Handling Challenges in Complex Systems", *International Public Management Journal*, Vol.8, No.3, pp.417–424.

Taleb, N.N. (2007), *The Black Swan*, Penguin, London.

Taleb, N.N. (2012), *Antifragile*, Penguin, London.

Taleb, N.N., Goldstein, D.G. and Spitznagel, M.W. (Oct 2009), "The Six Mistakes Executives Make in Risk Management", *Harvard Business Review*, pp.78–81.

Taylor, P.M. (1989), *The Hillsborough Stadium Disaster 15 April 1989 – Interim Report*, HSMO, London.

Taylor, P.M. (1990), *The Hillsborough Stadium Disaster 15 April 1989 – Final Report*, HSMO, London.

Thompson, J.D. (1967), *Organisations in Action*, McGraw-Hill, New York.

Todd, P.M. and Gigerenzer, G. (2003), "Bounding Rationality to the World", *Journal of Economic Psychology*, Vol.24, Iss 2, pp.143–165.

Toft, B. (2001), *External Inquiry into the Adverse Incident that Occurred at Queen's Medical Centre*, Nottingham, Department of Health, London.

Toft, B. and Reynolds, S. (2005), *Learning from Disasters: A Management Approach*, 3rd edn, Palgrave Macmillan, Basingstoke.

Tuchman, B. (1984), *The March of Folly*, The Folly Society, Bury St Edmunds.

Turner, B.A. (1976a), "The Development of Disaster – A Sequence Model for the Analysis of the Origins of Disaster", *Sociological Review*, Vol.24, pp.754–774.

Turner, B.A. (1976b), "The Organizational and Interorganizational Development of Disasters", *Administrative Science Quarterly*, Vol.21, pp.378–397.

Turner, B.A. (1978), *Man-made Disaster*, Wykeham, London.

Turner, B.A. (1994), "Causes of Disaster: Sloppy Management", *British Journal of Management*, Vol.5, pp.215–219.

Turner, B.A. and Pidgeon, N. (1997), *Man-made Disasters*, Butterworth-Heinemann, London.

US DOE Standard 1028 (2009), *Human Performance Improvement Handbook Volume 2: Human Performance Tools for Individuals, Work Teams, and Management*, DOE, Washington.

Van de Ven, A.H. (1989), "Nothing Is Quite So Practical as a Good Theory", *Academy of Management Review*, Vol.14, No.4, pp.486–489.

Van de Ven, A.H. (2007), *Engaged Scholarship*, OUP, Oxford.

Van de Ven, A.H. and Poole, M.S. (1995), "Explaining Development and Change in Organizations", *The Academy of Management Review*; Vol.20, No.3, pp.510–540.

Vaughan, D. (1996), *The Challenger Launch Secision*, Chicago Press, London.

Vaughan, D. (1997), "The Trickle-down Effect: Policy Decisions, Risky Work, and the Challenger Tragedy", *California Management Review*, Vol. 39, No.2, pp.80–102.

Vaughan, D. (1999), "The Dark Side of Organizations: Mistake, Misconduct, and Disaster", *Annual Review of Sociology*, Vol.25, pp.271–305.

Walker, D. (2009), *A Review of Corporate Governance in UK Banks and Other Financial Industry Entities – Final Recommendations*. The Walker review secretariat, London.

Ward, S. and Chapman, C. (2003), "Transforming Project Risk Management into Project Uncertainty Management", *International Journal of Project Management*, Vol.21, No.2, pp.97–105.

Ward, S. and Chapman, C.B. (2002), *Managing Project Risk and Uncertainty: A Constructively Simple Approach to Decision Making*, Wiley, Chichester.

Waring, R.H. and Glendon, A.I. (1998), *Managing Risk: Critical Issues for Survival and Success into the 21st Century*, International Thomson Business, London.

Weick, K.E. (1987), "Organizational Culture as a Source of High Reliability", *California Management Review*, Vol.29, No.2, pp.112–127.

Weick, K.E. (1988), "Enacted Sensemaking In Crisis Situations", *Journal of Management Studies*, Vol.25, No.4, pp.305–317.

Weick, K.E. (1989), "Theory Construction as Disciplined Imagination", *Academy of Management Review*, Vol.14, No.4, pp.516–531.

Weick, K.E. (1993), "The Collapse of Sensemaking in Organizations: The Mann Gulch Disaster", *Administrative Science Quarterly*, Vol.38, No.4, pp.628–652.

Weick, K.E. (1997), "The Challenger Launch Decision: Risky Technology, Culture, and Deviance at NASA", *Administrative Science Quarterly*, Vol.42, No.2, pp.395–401.

Weick, K.E. (2004), "Normal Accident Theory as Frame, Link, and Provocation", *Organization and Environment*, Vol.17, No.1, pp.27–31.

Weick, K.E. (2005), "Organizing and Failures of Imagination", *International Public Management Journal*, Vol.8, No.3, pp.425–438.

Weick, K.E. (2010), "Reflections on Enacted Sensemaking in the Bhopal Disaster", *Journal of Management Studies*, Vol.47, No.3, pp.537–550.

Weick, K.E. and Sutcliffe, K. (2007), *Managing the Unexpected: Resilient Performance in an Age of Uncertainty*, 2nd edn, Jossey-Bass, San Francisco.

Weir, D. (2002), "When Will They Ever Learn? The Conditions for Failure in Publicly Funded High Technology Projects: The R101 and Challenger Disasters Compared", *Disaster Prevention and Management*, Vol.11, No.4, pp.299–307.

Westrum, R. (1982), "Social Intelligence about Hidden Events", *Knowledge: Creation, Diffusion, Utilization*, Vol.3, No.3, pp.381–400.

Whyte, W.H., Jr. (March 1952), "Groupthink", *Fortune,* Vol.142, Iss.146, pp.114–117.

Woods, D.D. (2009), "Escaping Failures of Foresight", *Safety Science*, Vol.47, pp.498–501.

Woolf Committee (2008), *Business Ethics, Global Companies and the Defence Industry,* The Duncan Print Group, Welwyn Garden City.

Woolgar, S. (1980), "Discovery: logic and sequence in scientific text" in Knorr, K.D., Krohn, R. and Whitley, R. (Eds), *The Social Process of Scientific Investigation, Society of the Sciences*, Reidel, Dordrecht Vol.4, pp.239–268.

Yin, R.K. (2003), "The role of Theory in Doing Case Studies", *In Applications of Case Study Research* (3rd edn), Sage, London.

Zwetsloot, G.I.J.M. (2009), "Prospects and Limitations of Process Safety Performance Indicators", *Safety Science*, Vol.47, pp.495–497.

Index